Chalk Lines

Chalk Lines

The Politics of Work in the Managed University

Randy Martin, editor

Duke University Press   Durham and London   1998

Designed by C. H. Westmoreland

Typeset in Quadraat by Tseng Information Systems, Inc.

Library of Congress Cataloging-in-Publication Data

appear on the last printed page of this book.

The text of this book was originally published without

the present introduction, index, and essays by Currie

and Vidovich, Montgomery, Harney and Moten,

and Vaughn, as well as the present version of

the essay by Meyers, as Social Text 51, vol. 15, no. 2 (summer 1997).

Contents

Acknowledgments

This book got its start as a special issue of *Social Text* (number 51, summer 1997). Eight of the essays were published in that volume, and four appear here for the first time. That issue followed the journal's coverage of the Yale Strike (number 49), which is now elaborated and published as *Will Teach for Food*, edited by Cary Nelson.

Social Text has been an intellectual home for more than a dozen years, and I drew enormous support in this project from the editorial committee. The idea for the project was first proposed by Andrew Ross, and his efforts in bringing it to fruition have been unsparing and inspiring all along. Bruce Robbins was extremely generous and acute in his review of the journal material. Monica Marciczkiewicz, managing editor, provided always impressive editorial clarity and organizational acumen that brought the issue together. José Muñoz and George Yúdice provided much appreciated editorial input. Toby Miller offered incisive readings of the new chapters, including particularly useful comments to my introduction. The various contributors themselves were a pleasure to work with, cooperative and responsive throughout. At Duke University Press,

Ken Wissoker and Richard Morrison have been steady guides, and Jean Brady, Anna Haas, and Nicole Cosentino have been a pleasure to work with. Once again, I have been the beneficiary of Nancy Malone's extraordinary editorial talents.

For myself, *Chalk Lines* represents a return to my first interest in sociology, amalgamated with the changes to the industry I have been part of since then. Twenty years ago, as an undergraduate with marxist inclinations, I entered the shop floor and joined the International Ladies' Garment Workers Union, and then the International Brotherhood of Paintmakers, to find out what labor was really like. The militancy I sought in those factories during my years at Berkeley, I encountered as a graduate student in Madison, Wisconsin, during the Teaching Assistants Association (TAA) strike of 1980. The strike was crushed, and I stood accused of fomenting a cheating scandal while on the picket line in the class for which I was a TA. Unable to secure further funding, I left Wisconsin (with the master's thesis I had finished there on worker resistance in a garment and a paint factory) for New York to try my hand and feet at professional modern dance. After a year, I returned to graduate school at the City University of New York and applied my ethnographic training to a dissertation based on my experiences in dance. In 1984, Ph.D. completed, the academic labor market had yielded a continuation of the position I had held the two prior years teaching a couple of courses as an adjunct at Queens College. Subsequently, the jobs I obtained followed no clear pattern of ascent in the occupational hierarchy. Over the next several years, I moved from a tenure-track position to a visiting one-year position as assistant professor, then another as lecturer as I toured the country from Memphis to upstate New York. In 1989, I gained another tenure-track appointment at Pratt Institute, one of a relative minority of private universities with a faculty union (representing both full- and part-timers—the latter composing some four-fifths of this professionally oriented school). I am now professor and chair of the Department of Social Science and Management, responsible, among other things, for hiring adjuncts and local execution of the school's strategic plan. From these commanding heights, I have learned a great deal about the organizational machinations of the institution and have seen how quickly the tables can turn.

This biographical sketch is offered less as a midcareer review than as an effort to situate my own path within the events and forces that have led to this book. The study of labor and the teaching of work's travails can no longer avoid understanding themselves. The self-awareness of the academy as an industry and labor's place within it should not exhaust academics' organizational energies. Quite the contrary, a fuller grasp of the academy's internal dynamics should make affiliations and interventions beyond it more possible. This, at least, is one lesson I have taken away from this book to fuel my passions for what I can teach. In this endeavor as a teacher, Ginger Gillespie has ridden along the learning curve with me since I first hopped into a classroom more than fifteen years ago, and for that journey I am most grateful.

Introduction

Education as National Pedagogy

Randy Martin

S ome twenty-five years ago, labor militancy in this country increased dramatically with a near record number of strikes in 1974. Amid other shifts in the world's division of labor, a countersiege of global proportions ensued, one that marshaled a variety of weapons against labor organizations: plant closings and subcontracting, sometimes to sources outside the country; erosion of the government mechanisms for arbitration and other protections of workers' rights; and various free-trade agreements and policies that abetted the movement of capital. Union membership was cut in half, and most people saw their real incomes decline between 1974 and 1994. With the August 1997 Teamsters strike against United Parcel Service as a benchmark, only now is the labor movement in the United States showing signs of revival. Among the promising indicators are new national leadership (that has benefited from insurgencies), refined strike tactics (such as the series of shutdowns at single General Motors plants that have caused parts shortages throughout the production network), spirited national media campaigns, and the enlistment of students in organizing drives (as in the [A F L-C I O] Union Summer Projects).

The current reflorescence of unionism on many North American campuses may turn out to echo the militant campus activism of the mid-1970s. Responding to the crisis at the City University of New York (C U N Y) in 1974, a group of faculty activists described the situation thus: "At this very moment C U N Y students and faculty are under the gun. People everywhere are being fired. Financial aid is being slashed. Courses are being chopped. Class sizes increased. The state is moving to impose tuition, which will drive huge numbers of students out of school." [1]

As these words remind us, the promise of universal access to higher education had barely survived its first decade before it began to come under serious and by now familiar attack from the very government sources that were responsible for assuring that the dream was indeed realizable. At the time, the C U N Y emergency might have appeared to have been the outcome of a failure in local revenue mechanisms. By now, however, government pronouncements of "fiscal crisis" have become virtually universal and normalized. Ironically, actual deficits are typically in decline, and many municipalities and states report surplus revenues — frequently, already earmarked "return to sender." Absent is the political will. Broken is the old social contract. "We can't" is restated as "we shouldn't." The current shake-up of academic labor is not a simple replay of the local as the national, nor is the activism it has inspired merely a continuation of the spirit of earlier times. There is no doubt that we need to take a fresh look at what is fueling the fires on campuses today.

Discipline and Finance

To hear the president of the United States tell it in his State of the Union Address of February 4, 1997, these are auspicious times for education, his "number one priority." Clinton's ambitions for education are great: "to prepare our people for the bold new world of the 21st Century." [2] As education is to be a sort of antidote for the "challenges" presented by globalization, it is worth reflecting on the ideological work it is being asked to do. Surely, this speech is but one of many, and its proposals are not guaranteed implementation. But it does condense the state of the administration's self-understanding, as much as it reports on the national condition. For the country's featured course of action, the sums of money involved are modest when compared with those for such initiatives as the savings and loan bailout ($200 billion) or the Mexican peso stabilization (less than $20 billion).

The Department of Education itself stands as the federal government's smallest cabinet-level bureau, with a staff of fewer than five thousand. Its budget is less than $30 billion. This is hardly a vehicle for major government intervention—unless that is precisely the point to achieve Clinton's demonstration effect of how little the government needs to spend to align models of citizen, consumer, and worker in the figure of the student. Most of what is devoted to higher education consists of financial aid and the recently acquired responsibility for direct student loans ($5.3 billion to students, and nearly $1 billion more in subsidies to banks, with $5 billion more going to academic institutions for various programs). Still, in all, the federal government contributes roughly $70 billion to the $529.6 billion that was spent on education in 1996, of which $211 billion went into postsecondary schooling. The Department of Education was first established by an act of that name in 1867. It subsequently became the Office of Education, and then in 1980, a cabinet-level department separate from health and human services. Federal policy coordinated through these various offices has aimed to shape how the rest of that money is expended and to influence how people think about education. In the eighty years after the department first made its appearance, ten acts were passed, geared largely toward promoting agricultural and industrial education that would span the nation. During the next forty years (1941–81), over seventy pieces of legislation were passed that extended access, secured financial assistance, and underwrote research. In the last fifteen years, purportedly those of diminished government intervention, nearly eighty bills have been signed into law. This unprecedented legislative intensity has been oriented in the main toward restructuring finance and regulating evaluation.[3]

In privileging education as the vehicle of success in the post–cold war era, Clinton is doing no less for how the people of the United States are to think of themselves as citizens, consumers, and workers. With this emphasis, Clinton is marking a break from the Reagan-Bush years, at the same time extending and deepening their supply-side economics. Budget balancing and tax relief can end government as we knew it, while enlarging the disciplinary operations of the state. The interpellation of fiscal constraint for much of the citizenry is thereby twinned with newfound freedom of movement for financial instruments. For those toiling with campus politics, this larger context for what education is being asked to do is crucial, both to anticipate the kinds of forces that will be brought to bear on the academy and to recognize the strategic linkages available between the university and the larger political arena. What Clinton means to signal is that educational access and attainment are, henceforth, to link labor and citizenship in a renewed covenant of the sovereign subject. With all the precision of financial planning, people are, through their actions, to become the masters of their own destinies. In more prosaic terms, there is still room aboard the ship of success said to unite these states, if one only prepares oneself adequately for the passage.

Whereas Reagan had argued early on that this preparation for self-directed advancement entailed inviting the unemployed to work for lower wages, Clinton's version of labor supplying its own opportunities for employment is to create "national standards, representing what all our students must know to succeed in the knowledge economy of the 21st Century." Study is the supreme form of information management, where the individual worker is the site of accumulation. The promise of universal access to higher education, which had gone missing in past administrations, derives from this refurbished idea of *homo economicus:* "every 18 year old must be able to go to college; and every adult American must be able to keep on learning for a lifetime." The reason that education itself must be a focus of national mobilization is that globalization, Clinton's no longer brave but now "bold new world," presents a novel kind of security risk. The president makes this explicit when he explains the significance of his policy. "One of the greatest sources of our strength throughout the Cold War was a bipartisan foreign policy because our future was at stake." We now need "a new nonpartisan commitment to education because education is a critical national security issue for our future, and politics must stop at the schoolhouse door."[4]

Here, political and economic security become amalgamated, and Clinton is attempting to curtail the uncivil culture wars (in which he has been a willing combatant—as, for instance, in his attacks on Sister Souljah in the 1992 presidential campaign) that had been used to demonstrate that the university was a holdout against rationalization, economic and cultural. In Reagan's day, the arguments over who or what was entitled to speak from a position of being universal (political correctness) drew the limelight, while a series of laws were passed to elaborate the traffic in intellectual property rights, on campus, and in the world. Now that campus life has been thoroughly subjected to business regimen, it is to be increasingly used to demonstrate a different effect, that multiculturalism is not politically disruptive but simply another economic input. As Clinton begins to wind down his speech, he says, "We must never ever believe that our diversity is a weakness—it is our greatest strength"; we must "live and advance together across differences."[5] Through this lowering of the temperature on campus, this revelation that there, difference makes no difference to what one knows or the uses to which knowledge is put, the university passes from a den of inequity where the meek threaten to inherit, to an exemplary site of personal responsibility for all who venture self-constraint.

The access that Clinton is trumpeting for his subjects could be seen as another nail driven into the coffin of humanism, a model of knowledge for its own ends whose availability was historically restricted to those of means. Clinton's universal is of a rather restricted variety. The promise of four years of liberal arts education has been downsized to two years of community college. This is something vaguer than the vocational programs of dubious success in landing actual employment that have been cut back in recent years. Instead, the guarantee of community college represents efforts to solidify the vocational link between learning and work.[6] But while there is little in recent legislation to reverse the historic failure of narrowly focused vocational training to generate well-paying jobs, it does help set a clear example for college administrators that, henceforth, education means business. The competitive edge in this reinvented market ideology does not guarantee jobs; it insists only that work be the end(s) of education. To the extent that education will also provide the means, it is as a model, now supposedly available to all, of the managed self, a disciplinary program in which financial planning usurps other modes of surveillance designed to assure that the self is being properly cared for.

The announcement of new policy allows Clinton to use his "bully pulpit" to articulate a more general account of worker self-management than that associated with control over the shop floor. This amounts to a vision of citizenship based on financial planning that is evident not only in the State of the Union Address but also in recent policy initiatives. One such initiative is the Goals 2000: Educate America Act, signed into law on March 31, 1994. The bill, funded at over $500 million for 1996, based on premises developed in the Bush administration, is part of the broader scheme to shift fiscal responsibilities for social services from the federal government to the states, a process called "devolution." The state assembles a "planning panel" that allows businesspeople to mix with educators, all of whom are charged with meeting national education standards, increasing student discipline and school safety. One of the principal features of the legislation is to provide grants directly to local school districts to engage in processes of community planning that involve parents, teachers and administrators, and business, in something like a supercharged version of the Parent-Teacher Association (PTA).

Business, given a place at the table by government, is a key component of these new voluntary associations touted as civil society, a domain described as beyond either market or polity.[7] Among the components of the plan's goals is the introduction of mechanisms for each school to "align responsibility, authority, and accountability throughout the education system, so that decisions regarding 'how to move all students toward the state's high standards' are made closest to the learners."[8] Perhaps there is some appeal to this populism that teachers and parents (those "closest to the learners") and their organizations could seize on without contributing to the sense that students are to be made the objects of greater efficiency. Yet not only does this planning process introduce management models of decision making into education, but it is also itself an accounting system in which accomplishments are measured in relation to goals as in a ledger of debits and credits. While aimed at channeling popular participation and local control, the dissemination of standardized patterns of decision making is meant to define what constitutes community modeled on corporate protocols. By this reckoning the federal government is seeking to devolve the public to the private, in the dual sense of discharging its social responsibilities to personal initiative and rendering the propriety of profit the ultimate arbiter of individual decorum.

In this, the state does not diminish its role but invests itself more firmly in promoting an alignment of human initiative with business interest (thereby risking that student defiance in learning to labor will be less toward education than toward managerialism as such). There are hints in Goals 2000 that some will find its regimen distasteful or themselves excluded from the communities that are being operationalized. This is met with a confidence that diversity can be directed toward a unitary conception of citizenship. For example, in the act's title 7, "Minority Focused Civics Education," diversity, here a property of minorities, requires that its fidelity to government be affirmed so as to "improve minority and Native American student knowledge and understanding of the American system of government."[9]

It may seem curious for the United States government to be spending a half billion dollars on planning, but at less than two dollars per citizen, this sum is not likely to go very far in disciplining the self to a renewed regimen of finance. Because they are already community institutions and the barriers to participation in terms of expertise are taken to be low, schools become an easy mark for social experimentation. The call for universal access to secondary education, made in Clinton's address, has taken legislative form in the Hope and Opportunity for Postsecondary Education (HOPE) Act of 1997. At first glance, its central provision appears to be no more than a modest tax credit for schooling of fifteen hundred dollars. By all measures, its modesty is meant to be its virtue. The innovation intends to provide tax relief to those who don't make enough money to itemize deductions, thereby extending to lower-income families perquisites hitherto enjoyed only by those on the higher end of the wage scale. Tax abatement is now the currency of the realm in terms of government benefits and is what united supply-side notions across the economic spectrum.

At a time when the vaunted middle class appears to be another category of persons "at risk," the redistribution of tax benefits downward has a certain equivalence to the government's role in creating conditions for home ownership after World War II, which constituted that particular version of the American dream. The corollary legislative piece was the Serviceman's Readjustment Act of 1944, better known as the G.I. Bill, which tied together education benefits with housing subsidies in the form of mortgages and infrastructure assistance to building contractors. The savings and loan industry, which so infamously collapsed in the eighties, with the encouragement of deregulation, was created to support the material underpinnings of the trappings of middle-class life.

What rose and fell during these fifty years were the assortment of government policies, known most broadly as Keynesianism, intended to aid and abet the production of demand for consumer goods. The presumption that mass consumption was the handmaiden for maintaining profitability in industrial production (Fordism) spun the social contract of union-driven wage increases and economic growth that stitched labor into middle-class garments and encouraged further social spending. The cold war response to Communism (here the 1958 National Defense Education Act is emblematic) established a delimited social economy, still highly variegated in terms of race, gender, and citizenship. The claim that the principal assistance that government intervention offers to a capitalist economy is control of inflation through monetary policy, rather than stimulus of demand through "pump priming," converts Keynesianism to monetarism.

In practice the state still acts to shape demand (think of its role in restructuring the defense industry), these actions are disavowed in favor of a new common sense. Strictly speaking, the tight control of the monetary supply on the part of the Federal Reserve, the bank that lends to banks, was associated with Paul Volcker's leadership between 1979 and 1982. In more general terms, the operating principles of monetarism have expanded.

Reagan, Bush, and Clinton have participated in dismantling the institutional supports of the Fordist social contract, in no small measure through attacks on subalterns, while helping to free business from a unionized workforce. Given the enormous attentions applied to deunionization, organizing workers may have more significant effects than it could have had two decades ago. Perhaps in anticipation of this, Clinton is pursuing mechanisms for a monetarist reinvention of that basis of refracted participation in economic expansion known as the middle class. The significant difference this time around is that rather than participation in home ownership, citizens hitherto too poor to qualify can now become the masters of their own credit and debt. The HOPE Act recommends that financial planning for children's education begin at age twelve with investments in the appropriate portfolio of tax-deferred annuities.

The future is paved with financial planning, in which sufficient savings becomes the goal to be met. In the face of skyrocketing tuition costs, schools can themselves reduce financial aid awards and meet the challenges of students trading aid packages for the best bargain. Whatever the connection between financial strain and social unrest, no one watching the escalating volume of consumer debt (underwritten by government-supported habits) can fail to see the instabilities to financial institutions that could ensue. For those to whom consumer credit has been made available in the last decade, borrowing has compensated for lost wages. In 1995, over $900 billion was spent on servicing this debt, an amount equal to 16.7 percent of after-tax earnings for households in the United States.[10] For students, borrowing to pay for college increased 22 percent per year between 1990 and 1994, amid tuition increases and cuts to state and federal aid programs.[11] Rather than prepare for a bailout of credit card companies when too many of these households default, the pedagogy of financial planning aims to introduce the appropriate rigors of lifetime self-discipline.

Children reared as disciples of such planning will be able to put it to work as soon as they enroll. While increased productivity and higher wages are the promised outcomes of higher education, school attendance itself is to be disciplined by "learning productivity," a principle coined by the former State University of New York (SUNY) chancellor Bruce Johnstone, who entreats students to "assume greater personal responsibility for their learning." The gist of the concept is to "achieve higher levels of skill and knowledge attainment at lower cost." Savings are to be realized by "distance learning," replacing classroom experiences with computers, which students will be encouraged to purchase, and limiting the credit hours that can be subsidized.[12] The computerization of education, which runs throughout Clinton policy, comes at a time when demand for personal computers appears otherwise saturated. With placement of the emphasis of competitiveness on whether or not technology is current, education can take on more directly machinic comparisons as corporations reap a larger share of educational expenditure without having to worry about the direct costs of managing universities. Presumably after all this planning, saving, investing, and purchasing, the student's own course of study will be securely predetermined.

The Reorder Within

If participation in a system of tax relief is now to be made universal so that all have equal access to education, it should be clear that the academy itself has been retrenched from its own universal ambitions. This is the presumed result of strategic planning: the conversion from the campus that does it all to one that excels at niche marketing. Private consultants and special commissioners, whose recommendations about which programs to eliminate and which initiatives to invest in help cast the terms of engagement for schools' corporate self-identification, tell us that each campus should focus on a "core business . . . by adopting a strategy of 'selective excellence.' "[13] Restructuring, downsizing, reengineering, and strategic planning have been the rubrics for eliminating programs and personnel in some two-thirds of the institutions of higher education in the United States. This upsurge in corporate-type planning has been the legacy not only of the guardians of the universities' portfolios but of government-induced fiscal crisis as well. The rule of austerity invokes as its authority the newly self-evident truths of capital's global investment prerogatives, which entail unhitching social services from government stewardship, cutting taxes on wealth (which in turn swells budget deficits), and reducing public debt to better amass private credit. The launch of Sputnik from within a planned economy prompted legislators' calls for "universal opportunity" in higher education. Thirty years later, the fall of the Berlin Wall and the presumed discrediting of "the plan" in favor of "the market" appear to have unleashed an avalanche of planning portfolios in education to mask the effects of unbridled niche marketing.

In the light of these proposals to link learning directly to fading career prospects, the vast educational capacity generated over the past decades now appears to have encountered its own crisis of overproduction—a gap between the kinds of commodities available and the ability to pay for them. Despite the historically relative abundance of trained professionals and teaching infrastructure, the act of limiting the goals of education makes these things seem eternally scarce. At the same time, to complete a vicious circle, university managers inform us that the best way of stemming the internal hemorrhaging is to narrow curricular content and access.

On many campuses, the old math of classroom head counts is no longer enough to secure budgetary allocations. Increasingly, profitability beyond the university enters into the fiduciary calculus and forces all concerned unequal players into an ever more competitive gambit. Universities' adoption of corporate reengineering has meant putting the squeeze on the very way resources are distributed downward in the organization better to enable control over their upward flow.[14] This, in turn, is reflected not only in the growing ranks of administrators but in their regulation of admissions, retention, scholarships, discretionary accounts, and hirings as well. These shared conditions have also allowed all who labor at the university to see it as their common workplace.

If Clinton's ambitions were to lower the heat on campus as he upheld the mantle of the "center" he has helped to destroy, the rash of labor responses across the country hint at a different result. The efforts to present the business talk on campus as a de-ideologized newspeak do suggest certain paradoxical effects. In the lexicon of strategic planning, departments and every other type of staffed office or service may equally become "responsibility centers" that set goals and take "action steps" meant to calibrate their hitherto disparate identities into a shared economic language of self-representation. All this talk of exchange—of what is needed by the "responsibility center" and what goods it must deliver—at least has the potential to slip uneasily between competition over monies from a shrinking pot and the realization of mutual interest in who controls the plan. At a very minimum, this instrumentalizing of education allows it to be treated as a means to a different end. The neoliberal attack on the liberalism of education leaves the defense of the pristine halls aside so as to pose the question in a less idealized yet perhaps more comprehensive way of who works in these corridors and to what purpose.

Nor should the promise of universal access to higher education, however compromised or compacted, be dismissed out of hand for its disingenuity (after all, primary and secondary education were once also restricted forms). Quite the contrary, the burden of committed analysis is to show where the promise is deficient in order to widen the opportunity. Substantive entitlements that attach to citizenship are too rare in the present context to bypass, and here an expansive attitude to education could be extended to other domains. The argument that higher education enhances productivity can certainly be extended to health care and housing as well. And the claim that an educated labor supply adds value that is measurable in wages presupposes expanding the kinds of employment that require such enhancement.

Yet without abandoning these sorts of economic argument, it is also important to move beyond their constricted parameters. The presumption that education is only for employment still assumes that the latter is a scarce item that one must be relieved or somehow grateful to receive. By this reckoning, education is merely an extension of labor-market discipline. Yet, after six years of economic recovery, with minimal inflation and twelve million new jobs, two-thirds of the states and many municipalities were reporting budget surpluses. Although it is easy to say that these monies are only short-term surprises that won't address structural problems, their appearance can be used to challenge the united front of scarcity we have come to expect from government precincts. Politicizing these surpluses entails insisting that they are social resources for general betterment, rather than an aggregate of private property in need of individuated redistribution.

Retaining the narrow focus on employment also leaves education itself much impoverished. If Clinton has sought to neutralize the charged climate around curriculum, he has also raised the specter of an educational opportunity without intellectual content. The sense of a life-enhancing project beyond sheer employment used to be captured by the term "career." Displacement and downsizing give a cynical cast to such claims. All the more reason, then, to think of education as a kind of ongoing surplus, a sense of what's left over when the demand for production has been met. In this regard education is a rejoinder to the pronouncement that all activity serve the market. From this perspective education prepares one in a very different way to deal with the predicament of having to work for a living. Emphasis on this role for education could give voice to that side of the multiculturalism debate silenced by the accusation of political correctness. But above all, it suggests that a strategic linkage between campus organizing and other forms of social activism lies in how those who work in the academy pin their own fortunes to these larger issues in a way that reverses the common accusations of unions as somehow a special interest. As I suggested at the beginning of this introduction, unions have come to bear a more general burden for righting the ills that face a society in which the conditions of work and the general conditions of social life seem less easy to extricate from each other than they might have in the recent past. The public sympathies that unions can now muster, whether for particular work actions or "fast-track" trade policies, the sense in which they have become a voice against the economization of life as we have known it, can only further the resurgence of organizing activity.

Beyond the onslaught of managerialism, just what are the conditions for unionizing the academy? No express train shuttles people from what is done to them to what they do with their circumstances, but the particular consequences can still benefit from a map. There are real risks involved in speaking of central tendencies among the 2.6 million workers in the academy (43 percent of whom are faculty or teaching assistants) given that, on average, polarization and diversification of experiences are the order of the day. For all practical purposes, stars and adjuncts are not in the same labor market. Nor are Ph.D.'s in physics, English, or business, fields which each generate roughly 1,300 doctorates but in which undergraduate degrees number around 4,000, 54,000, and 250,000, respectively.[15] Yet despite the very visible exceptions, academics share something with the great majority of workers in other fields: longer hours for less pay. When controlled for inflation, faculty salaries lost 17 percent of their purchasing power in the seventies and have only partially recouped that loss in the eighties, with the gaps widening the further down the ranks one goes and between men and women.[16] By contrast, those faculty with collective bargaining agreements average over six thousand dollars more than those without them.[17] Full-time faculty now work an average 52.5-hour week, while part-timers labor for 33.8 hours (at private research institutions, where the category is most strained, the part-time workweek exceeds forty hours).[18]

Yet clearly the number of hours worked is not the best measure of what divides full- and part-time faculty, any more than it can be folded neatly into that often spurious concept of productivity. Seventy-five percent of part-timers make under ten thousand dollars a year, whereas the average full-timer's salary approaches fifty thousand dollars. Academic stars and senior administrators have salaries in excess of one hundred thousand dollars.[19] Compared with other U.S. businesses (whose chief executive officers average one hundred fifty times the pay of line employees), the professorial pay structure appears almost egalitarian or, conversely, close enough actually to make it so. More to the point, part-timers are largely without representation in a field in which full-timers can boast of robust union participation. Ten years ago, when part-time employment began to increase at a significantly faster clip (than it had in the past and than did full-time positions), only 9 percent of institutions had bargaining units for their contingent workers.[20] But casualization of the workforce has itself increased dramatically of late. In 1991, 536,000 faculty were full-time, and 291,000 worked part-time. Two years later, those numbers were 546,000 and 370,000, respectively.[21] While the portion of full-time faculty who are tenured has remained over 60 percent for the past twenty years (though this figure says nothing about turnover as a function of the rates at which faculty are denied tenure or about the cut from 60 percent to 40 percent in the past twenty years of those who are eligible to apply), the increase in adjuncts has brought the overall figure down to a quarter of the professoriat.[22]

This growth in the professoriat during otherwise bleak times for education has been driven by an enormous increase in demand. Enrollments increased 20 percent between 1974 and 1984, and almost as much over the next ten years, to reach a total of 14.3 million students, with large increases in students over twenty-five and even bigger gains in graduate enrollment.[23] Consequently, the number of doctorates granted has increased from one in 1870 to 32,107 in 1970 and to over 43,000 in 1994. Much of this recent increase reflects a feminization of graduate education, which is in turn reflected in the rolls of part-timers.[24] In 1973, 1,258 men and 677 women earned doctorates in English. Twenty years later, degrees were conferred to 568 men and 776 women. Even in business, the number of male Ph.D.'s declined from 1973 to 1993, whereas that of women increased sevenfold.[25]

In the annals of labor history, supply and demand alone have never been sufficient to determine the degree of control over conditions of employment exercised by unions, guilds, and professional associations. Where these are weak or nonexistent, limited availability of workers, typically measured as low rates of unemployment, boosts salaries only in the rarefied sectors of finance and related professions. This is why the denial that graduate students work and the disavowal that the life of the mind is a kind of labor have such enormous ideological implications—for here, exceptionalism is offered as a rule. Of newly minted Ph.D.'s, more than a fifth were seeking employment, and less than half had "definite employment."[26] These statistics compare miserably with what are considered low national rates of under 5 percent of the total civilian workforce and look worse when set next to postbaccalaureate unemployment (2.4 percent). They also argue for the failure of market forces to match persons with places, which is where, historically, union control has bested the "invisible hand" of the market. At the same time it is worth exercising caution against too narrowly vocational a conception of what graduate education is for. It would be an irony if the voices who championed education as an end in itself fell victim to self-applied instrumentalism.

One potential resource for organizing this workforce is the incredible concentration of the industry. Schools can be readily tagged by their wealth—120 of them control more than two-thirds of the nearly $100 billion total endowment.[27] Although there are several thousand college campuses in the United States, the large, mainly public ones (the 11 percent with over ten thousand students) have half the total enrollment. Production of doctorates is particularly concentrated, with sixty schools turning out almost two-thirds of all Ph.D.'s. Among these, the three largest—the University of California, Berkeley; the University of Wisconsin, Madison; and the University of Illinois, Urbana-Champaign—have graduate employee organizations.[28]

Indeed, faculty unions are themselves quite concentrated in the public sector (only 10,000 of 250,000 unionized faculty teach at private schools), as they are geographically, with half of the 1,115 campuses in New York and California. Contrary to the rest of the workforce, the professoriat has continued to unionize since the seventies, albeit at a modest rate; in 1995, all four certifying elections were won, and in the previous year, eight of eleven efforts were successful.[29] Strike activity, on the other hand, had decreased during these years. Between 1966 and 1994 there were 163 actions, with 78 in the 1970s, 54 in the 1980s, and 13 in the first half of the 1990s. Most of these occurred at two-year colleges in Michigan, New York, Pennsylvania, and New Jersey, and only a quarter, at private schools.[30]

It should come as little surprise that the further industrialization of education has led to the heightened awareness that what goes on at the university is *work*—and a highly organized division of labor at that. Notoriously, this revelation seems to have come late to many tenured faculty, but where organizing efforts have broken out, they have succeeded in displaying to all the unusually high stakes of this shared consciousness. They have also shown how important it is to integrate the panoply of issues that administrations are learning to triage and contain—from who teaches and what is taught to who is learning and the physical conditions under which learning occurs. What might have been unforeseen just a few years ago is that unionization drives would become the vehicles to integrate the infamous divide between issues of identity and matters of political economy, would generate solidarities across occupational lines and internal hierarchies, and would serve to link battles at particular sites with a larger sense of national political possibility. The organizing efforts at places such as CUNY, the Universities of California, Illinois, Iowa, and Minnesota, New York University (NYU), Yale, Central Washington State, Florida A&M, the College of the Desert in California, and John A. Logan in Illinois suggest that actions initiated by any sector among those who toil at the academy—clericals, graduate assistants, or faculty—can launch more than one ship. Campaigns that had languished for ten years,

16

such as the one at Southern Illinois at Carbondale, got 60 percent of the faculty to sign union cards within a month. A unionist from the National Education Association (NEA) who reports a "tremendous resurgence" in activity over the past few years is in the midst of five organizing drives, with faculty from all over the country calling.[31]

This is not a perception that is universally shared among union staffers, and for sound reasons. Contract negotiations are in a sorry state on many campuses, with some faculty continuing to work without them. The nation's largest bargaining agent in higher education, the American Federation of Teachers (AFT), is witnessing little new organizing activity. Full-timers with job security can see scant gain and much to risk by mobilizing, and adjuncts can be engaged with full-time employment elsewhere. Incumbent union leadership at CUNY and the Fashion Institute of Technology of SUNY were recently reelected by wide margins in the face of insurgent challenges. Faculty at the University of Minnesota, pushed to the brink by their administration, were still unable to gather sufficient support to gain union representation. All this would appear to suggest that the present augurs more of a "holding pattern" than forward motion.[32] While there has been media attention, little has changed in legislative terms that would facilitate unionization, although the merger under negotiation between the NEA and the AFT should provide some of the muscle necessary to create the required statutory support to shift the present interest into action.[33]

Beauty here is not simply in the eyes of the beholder. Although the specter of discrediting disappointment awaits those who would inflate the prospects of success, immobility can lie in store for those who make too little of otherwise inchoate possibilities. What makes the matter more complex is that such alternatives are not freely chosen but shaped by the immediate circumstances of the project in which one is engaged. Yet part of what is up for grabs are the very criteria we use to evaluate progress when standard means of assessment may suggest that our efforts at change are insufficient to the magnitude of the problems we face.

In 1960, none of the academic workforce was unionized. Today, in the public sector in which nearly three-quarters of the professoriat is employed, 63 percent of full-timers are unionized, as are 44 percent of all college teachers, a rate that exceeds three times that of the total workforce in the United States.[34] And whereas early faculty unionization efforts, such as CUNY's Legislative Conference, sought to segregate full- and part-timers into separate bargaining units, the New Caucus, which has run an alternate slate of candidates, attempts their integration.

Among the significant challenges to unionization efforts that can capture a broader spectrum of issues pertaining to education is how to expand the craft conception of faculty unions without undermining their success. Until now, seniority, workload, salary, and benefits have typically been taken to be self-contained with respect to other campus constituencies, most pointedly, graduate students and adjuncts. The key legal moment in this partition was a 1972 National Labor Relations Board decision disallowing graduate students in the faculty bargaining unit because they are "*primarily students* and do not have a sufficient *community of interest* with regular faculty to warrant inclusion in their unit."[35] In this instance, the university sought inclusion against the wishes of the faculty union. The Yeshiva decision has been taken as equally fateful for unionization of independent institutions, with seventy-five schools using it to challenge faculty efforts and many more developing "employee involvement schemes" as parallel governance structures.[36]

One relevant question is whether the rise of managerialism in the past twenty-five years, both within and beyond the university, has expanded the community of interest sufficiently to consider different lines of alliance. The centrality of higher education in the constitution of the citizen-subject raises the prospect that labor organizations can amalgamate issues that have of late been treated as beyond their grasp. This would entail rethinking not only the craft-industrial union divide but the very nature of academic labor as well. The Yale graduate student strike was significant not only because an elite institution was being forced to confront its own hypocrisy as a locus of opportunity but also because it forced recognition that a category of human activity was, in fact, labor. True to form, the graduate students got very little sympathy from their mentors, but part of the national attention that the strike drew was support from tenured faculty elsewhere.[37]

The point is not simply that the unpaid and undercompensated should receive their just rewards—though clearly they should. Nor is it sufficient to suggest that people who demonstrate competence through their qualifications should be able to find meaningful employment in the fields of their choosing. At some point, the foregrounding of education in the national imagination must be used by activists on campus and off to move beyond the parameters of value-added calculations and paeans to meritocracy. As long as some failed or were denied access, the correlations between credentials and wages could be positive (except, perhaps, for academics themselves). Universalizing higher education, like any all-inclusive agenda, proposes what it means to act together as a "we." Insofar as we continue to invest in the mythos of academic hierarchy—the faith that a few places confer identity and the rest anonymity—opportunities that are adequate to expectations will appear eternally scarce, and we will continue to be implicated in the manufacture of our own relative surplus population. This would in turn require a consideration of the question of value more broadly, of what counts as usefulness in a world defined by profit-taking exchange.

We must learn to diversify what education is for if we are to use it to organize both for work and for life. If the humanism that now no longer seems to require a defense has been replaced with a universalizing managerialism, it is incumbent on us to interrogate the nature of the universal this time around. At stake is not only access to increased disciplinary requirements but also what forms of human association, cooperation, affiliation, and collective fantasy can be accessed through education. Although it may seem a throwback to what has been treated as a fading technology (a bit like labor organizing itself), we should not forget that some of the lines between us are drawn in chalk. They have been, and they can be, creatively redrawn.

The Present Work

The twelve essays published here are by no means exhaustive, but they do cast a wide net over the current situation of academic labor in the United States, with a nod toward how this impacts the rest of the world. Eight of them appeared originally in a special issue of *Social Text* (number 51, summer 1997), and four others are published here for the first time. The essays are divided into three parts in which their authors examine the implications of managerialism, the status of academic labor, and avenues of organizational response.

In their previous work, Sheila Slaughter and Gary Rhoades have drawn the linkages between laws, such as the Bayh-Dole Act of 1980, that allowed universities to act as purveyors of intellectual property, and the juridical framework that facilitated the globalization of this commodity form over the next fifteen years.[38] In their contribution to this book, the authors examine the restructured university—not only where and how resources are applied but also how the organizational fabric of the institution itself has been transformed. They frame the central tendency of this great transformation and describe countermovements and tensions between its economic, political, and ideological aspects. For example, while universities have assimilated more of the protocols of profitability touted by the U.S. corporate sector, the academy, unlike many of the industries it would imitate, remains globally dominant, even if it acts as a supplicant to failed models of competitiveness.

Although the university has long been a student of corporate ways, it is important to remember that the business model itself is by no means unitary. Management's perennial question of how to extract the most product from the smallest magnitude of labor still awaits its definitive reply. Even Frederick Winslow Taylor, the godparent of reengineering and developer of the principles of scientific management at the turn of the last century, recognized the need to enlist the participation and knowledge of workers in their own exploitation. The tensions between the administration of people and of things continue apace, even when that most scientific principle, accounting, achieves ascendance in the habits of corporate control, as it has after World War II. The result, as those who work within universities have learned with a vengeance, is that budgeting becomes the ruling organizational idea. California's vast educational enterprise is the home of Clark Kerr's multiversity, government-mandated classroom access of a percentage of the state's potential student population, and, more recently, a sustained budget crisis prompted by tax cuts and capital flight, as well as the dismantling of affirmative action. This past and present makes the Golden State a particularly useful site to examine these contested managerialisms in formation, which is what Christopher Newfield does in his essay. In the corporate version of workers' self-management, now becoming popular in certain boardrooms, Newfield identifies a limited critique of its brethren's slash-and-burn approach. He suggests how this rejection of tyrannical management techniques can be amplified to envision a broader front of opposition that nonetheless makes use of the antinomies within the seemingly impregnable business imaginary.

In the town where I live, Columbia University is the third-largest and NYU is the sixth-largest private employer (at 14,811 and 13,692, respectively). Both added jobs when their larger brethren (the Chase Bank and Nynex) were downsizing, and each saw a healthy increase in revenue over the previous fiscal year (Columbia's 1995 income increased 6.3 percent to just under $1.2 billion, and NYU, with a larger student body, saw an 8.2 percent gain to over $1.5 billion).[39] But these academic firms are in no way typical. In her contribution Zelda Gamson allows us to think about the academy as a highly stratified industrial sector, illustrating some of the disparities between those institutions which assume the mantle of the "elite" and those which harbor the mass of the student body. She examines the rise and fall of "research culture" as a generalized model for academic work and invites us to reflect on how well this shoe really fits.

Just how generalizable these tendencies toward managerialism are beyond the United States enables us to apply some specificity to the mantra of globalization that typically gets used as a stick in reengineering the academy at home. In the face of these impersonal forces of the world market, much is rationalized as necessary and unstoppable. Among the points that get lost in this account is how influential homegrown models are elsewhere. Of the seventy-eight million students enrolled in higher education worldwide, just over one-half million are visitors to the United States from abroad.[40] The models travel more readily than students, and to greater effect. Jan Currie and Lesley Vidovich examine three Australian and three U.S. universities that have sustained restructuring initiatives. The centralized Australian system could assimilate and disseminate the rubric of managerialism more rapidly than the country that inspired it.

The authors draw on hundreds of in-depth interviews to give voice to faculty responses and to reveal the complexities that attach to these various decision-making schemes.

Managerialism aims to inhabit all the fleshy parts of labor, at the same time that work is to be recognized the way management sees itself, namely, as an endless stream of decisions taken. While accountability and efficiency are the watchwords of these quality controls, the attention to detail such responsibility promotes can readily overwhelm the appreciation of the ends to which managerialism is put. David Montgomery is a distinguished Yale professor noted for his fine labor studies and his support of striking graduate students. In this transcription of his speech at the "Between Classes" conference held at New York University in November 1996, he is quite pointed in stating the aims of the present restructuring. His example of impoverishment against the enormous concentration of wealth that has been accomplished through managerialism's fiscal responsibility refers not simply to well-endowed universities but also to the country as a whole. The gauntlet he lays down concerns both the disidentification of financial health with common interest and the reinvestment in public life that supporting labor's conditions in academia and elsewhere presupposes.

In the face of reports to the contrary, affirming that the academy runs on labor is an important step to take, but others must follow if the selfless faith in an academic calling that can appear to transcend worldly travail is to take a more self-critical turn. Effort is applied to materials that yield a socially useful entity. The ability to subsist through engaging in this activity is contingent on contractual relations to which the producers are subject. Time is treated as a measure of the endeavor and is calibrated for exchange in the form of a wage. The value of what is created exceeds the compensation. In all these aspects, academic labor is conventional. Yet in other regards, academic labor confounds received categorization. Knowledge, if that is what is being produced, is a slippery thing. It is at once local and in defiance of locality. Wages for thought jostle uneasily between what is paid for and what is not. Product, whether as successfully completed credit hour or publication, cannot straightforwardly be seen as containing the value attributed to it. Appropriation, which names learning as much as it does teaching, generates kinds of surplus that are not necessarily commensurate with one another. These problems urge a more thorough unpacking of what academic labor entails, which Stefano Harney and Frederick Moten venture in their contribution. They reveal the uneasiness with which social categories of labor coexist with the mists of meritocracy and explain why affirmative action becomes so crucial in displaying and managing this tension.

Stratification pertains to resources allocated to students within and across different kinds of college campuses and to the highly segmented character of the academic labor market as well. The public-funded expansion of the university-industrial complex corresponds to that moment in U.S. history considered a turning point in the social compact between labor and capital. Vincent Tirelli places his study of adjunct labor in the context of post-Fordism: the displacement of workers from stable employment and "flexibility" as a managerial rallying cry. The opening up of student admissions, like other instances of mass marketing, was administered through the expansion of a part-time and casualized labor force in the form of contract laborers without benefits, subjected to ideologies of self-motivation and sacrifice. In so doing, the university developed a managerial model of subcontracting that would become the envy of other industrial sectors (which had hitherto ridiculed academics for their laxity in the habits of the real world). Tirelli pursues the implications for organizing that inhere when workers such as adjuncts are no longer marginal but central. As a result, the university may offer a prototype for the initiatives of labor in addition to those it has provided for management.

The percentage of full-time faculty (tenure-track and non-tenure-track) has declined over the past decade (one study reported a decline from 60 percent in 1987 to 53 percent in 1992—about the same as the 1974 rate of 54 percent), and gaps along lines of race and gender have persisted or increased accordingly.[41] Between retrenchment, nonreplacement, contingency, the derogation of such principles as academic freedom, job security, stabilization of institutions, and labor markets, it may still be possible to debate the point at which tenure can be declared an endangered species. Rather than simply arguing over numbers, however, it is worth dwelling on the nature of the beast that we wrestle with. Stanley Aronowitz, in his autoarcheology of professorial work, makes plain that the question of academic labor should address the very conception of our relation between work and life. Flexibility from the perspective of labor raises its own issues of control over time and, with this, the ability to re-negotiate the boundaries between work and leisure, public and private, that are said to assign human activity its value and its just compensation. The well-examined and self-regulated life need not be confined to the precincts of privilege. And if it is, then the battle for the future of academic labor risks being relevant for only a few.

If the lessons of academic labor are to be applied most generally, then the problem of access to institutionalized learning must also be considered. Workfare raises the most dramatic specter of a dire alternative to education *and* edifying work. Adult education programs were one legacy of the 1960s promise codified in the Adult Education Act (1966) to make education universally accessible. For critical educators who work in this area, such as Emily Hacker and Ira Yankwitt, literacy is not a passively acquired technique but a means of "self-transformation." They thus find themselves at odds with the new policy demands that adult education programs do job placement and surveillance while sorting out skills training curricula for workers from coursework allocated to the nonworkers who will be the grist for the workfare mill. Such programs may help close the $2 billion New York City budget gap by replacing unionized city workers and making possible the continued subsidy of wealth through tax abatements, but they also constitute a Slim-fast tonic for the already impoverished student body. The cleaners in civic places who wear orange aprons as a mark of their common sin of poverty offer a cautionary tale. The dream of mobility through educational opportunity is being displaced by the spectacle of public penitence.

The attack on students takes many forms: workfare, tuition increases, scholarship cuts, increased class size, and, when they dare to challenge these, the stiff arm of the law. Students and faculty at CUNY who organized one such response to these attacks received direct instruction in the rougher side of crowd control from some of the police assigned to monitor their march. Yet state violence has not been the only use of government, as the CUNY faculty union found in its successful court challenges to the cuts in funding that have themselves been the grounds for various retrenchment plans on the basis of budgetary-induced fiscal exigency. Bart Meyers makes the linkages between student militancy waged in defense of access to campuses and curricular content, and faculty access to their own organizational structures. As has occurred in other well-established trade unions in this country, a labor insurgency has developed among C U N Y faculty over the union's direction and leadership. For the New Caucus, calls for increased participation have meant greater inclusion of the needs of part-timers in the priorities of collective bargaining and stronger alliances with student activists.

The strength of student activism is not a topic that receives much attention these days, lending credence to the self-serving pronouncements about youth indifference by those who would have young people accept more of less in the distribution of social resources. The warm autumn of 1996 yielded not only a series of labor actions by graduate students and clericals but also a burst of hybrid conference-rallies engaging academics and labor at Columbia, N Y U, and Massachusetts Institute of Technology (M I T). This last meeting was put together by the Cambridge-based Center for Campus Organizing (C C O), a national clearinghouse by and for student activists. In recounting his experiences with the C C O and fleshing out its project, Jeremy Smith challenges the image of an apathetic student body when he discusses the difficulties faced by students who undertake as part of their charge the organization of faculty. He underscores as well the importance of faculty input in student organizations as a form of campus activism. The essays in this book leave no doubt that the future of academic labor rests on such alliances.

While the waves of managerialism have extended the bases for such alliances, ultimately it is organizational form that will sustain them. For the dozens of campuses that are engaged in union organizing, especially among graduate students, this becomes part and parcel of the way in which professionals are socialized. William Vaughn, one of its key organizers, offers a vivid portrait of a graduate student union under construction at the University of Illinois. He indicates the kinds of substantive ties that are forged through organizing activity and helps us imagine all the varied careers for which organizing prepares us. No less than medical residents, who are also beginning to unionize as the power of the last guild in this country erodes and who face uncertain prospects as well, the professional-managerial strata may begin to deconsolidate their community of interest. Workers with various designations of skill and credential may find themselves assigned to read the same manuals of reengineering and accountability, written by authors they commonly see as alien to their ranks. The confusion of mission between public and private institutions—where these distinctions still apply—introduces the potential that organizations on behalf of a genuine social interest can forge combinations of hitherto unforeseen scope. It is not difficult to detect the design of national pedagogy being taught on campus as nothing short of a financial calculus of the self that eclipses labor's actual opportunities. Yet the schooling of life offers other lessons of how people may associate. Higher education is also providing clues to this other principle of organization.

Notes

1 Newt Davidson Collective, epigraph to *Crisis at CUNY* (New York: Newt Davidson Collective, 1974), i.

2 All quotations from the State of the Union Address, February 4, 1997, taken from the official transcript downloaded from the United States Department of Education web site, http://www.ed.gov.

3 For a complete listing of federal education legislation since the first land grants of 1787, see "Federal Programs for Education and Related Activities," in *Digest of Education Statistics* (Washington, D.C.: U.S. Department of Education, National Center for Education Statistics, 1996), 367–78.

4 Clinton, State of the Union Address, February 4, 1997.

5 Ibid.

6 E. Gareth Hoachlander, "New Directions for Policy on Education for Work," *Education and Urban Society* 27, no. 3 (May 1995): 353–62.

7 For perhaps the most complete, more recent discussion of the civil society concept from a left perspective, see Jean Cohen and Andrew Arato, *Civil Society and Political Theory* (Cambridge: MIT Press, 1992). Yet the political pedigree of this concept, like others that have found their way into the Clinton lexicon, is particularly difficult to pin down.

8 Kirk Winters, *An Invitation to Your Community: Building Partnerships for Learning*, a Goals 2000 pamphlet (Washington, D.C.: U.S. Department of Education, 1995), 38.

9 "Goals 2000: Educate America Act, March 31, 1994, P.L. 103-277," in *United States Code Congressional and Administrative News 103rd Congress—Second Session* 1994, vol. 1 (St. Paul, Minn.: West Publishing, 1995), 209.

10 Doug Henwood, *Wall Street* (London: Verso, 1997), 65.

11 William Zumeta and John Fawcett-Long, "State Fiscal and Policy Climate for Higher Education: 1996," in *The NEA 1997 Almanac of Higher Education* (Washington, D.C.: National Education Association [NEA], 1997), 99.

12 James R. Mingle, "Goals for Federal/State Policy in the 21st Century: Affordability, Mobility, and Learning Productivity," paper presented at the U.S. Department of Education conference "Financing Postsecondary Education: The Federal Role," College of Charleston, Charleston, S.C., October 8–9, 1995, n.p.

13 Clyde W. Barrow, "The New Economy and Restructuring Higher Education," *Thought and Action* 12, no. 1 (spring 1996): 42.

14 David M. Gordon, *Fat and Mean: The Corporate Squeeze of Working Americans and the Myth of Managerial "Downsizing"* (New York: Free Press, 1996).

15 These figures are taken from the *Digest of Education Statistics*, 259–63.

16 Ibid., 243.

17 John B. Lee, "Faculty Salaries, 1995–96," in NEA 1997 Almanac, 7.

18 *Digest of Education Statistics*, 234–35.

19 David C. Montgomery and Gwendolyn L. Lewis, "Administrative Staff: Salaries and Issues," NEA 1997 Almanac: *Digest of Education Statistics*, 129–50.

20 Gary Rhoades and Rachel Hendrickson, "Re(con)figuring the Professional Workforce," in 1997 NEA Almanac, 63–82.

21 *Digest of Education Statistics*, 231.

22 Brent Staples, "The End of Tenure? When Colleges Turn to Migrant Labor," *New York Times*, Sunday, June 29, 1997, E14.

23 *Digest of Education Statistics*, 167.

24 Karen Thompson cites a 1993 figure of 51 percent part-timers being women. See her "Alchemy in the Academy: Moving Part-Time Faculty from Piecework to Parity," in *Will Teach For Food*, ed. Cary Nelson (Minneapolis: University of Minnesota Press, 1997).

25 *Digest of Education Statistics*, 267–76.

26 Ibid., 308.

27 Ibid., 361.

28 Ibid., 312.

29 Richard Hurd and Amy Foerster, with Beth Hillman Johnson, *Directory of Fac-*

ulty *Contracts and Bargaining Agents in Institutions Of Higher Education,* 1995 (New York: National Center for the Study of Collective Bargaining in Higher Education and the Professions, 1955), v–ix.

30 Frank Annunziato, "Faculty Strikes in Higher Education," in *Newsletter of the National Center for the Study of Collective Bargaining in Higher Education and the Professions* 22, no. 4 (November/December 1994): 1.

31 Rachel Hendrickson, NEA higher education staff member, personal communication, July 28, 1997.

32 Frank Annunziato, Professional Staff Congress of CUNY, AFT, personal communication, July 29, 1997.

33 Joel M. Douglas, professor in the School of Public Affairs at Baruch College, CUNY, personal communication, July 30, 1997.

34 Clark Kerr, *The Great Transformation in Higher Education, 1960–1980* (Albany: State University of New York Press, 1991), xiv; Gary Rhoades, "Retrenchment Clauses in Faculty Union Contracts: Faculty Rights and Administrative Discretion," *Journal of Higher Education* 64, no. 3 (May/June 1993): 312–47, and the essay by Gary Rhoades and Sheila Slaughter in this book.

35 Frank Annunziato, "Graduate Assistants and Unionization," *Newsletter* NCSCBHEP 22, no. 2 (April/May 1994): 1.

36 Joel M. Douglas, "An Investigation of Employee Involvement Schemes and Governance Structures in Professional Employment," in *Newsletter NCSCBHEP* 23, no. 4 (November/December 1995): 1–8.

37 As a document of that support and a documentation of it, see the essays collected in Cary Nelson's edited collection *Will Teach For Food.* See also Nelson's collection of his own essays on the subject, *Manifesto of a Tenured Radical* (New York: New York University Press, 1997).

38 Sheila Slaughter and Gary Rhoades, "The Emergence of a Competitiveness Research and Development Policy Coalition and the Commercialization of Academic Science and Technology," *Science, Technology, and Human Values* 21, no. 3 (summer 1996): 303–39.

39 "New York Area's Largest Employers, Ranked by Number of City Employees," *Crain's New York Business* 12, no. 53 (January 1997): 38.

40 *Digest of Education Statistics,* 428.

41 Philo A. Hutcheson, "Faculty Tenure: Myth and Reality, 1974 to 1992," *Thought and Action* 12, no. 1 (spring 1996): 7–22. Tenure rates vary over 10 percent between public and private schools. In 1992, among all full-time faculty, people of color made up 14 percent of all full-time faculty, whereas roughly a third were women. While the proportion of women to men who had tenure

rose between the mid-1970s and the mid-1980s, by the early 1990s it was on the decline for all but public universities, where it remained unchanged. Relative to whites and with the exception of Hispanics, proportionately more people of color held non-tenure-track, full-time appointments. This status was held by 32 percent of Asians, 30 percent of blacks, 32 percent of American Indians, 24 percent of Hispanics, and 26 percent of whites.

I

The Whole Business

Academic Capitalism, Managed Professionals, and Supply-Side Higher Education

Gary Rhoades and Sheila Slaughter

The political-economic context of higher education—whether global, regional, national, or local—is changing. So, too, the organizational sites, terms of academic employment, and nature of the professional workforce in higher education are being restratified, restructured, and reconfigured. In the process, the content of work in the academy—of curriculum development, research, and service—is shifting and being redefined. We characterize these trends as the emergence and growth of academic capitalism, of increasingly managed professionals, and of supply-side higher education focused on economic competitiveness.[1]

We begin our essay with excerpts from four cases drawn from our work on restructuring. Academic capitalism, the increased management of professionals, and supply-side higher education policies are not dis-embodied systems and structures. They are lived experiences, deeply embedded in people's daily worlds in colleges and universities. All the practices described in the cases below are not just real but legal as well. They occur to varying degrees across the full spectrum of higher education, from community colleges to research universities.

In the rest of the essay, we analyze the structural patterns of capitalism, management, and supply-side policies that play out in the cases below. We then go beyond these analyses to explore the subtexts of disjuncture realized in any process of social construction. We also explore alternatives, noting and proposing hybrid forms of higher education organization and activity.

Case 1: An increasingly part-time profession. At Eastern Oregon State College, program restructuring enabled the institution to rehire fired full-time faculty on a part-time basis. Professor Carol E. Rathe, music education, was one of four faculty members terminated in program reduction. Initially, she was kept on as a part-time tenured faculty member and paid for a fraction of her tenured appointment. She was then reduced to a "teach only" basis. This new status meant that she was rehired to teach part of her former load, but on a per-course basis that amounted to a fraction of her former salary. The rationale was that she was not engaged in student advising, curriculum planning, supervising, or research. Finally, she was let go entirely.[2]

Case 2: An increasingly managed profession. In early 1982, in response to declining enrollments, the president at Sonoma State University announced that he was restructuring existing programs to deal with students' shift in interests. To inform the faculty of the dimension of the restructuring proposed, he issued a "jeopardy list" that named fifty-three faculty members as candidates for termination. The professors at risk were on the list because their Teaching Services Area (TSA) faced "lack of funds or lack of work." Although the president claimed to honor seniority in dismissals, the flexibility of the unit of retrenchment made determination of seniority difficult. A professor's TSA was determined by the administration, either in individual negotiations with faculty or unilaterally. TSAs were not coterminous with departments. For example, in biology the administration could define a TSA in molecular biology and a TSA in botany, and decide to keep the former and eliminate the latter. The TSA was essentially a mechanism that allowed the president to consider each faculty member individually. Professor William Crowley, chair of geography, publicly disagreed with the president about issues pertinent to the football program. Crowley was fourth in seniority in his TSA, and the president decided to keep only three tenured faculty. Crowley was terminated even though one of his junior colleagues escaped dismissal because the untenured professor was able to transfer from geography to the "safe area" of computer science. Using the TSA as the unit of retrenchment, the administration was able to rid itself of a senior member of the department who acted as a critic and keep a junior professor deemed more valuable.[3]

Case 3: An increasingly capitalistic profession, globally. At New Wave University in Australia, Ronald Collins was head of the Water Systems Institute, a self-sustaining group run by academic professionals. Collins used research grants, royalties, and direct product sales to support his group. His strategy was diversified: at the low technology end, he focused on services and simple product development supplemented by consultancies; at the high end, he tried to develop patents and intellectual property. At the low end he created products that were made in small batches by local manufacturers. At the high end he developed sophisticated electronics, dependent on two chips, produced for him in small quantities by a foreign manufacturer. Collins used the chips in a complex system that he offered to state agencies. Unlike most other centers, the institute generated more money than the university or government agencies put into it. It had no students. Moreover, its entrepreneurial activities called for the addition of more and more professional staff and technicians rather than faculty and graduate students.[4]

Case 4: Increasingly commodified faculty–graduate student relationships. At Nouveau University, faculty were quite explicit about the disruption of faculty-student relationships resulting from increased commercialization of intellectual property. In discussing a program in which management graduate students developed business plans for inventor-scientists who thought they had a discovery with commercial potential, one faculty member noted:

The faculty started becoming reticent with how much information they were gonna give them. . . . [I]t became a source of increased problems, plus the students were starting to see some real payoffs, they were discovering some real market potentials. . . . There was no willingness to sort of get them [faculty] to share with them [students] in an equity sense . . . so now before we get our students involved in these projects . . . we try to minimize the possibility of surprises. . . . [W]e have the faculty member meet with students and we're there, and we have a business person from the outside who is familiar with writing contracts, or letters of intent or whatever, to get the thing laid out. (Andrew Koepplin, professor, information and policy sciences professional school)

Another faculty member said:

But if a student is really committed, if a student is really involved in the project, it becomes their baby and they want a piece of it. . . . I've had friends who've had students who they've had fights with over nonexistent royalties, over the possibility of royalties. (Michael O'Reilly, professor and head, interdisciplinary science unit) [5]

The inequities and inequalities in people's material existence in higher education are vast and expanding. The number of part-time faculty has increased to 43 percent of the total faculty workforce. The percentages vary by field, however, with those fields (and institutions) that teach the largest numbers of undergraduates having the highest percentages of part-time faculty. For instance, 41 percent of faculty in English are part-timers, versus 24 percent in engineering. Similarly, the likelihood of retrenchment (layoffs) varies by field. It is more likely in less prestigious fields, in fields that are perceived to be distant from the "market" — for instance, in education, arts, and social sciences versus in science and math.[6] Ironically, much academic capitalistic activity of the type described in our cases is subsidized by the state. For example, in the 1980s the National Science Foundation (NSF) funded dozens of engineering research centers, which were designed as "partnerships" between business and higher education. Although the intention was to leverage more private support for research, the centers continue to be underwritten largely by the NSF. Essentially, they are state subsidies for entrepreneurial academics and large private corporations. Many universities are increasingly investing in technology transfer activities despite the fact that most such operations fail to generate the revenues they expend.

In short, even as faculty and students in some fields experience reduced support and declining resources, low salaries, and limited employment opportunities, others enjoy increased support and growing resources, high salaries (often triple the mean U.S. salary for a family of four), and a wide range of public and private employment opportunities. In fact, the resources devoted to recruiting and supporting *graduate students* in some fields exceed those devoted to recruiting and supporting *tenure-track faculty* in others. For example, a recent issue of *Academe* focused on the plight of prospective faculty in the Modern Language Association. In some cases, candidates are forced to pay for their interview costs (travel, accommodations, and so forth) if they receive a job offer and do not accept the job. By contrast, prospective graduate students in some fields of engineering are *paid* to visit a department as part of its recruitment activities.

More than just resource inequities, the patterns we point to involve highly differentiated functions and levels of job security for faculty. Even as some units and faculty have increased responsibility for undergraduate teaching accompanied by the layoffs of colleagues replaced by part-time employees, others (as in the physical sciences and engineering, which are experiencing declining undergraduate enrollments) are directed to engage in more and commercially relevant research, accompanied by the hiring of additional peers and nonfaculty professional support staff.

We now turn to three interrelated patterns that are expressed in the cases we described above. In this essay, we separate academic capitalism, managed professionals, and supply-side higher education policies for analytic purposes. However, we regard these economic, political, and ideological dimensions as being, in their concrete practice, all of a piece. They are embedded in a world of increased global economic competition, managerial control, and neoconservative public policy.

Academic Capitalism

In *Academic Capitalism*, Sheila Slaughter and Larry Leslie argue that capitalism is permeating public research universities. The pattern of an academy that is increasingly and explicitly integrated with the service and character of monopoly capital matches a pattern of increased challenge to and crisis of U.S. monopoly capital's competitive global position. We take as "a convenient marker" of the shift the worldwide recession originating in 1973.[7] Since that time, public, block grant support for universities has declined as a share of institutional revenues. In the United States, that translates into a decreased rate of growth in state appropriations and in such appropriations' share of institutional monies, from about 50 percent in 1973 to nearly 33 percent in the 1990s.[8]

What revenue streams have increased their share of university revenues? Tuition and fee increases have outpaced inflation and have increased as a share of institutional monies—from about 15 percent in 1973 to about 22 percent currently. So, too, in public research universities, revenues from grants and contracts have increased, with the greatest share of increases coming from the private sector and from the institution itself (in absolute terms, of course, federal support dominates the grants and contracts portfolio of universities). Universities have increasingly moved to applied and entrepreneurial science to generate revenues, establishing research parks and technology transfer offices. Finally, public universities have turned more and more to fund-raising activities, establishing development offices and foundations within the past ten to fifteen years. Campaigns to raise millions of dollars have become commonplace in a sector where twenty-five years ago fund-raising was simply a matter of alumni contributions.

The revenue mix and the character of the revenue streams have changed considerably for public higher education. The move toward academic capitalism is partly a move toward higher tuition (in competition with other institutions in the academic marketplace), more competitive grants and contracts, more solicited private gifts, and other sorts of competitive monies.

Yet academic capitalism is more than that. Not-for-profit institutions in the academy are taking on the characteristics and activities of profit-making organizations. Universities are not just servants of or suppliers to the marketplace. They are active players in the marketplace. For example, universities are investors and equity holders in their faculty members' start-up companies. They are developers and owners of commercial products (patents) that they financially help bring from the lab to the market, with technology development corporations which may be at "arms length" but which are clearly attached to the university. Universities are parties to and partners in contractual arrangements in which they sell the rights to their employees' activities, knowledge, and products to private enterprise. Universities, public and private alike, have gone way "beyond the ivory tower," participating in privatization, deregulation, and commercialization to a greater degree than any public institutions other than the federal laboratories.[9]

We are witnessing, in higher education, the "privatization" of yet another public domain. To a remarkable degree, there has been a dramatic inversion of not-for-profit universities' ideological underpinnings. In the past, the belief system surrounding the public interest has been that public entities (and actors) must be kept separate from the private domain and that the public interest is best served by preventing conflict of interest. Now, the public interest is said to be served by directly involving public entities in the private sector and by fostering the pursuit of private profit. So, for example, state conflict-of-interest laws for public employees have been changed to exempt public university professors engaged in technology transfer activities. The shift strikes to the heart of professional ideology—professionals no longer are believed to act simply out of commitment to the intellectual enterprise and to the welfare of society (and of clients). Faculty/inventors need a material incentive to develop and transfer knowledge from the lab to the marketplace. So, too, with organizations. Public universities have redefined public service, from service for free to services (often renamed as outreach) for a fee.[10]

With regard to students, the ideology of the marketplace rules as well. Promoters and translators of Total Quality Management (TQM) in higher education have the language right but the players wrong. Students are neither "customers" or "consumers." They are the "industry's" "inputs" and "products." The purchasers of the products—private, corporate "employers"—are the customers. The push, then, is to improve (standardize) the product by "improving" the input, a strategy that has clear implications (and no place) for access and affirmative action.

Subtexts

The dominant text we have mapped out thus far should be amended with various subtexts of divergence and disjuncture. For example, the language and pattern of academic capitalism suggest that academic institutions (and professions) have become capitalist entrepreneurs. The "risks" undertaken by such academic capitalists, however, are publicly underwritten. Although in the private-sector marketplace there are state subsidies for capital as well, universities and colleges are far less likely to go "belly up" than are entrepreneurial enterprises in the private economy. For all the talk of private colleges and universities going bankrupt, the mortality rate of enterprises in higher education as an organizational field is quite low. That is even more true in the case of public colleges and universities, where any entrepreneurial activity is state-subsidized.

Moreover, much of the "competitive monies" that institutions are increasingly relying on are actually public-sector monies. Consider the case of tuition. Colleges and universities compete for the tuition dollars of prospective, private consumers of a college education. Yet there have been no "tuition wars" evidencing competitive pricing in this industry. The recent history of tuition increases has more the flavor of monopolistic practice or of an "artificially" state-supported price structure. To some extent in higher education, not unlike in the health care industry, costs have been inflated by state subsidy. A large proportion of tuition monies, particularly in expensive private colleges and universities, are underwritten by a massive set of institutional, state, and federal subsidies in the form of fee waivers, loans, grants, and fellowships.

Similarly, consider research monies. The overwhelming proportion of these monies continues to come from the federal government. To become more competitive in obtaining such grants and contracts does not mean turning to private markets and competing for private monies. By and large, it means working more successfully toward obtaining another kind of public money. For all the courting efforts of universities, private enterprise has never been willing to substitute its monies for those coming from the federal government (with the exception of biotechnology). The private sector's share of support for university research has increased, but it remains quite small in relative terms—about 8 percent.[11] Colleges and universities' revenue portfolios are becoming more diverse and competitive, but only very slightly more privatized. Change is at the margins.

There is an irony in higher education's courtship of business. Higher education is playing supplicant to an industry with an inferior performance record. Unlike private business, U.S. higher education, as an "industry," has an excellent record in terms of its global competitiveness.

Arguably, it is globally dominant, not unlike corporate America's position in the early post-World War II years. U.S. graduate education and research have not only long been dominant in terms of production and quality, but other countries are increasingly modeling their doctoral education along U.S. lines as well. By contrast, in terms of quality across the board, undergraduate education in the United States has not been regarded as superior. Yet several major competitors at this level—for example, the United Kingdom, Australia, and many continental European systems—have experienced such fiscal distress and major structural change (mergers between traditional universities and "lesser" colleges) that they have lost ground relative to the United States. Moreover, if we shift the index from "quality" to competitiveness in "balance of trade" terms, the United States is clearly dominant: we attract far more international students than other countries attract U.S. students who study abroad.[12]

In addition, for all the criticism of American higher education, its value is stronger and higher than that of many central U.S. industries. Unlike the stock market, which experienced crashes during the past two decades, it has not seen dramatic drops in value. The "rate of return" on higher education continues to be high, even amid "massification." And colleges and universities have not gone bankrupt, as have so many savings and loans.[13]

Perhaps the most obvious way in which academic capitalism diverges from its private-sector counterpart is in its cost structure. In stark contrast to private industry, academic enterprises continue to be very labor intensive. Between 75 and 85 percent of most colleges' and universities' expenditures are in personnel costs. Academic institutions are not shipping jobs overseas and laying off tens of thousands of employees. (As we will discuss below, however, many of the practices utilized in the private sector to cut personnel costs—using part-timers, replacing workers with technology—are also being used in colleges and universities.)

Alternatives

The trend toward academic capitalism is associated with new organizational forms. In research universities the boundaries between public and private become blurred, permeable, and alterable. They are neither public nor private but are more (and less) than both. The dichotomies that shape our conceptions of universities in the organizational firmament—public versus private, state versus independent, regulated versus autonomous—no longer make sense.

Interestingly, such hybridity appears to be most dramatic in public colleges and universities, which may be the organizational exemplars of Reaganomics. In these public sites it may be easier to develop hybrid forms because of the traditional autonomy of higher education. (Public interest has always been linked to the economy. Land-grant universities were created to link higher education to the needs of agriculture and industry—the most significant public services they performed were economic, as in the extension services of agriculture colleges.) Higher education's set of "defenses" against external intrusion have traditionally been oriented to autonomy from state. They are ill-suited to prevent not-for-profit entities from adopting for-profit orientations. Thus, higher education may be at the cutting edge in melding public and private in hybrid forms.

The general revenue trends that we have mapped and the rise of academic capitalism are perhaps most dramatic for and relevant to the experience of public research universities. However, similar capitalistic hybridization can be found in other sectors of higher education. For example, public research universities are not alone among higher education enterprises in seeking to capitalize on the intellectual property created by their workers. Moreover, there is hybridization in the "tech prep" activities of community colleges and in academic programs directly "Taylored" to the needs of particular companies—contract education. Such educational activities go beyond the traditional servicing of the private sector to privatizing public-sector functions/services.

Such hybridization in higher education does not exist simply "at the margins." It defines the increasingly central activities of colleges and universities. And, as we shall show in discussing supply-side higher education, it also increasingly defines what is regarded as central in higher education.

Other forms are possible and, in our view, desirable. In particular, we would favor a hybrid form that bore the genetic imprint less of large, private, capitalist workplaces and more of community-based, public, democratically controlled social services. That might mean colleges and universities would produce and own property but that the proceeds would be disbursed and (re)invested in a publicly, democratically controlled process.

Our organizational preferences are grounded not just in the external distributive effects of these hybrid forms but also in their capitalist working conditions. In the ensuing section, then, we explore the implications of these hybrids for professionals' employment rights and for managers' employment practices.

Managed Professionals

Just as colleges and universities are becoming more entrepreneurial in a pattern of increased academic capitalism, so they are becoming more managerial in their governance and in their workforce. Faculty are increasingly "managed professionals," owing to extensive, growing managerial flexibility vis-à-vis employees. Moreover, faculty represent a decreasing proportion of the professional workforce on college and university campuses: the growth category is nonfaculty, "managerial" professionals.[14] Such trends are found in all higher education sectors.

In recent years, the discourse of executive administrators in higher education has been marked by a corporate "language of alterations." Colleges and universities are (pick your phrase) streamlining, downsizing, repositioning, reengineering, and restructuring. Academic programs are being merged, reduced, and reorganized. Faculty are, depending on one's rhetorical sensibilities, being retrenched, laid off, riffed, or reallocated. There is much talk of "tough choices," contrasted with a mythical recent past in which budget reductions were achieved by sharing the pain and cutting across the board. Now, however, faculty are told, not just by provosts, deans, and department heads but by many of their peers, that a continuation of equity-based cuts will compromise quality.[15] Thus the repeated campus exercises of assessing programs according to their "centrality," which has replaced merit/quality as the coin of the academic realm.

In the current context, there is a push for increased managerial "flexibility" in dealing with human resources, whether in hiring, firing, or re-allocating faculty (lines). Flexibility is a trope (and trump) for power. Its repeated invocation is a means by which to legitimate changing the balance of power between faculty and administration, altering faculty's professional terms of employment. Renewed challenges to tenure are a case in point. Such challenges are found even at the elite levels of the higher education system—public and private research universities. An example is the 1996–97 tenure battle at the University of Minnesota surrounding policy changes to enable executives to fire tenured faculty more easily by reorganizing academic programs. (More to the point, administrators already enjoy such flexibility in the current retrenchment policies of most colleges and universities—that is, program elimination and reorganization is a legal justification for retrenching tenured faculty. Such language is more far-reaching than the justification of financial exigency ever was.) Another instance is the recent lawsuit filed by basic science faculty at the University of Southern California's medical school. The suit charges that the school's renegotiation of faculty contracts violates their tenure. Changes include reducing the contract from twelve to nine months and a provision that tenure ensures faculty a position in the medical school but not a full salary. Faculty must raise most of their salary on their own—through grants and contracts or patient fees. In both these cases, academic capitalism has been accompanied by renegotiated terms of employment that accord managers in major research universities greater "flexibility" vis-à-vis tenured faculty, even in the most prestigious and lucrative parts of the institutions.

If such a pattern is found throughout higher education, the most extensive evidence of "managed professionals" is found in the nonelite sectors of higher education. A large proportion of such colleges and universities, particularly in the public sector, are unionized. Over 1,000 campuses and more than 240,000 faculty are represented by collective-bargaining agents. (The percentage of faculty covered—about 44 percent—is far higher than the percentage of workers in the economy that are unionized—16 percent.) About 60 percent of campuses and 63 percent of full-time faculty in the public sector are covered by faculty union contracts. A database of 212 such contracts (45 percent of the total) has been compiled on CD-ROM, enabling us to track faculty's terms of employment nationally in collective-bargaining agreements.[16]

Gary Rhoades has analyzed these agreements, focusing on managerial discretion as it is embedded in salary structures, retrenchment clauses, and in policies regarding the use of part-time faculty and of instructional technology and regarding outside employment and intellectual property. We think the patterns found in largely nonelite, unionized higher education are relevant for those of us who are not covered by collective-bargaining agreements. The growth and exercise of managerial discretion are paralleled in the two sectors, in quality if not entirely in degree.

Consider salary structures. Contrary to popular perception, unions are antithetical neither to merit nor to market mechanisms for determining faculty pay. Most four-year institutions have such structures embedded in their contracts. Of course, across-the-board salary increases are a central part of negotiated wages, as are salary scales that establish step increases for seniority and certification. Yet, in over two-thirds of the agreements, managers have the discretion to set initial salaries, according to merit or to market conditions.

Salary dispersion among faculty by field and by gender is extensive and expanding throughout higher education. It has developed to such an extent in unionized institutions—though less so than in nonunionized ones—that equity clauses are found in nearly one-half of the contracts in four-year institutions. (Such clauses are most commonly related to general or market-based, but not gender-based, inequities.) In higher education generally, the largest increases in the 1980s in average faculty salaries were in those fields which were already at the top of the salary hierarchy, and the smallest increases are found in those fields toward the bottom of the hierarchy.[17] Similarly, the gender gap in faculty salaries *increased* between 1972 and 1992, at a time when the gender gap in the general and professional workforces *decreased*.

The shifting balance of power in the politics of professional work is perhaps most evident in retrenchment clauses. The already extensive managerial discretion to lay off (tenured) faculty has expanded. Many contracts neither define nor identify conditions to justify retrenching faculty. In most contracts that do, such conditions include various noncrisis justifications, financial and otherwise, for layoffs. Very few contracts utilize the language of financial exigency, the rhetorical subject of much debate in the 1970s. Instead, the current rhetoric speaks to the reorganization or curtailment of academic programs. Such matters are not curricular decisions, resting in the academic domain, based on academic judgments about quality. They are, instead, strategic decisions, resting in the managerial domain, based on executive judgments about centrality and mission. Such retrenchment provisions are not unique to unionized institutions.

Most higher education institutions have gone through some campus exercise of strategic planning. National surveys suggest that nearly half have eliminated academic programs in the process, reallocating resources accordingly. This point is key. The most consequential reorganization lies not in firing fairly small numbers of faculty but in systematically reallocating faculty and other resources among programs. Unionized faculty, like faculty in nonunionized settings, have negotiated a range of structures and provisions—for example, for consultation, adequate notice of layoff, order of layoff by seniority, recall rights—that make it more procedurally and politically difficult than managers would like to lay off faculty. Managers, however, not only retain the final authority in virtually all such matters but also enjoy the flexibility to make exceptions to established procedures. (For example, they can violate the order of layoff if they believe that to follow such order would violate the quality or integrity of the unit.) Most important, managers have claimed and gained control over the determination of various strategic academic choices about where to invest the institution's resources.

One of the greatest sources of managerial flexibility in allocating faculty resources is the use of part-time faculty, who may be hired and released far more easily than full-timers. And managers are exercising that flexibility to hire increased numbers of part-time faculty. Throughout higher education, the proportion of part-time faculty nearly doubled from 1970 to 1991, increasing from 21.9 percent of the senior instructional workforce to 43 percent. And, according to a national survey of faculty, of those faculty hired in the past seven years, only one-third are full-time, tenure-track faculty. The rest are contract, contingent, and part-time faculty.[18]

In collective-bargaining agreements, there are relatively few (about 20 percent) workforce provisions that effectively control the proportions of full- versus part-time faculty, limiting the hiring of the latter. Moreover, on unionized campuses as on nonunionized ones, part-time and contingent faculty are marginalized. Indeed, many full-time faculty are content to contain them at the margins. Yet the hiring and workforce trends of recent decades are reducing the centrality of full-time faculty in the teaching workforce. Another source of growing managerial discretion is the use of instructional technology. Technology may not transform education, but it will affect social relations. It is another means by which managers can bypass faculty's bailiwick, the curriculum. It is a delivery system that can be staffed largely by part-time faculty. It is an area of academic activity in which state legislators and institutional managers are willing to invest. Ironically, much of that investment involves the hiring of technical support and nonfaculty professional personnel, as well as the buying or upgrading of equipment at a time when other instructional functions are being severely underfunded. If the ideal institution for faculty is one without students, the ideal college/university for managers is one without permanent faculty, a virtual university that is not only without walls but also without full-time, tenured faculty.

Despite the urging of national faculty unions, only a little over one-third of faculty contracts have provisions regarding instructional technology. For the most part, such provisions are limited efforts to protect current faculty against the involuntary use of and abuse from instructional technology. There is no effort to establish proactively involvement in or control of a range of decisions, educational and otherwise, surrounding the use of instructional technology. Faculty in nonunionized settings are if anything even less aware and collectively active.

We see faculty, including ourselves, as being technologically challenged, using the term as an adjective and as an adverb. In our field of higher education, as in the fields of most readers of this journal, we are stuck in an underfunded area of dirty blackboards and malfunctioning overheads. We need only walk around campus to find that more advanced technology, instructional and otherwise, exists in better resourced units of the university. Some such units are academic departments, and the budgets of our departments suffer the opportunity costs of investing in costly technologies elsewhere. Some are support units, however, not a few of which are focused on technologically enhanced instructional delivery. The model here is one of hiring various technicians, clerical personnel, and some nonfaculty professionals to staff these highly capitalized units. In unionized settings, managers are hiring more nonfaculty, nonbargaining-unit personnel to coordinate the delivery of an increased share of the instructional workload technologically and with the use of part-time faculty. In nonunionized settings, there may be variations on this theme of increasingly managed electronic subcontracting. In any case, full-time faculty are decentered, as part of the professional workforce and as producers and deliverers of the curriculum.

Subtexts

A minor departure from the general text is suggested by the case of outside employment and intellectual property rights clauses in collective-bargaining agreements. Part of the general theme of increased managerial discretion is that professional discretion is more likely to be compromised and even supplanted in less prestigious colleges and universities. This is consistent with our profession's assumption about the connection between faculty's expertise and their workplace autonomy. And it is consistent with the assumption, even among most critics of the system, from neo-Marxists and feminists to critical theorists and postmodernists, that faculty expertise is positively related to institutional prestige. (We are less inclined to apply the tenets of social constructionism to our own professional position than we are to the institutions and professions of others.)

Throughout the system, in unionized and nonunionized settings, there is evidence of increased managerial sway in regard to faculty members' time. Such is clear not just in contact-hour and course-load debates and in management pressures to increase our office hours and "mentoring" activities. It is also evident in outside employment and intellectual property rights policies. Yet in outside employment it seems that faculty in unionized settings enjoy greater control of their time than do faculty in research universities. For example, in research universities the standard provision regarding outside employment is the so-called one-day-a-week rule. Less than 3 percent of faculty contracts have such limits. It also appears that intellectual property provisions are more generous to faculty claims to "their own time" (to create property) and on their property in the contracts of two-year as compared with four-year institutions. In both cases, breaking from the general pattern, professional autonomy is greater in the less prestigious higher education institutions.

There are other divergences from the general pattern of increased managerial discretion. In contrast to the experience of unions in the private sector, the numbers of unionized campuses and of faculty members represented by collective-bargaining agents are growing. This despite the Yeshiva case, which, ironically, supported management's challenge to the faculty union on the grounds that academics are managerial personnel (and, indeed, that unionization is extremely limited in private higher education). Even part-timers are increasingly organizing.

Despite this growth, there is not the same full-blown managerial assault on faculty and their unions that is found in the private sector. (Yet there is a Republican assault in state legislatures on public-sector collective bargaining.) To some extent, this may have something to do with the relative quiescence of faculty unions. Well over half (58 percent) of the contracts have no-strike clauses (which apply during the terms of the contract). And from 1984 to 1994, there were only forty-eight strikes nationwide. Yet strikes and resistance on the part of faculty are usually minor variations on a dominant theme. Overall, in the academy's sociopolitical relations, executives are gaining greater discretion and flexibility in restructuring the faculty workforce.

Alternatives

Accompanying the pattern of increasingly managed professionals is a pattern of increased numbers of what Rhoades calls "managerial professionals." These employees do not fit squarely into the category of *faculty* or *administrator* but constitute an occupational type that bridges conventional categories. They share many characteristics of traditional liberal professions—a technical body of knowledge, advanced education (and in some cases certification), professional associations and journals, and codes of ethics. Yet they also mark a break with the liberal profession of faculty, being more closely linked and subordinate to managers and indeed being very much managers themselves. Such differences are plain in personnel practices—managerial professionals are hired, evaluated, and fired more by administrative superiors than by professional peers. Differences are also plain in their workday existence—a nine-to-five day and eleven-month contract pattern, marked by more contact with superiors and subordinates than with peers or clients.

Managerial professionals are the "middle management" of higher education, with two important inversions. First, in contrast to the large-scale layoffs of middle managers in private industry, managerial professionals are the growth category in higher education's professional workforce. From 1977 to 1989, their numbers increased by nearly 100 percent, compared with 19 percent for faculty and 37 percent for executives/administrators. That growth continues in a time of budget reductions in higher education. Not long ago, faculty represented the professionals on campus, accounting for 64 percent of that workforce. By 1989, they accounted for a little over half (55 percent) of that workforce, with the proportions continuing to decline. A second inversion is that managerial professionals are not "unproductive" labor. They are central production workers on campus. Some are directly involved in producing students (student services and instructional technology), research (research professionals and administrators, grants and contracts writers in administration), and service/outreach (technology transfer professionals). Others are directly involved in generating revenue for the institution (development professionals). In not just numerical but in functional terms as well, faculty are being decentered as the sole professional production workers on campus.

In some notable instances faculty are responding to increases in administrative power and being decentered by academic professionals by utilizing blue- and white-collar union political tactics and forming common political cause with nonprofessional groups. There have been few strikes of faculty, or cases of organized political resistance, in response to managers' workforce actions. However, a few cases pose the possibility and potential strength of collective action that extends beyond the faculty. Many readers will be familiar with the protests at the City University of New York that Bart Meyers discusses in this book. Less familiar, perhaps, is the case of San Diego State University, where in the early 1990s

President Tom Day proposed "deep and narrow" cuts, leading to the elimination of over 150 faculty positions. After considering and following traditional channels of politics, in the academic senate and in the form of grievances, the faculty union piggybacked on student protests and began working with them and with various political constituencies in the community. They challenged the president's actions not with the tools of the collegium or the contract but in the streets and in the press. Their efforts eventually won the day. The chancellor of the California State University system ordered President Day to rescind the layoff notices, and no full-time faculty were fired. A few years later, President Day resigned. Such cases pose the possibility, and possible success, of faculty joining forces politically with other groups in and outside the academy.[19] Such action points the way to an alternative text for faculty unions and for faculty in general in the politics of the professional workplace. This alternative was successfully pursued in previous decades by various white-collar, public-sector unions and professions such as nurses and social welfare workers. The effectiveness of such unions depends on strategic political alliances and mobilization, on framing negotiations in ways that go beyond the worker to the public agenda and public needs.[20]

Ironically, such collectivist social movement unionism has recently emerged in what was that most independent of professions, medicine. Physicians within a health maintenance organization (HMO) in Tucson voted in December of 1996 by nearly a 3–1 margin, to be represented by the Federation of Physicians and Dentists, an affiliate of the American Federation of State, County, and Municipal Employees. The spokesperson for the union framed the issue not in terms of salaries (which declined) or job security (which was eliminated in contracts that allow the HMO to lay off physicians at will) but in terms of the doctor-patient relationship and the quality/choice of medical care and procedures.

Faculty should take note. In our view, if faculty are to regain some influence over their work lives and workplaces, they must move beyond the ideological and political position of being independent professionals and connect their work and their professional ideology to the interests of the immediate communities and broader publics that they serve. To do so would engender a very different political discourse than that which continues to characterize policy discussions and decisions today.

Supply-Side Higher Education

In the 1970s, U.S. corporations experienced crises in profits and productivity. Globally, their dominance was challenged. In response, U.S. policies to regain position in world markets were marked by a decided shift to neoconservative, supply-side economics. These policies concentrated public monies on private-sector corporations, largely through changes in tax policy. The conviction was that tax incentives would lead to the creation of greater amounts of wealth, thereby stimulating the economy. The benefits of this wealth creation would then trickle down to all.

Reaganomics generally meant reduced funding for the state's welfare function. It meant incorporating various state functions that had the potential to generate and transfer wealth into the private sector through policies that promoted privatization, deregulation, and commercialization of public-sector entities, or of potentially lucrative elements of public-sector entities. In other words, it meant the creation of organizational forms that bridged public and private in the service of wealth creation.

As Slaughter points out, as with Reaganomics in the general economy in the 1980s, so with higher education.[21] Federal legislative changes overturned the university's traditional position toward intellectual property, in which such property was the byproduct of the quest for knowledge, and instead made knowledge embodied in products and processes for global markets the focus of science. In the 1980s, in a bipartisan effort, federal agencies, in concert with Congress, fashioned various policies designed to promote closer connections between the business world and higher education and to promote more commercially relevant research in research universities. The aim was to enhance U.S. corporations' economic competitiveness. A central aspect of the mechanism for attaining this goal is that federal (and state) legislation deregulated the organizational perimeters and parameters of universities, fostering and underwriting the emergence of forms that bridged the public and private worlds.

Indeed, federal funding patterns for university research reflect a supply-side approach, which directs monies to wealth producers or at least to those fields and units that are perceived as wealth producers. In the

1980s, universities realized an increased share of applied research monies and of development monies. Social science's share of N S F funding was cut in half (and was already low, at 6 percent). The National Endowment for the Arts was reduced. And monies for biotechnology and engineering have increased substantially.

Accompanying such revenue changes in the support of research is an interesting rhetorical shift. What was once referred to as *basic* and then *fundamental research* is now often referred to in reports as *curiosity-driven research*. It is not too far of a leap to transform that phrase into *curious research*, research that is a mere curiosity and certainly not as central as basic science.

Yet things get curiouser and curiouser in this supply-side world. The revenue patterns for research are in many cases inversely related to the flow of undergraduates. Most students are not in engineering and the physical sciences. In fact, math, engineering, and the physical sciences have experienced declines in undergraduate student numbers in recent years, matched by an increase in numbers of graduate students. No doubt Modern Language Association members, historians, and social scientists can guess what the pattern is in their fields: increased numbers of under-graduates and decreasing numbers of graduate students.

Over a twenty-year period the arts and sciences' share of total degrees declined, from 45 percent in 1973–74 to 34 percent in 1990–91. Traditional arts and sciences are no longer the curricular center of the university in particular or of higher education in general. During this same time, professional degrees rose, from 55 percent to 62 percent. In fact, such professional degrees even increased within liberal arts colleges, selective and unselective alike.[22]

Yet professional fields have not shared equally in the growth. Indeed, many professional areas are down in enrollments, including agriculture, education, library science, public affairs, and social work. Engineering is down in undergraduate enrollments but up in numbers of graduate students. The professional field that rules in this neoconservative period is, not surprisingly, business.

The picture is even more dramatic when we look at students' course-taking behavior. A national sample of students in the 1970s and 1980s revealed a significant shift away from education and toward business.

53

Clifford Adelman finds that in the 1980s the "empirical core curriculum," that is, the courses in which the largest numbers of students earn credit, is dominated by business fields.[23] Of the top thirty-five courses in the 1980s, six were in business and accounting, compared with two in the 1970s. Many arts and sciences fields that are traditional centers of general education decline in prominence in this empirical core: biology, chemistry, American (also English) literature, music, physics, psychology, sociology, U.S. history, and Western civilization. Of the six courses that dropped out of the core in these two decades, three are in arts and sciences—geology, geography, and German—and two others are in professional areas that have large numbers of women—education and nursing (the sixth is Bible studies).

The culture wars around the canon are mere skirmishes compared with this large-scale war of attrition. The proportion of students who earned bachelor's degrees who took courses in African American, Hispanic American, and Native American studies actually declined from the 1970s to the 1980s, down from 3.1, 1.3, and 2.9 percent to 1.9, .9, and 1.7 percent, respectively. Women's studies experienced a slight increase, from 6 percent to 7.1 percent, hardly one that suggests a feminist takeover that threatens curricular emasculation. All history courses are down. Western civilization lives—28.3 percent of students earning bachelor's degrees have earned credits in such a course—but is declining (down from 29.3 percent). U.S. history persists (at 37.9 percent) but is also down (from 42.1 percent). The story of the 1980s is perhaps most clearly revealed in English courses: literature is down, from American (23.1 to 18.6 percent) to English (16.5 to 13.4 percent) and general (31.1 to 24.5 percent); and composition and writing are up, from freshman composition (73.6 to 79.8 percent) to remedial writing (15.9 to 19.5 percent) and technical writing (7.8 to 16.7 percent). As against these numbers, keep in mind that computer science and computer programming more than doubled, from 8.4 and 10.2 percent to 22.2 and 25 percent. And the following business courses had share increases of greater than 10 percent: introduction to accounting (23 to 39.4 percent), marketing management (12.6 to 29.1 percent), general management (19.2 to 31 percent), finance (16.4 to 27.2 percent), business law (20.2 to 30.9 percent), general business principles (9.1 to 18.7 percent), and business correspondence (.5 to

10.8 percent). In short, canon battles are anachronistic. Canons are out-moded weapons, relevant and relegated to a colonial past, and not very effective in the face of a postcolonial, long-term, deeply entrenched pattern of business rule in a global economy.

What does this mean for students? It depends on which students you are talking about. The federal government's differential investment in fields and its supply-side policies shift the emphasis, in complex and differentiated ways, to distinctive conceptions of and policies toward students. Neoconservative discourse of the 1980s and 1990s focuses on quality and productivity, juxtaposing them to equity and access. Affirmative action for categories of students that historically and in an ongoing way have experienced discrimination is replaced by affirmative action for some students in key fields.

Public discourse is now filled with recriminations against those people, groups, and policies that seek to counter our ongoing history of discrimination as if efforts to challenge and change discrimination are the cause of tension and divisions in society. As a matter of policy and resources, our distribution concentrates public resources on those fields and students that are by virtue of private circumstance and support already relatively privileged. Policies driven by a concern with enhancing corporate competitiveness concentrate resources on fields that are seen as potential wealth creators, fields in which women and minorities are vastly under-represented.

The broad policy concern with corporate competitiveness transforms the ways in which students are conceived and thus are supported. Currently, a driving concern in reforming education is to better prepare students for "the workplace." Students are no longer as much individuals having a right to access or seeking upward mobility or both. They are, instead, future workers. More to the point, they are future cogs in the global corporate machine and economy. Thus, what is critical is that they be interchangeable, that they be standardized, that they be high quality, and that they be prepared in certain fields. (In an important divergence, in those key fields—science, math, and engineering—when there was a sense that supply was down, the NSF pushed for education reform to attract more students and for affirmative action because the demographics were such that there were not enough white males.)

Access, then, is no longer the driving emphasis of federal or state policy. In a period of attacks on governmental expenditures and of fiscal crises of states and of the state, less money is being devoted to ensuring access for those who are less well off. Although the policy discourse shifted to a combination of high tuition and high aid, the governmental resources did not follow suit. For example, although federal grant aid has increased in absolute terms, it lags far behind increases in college costs. Whereas the maximum Pell Grant award (the dominant federal award) in 1980 covered nearly 80 percent of tuition in public four-year institutions and nearly 40 percent of tuition in four-year privates, by 1994 the numbers dropped to 35 percent for publics and 15 percent for privates. Moreover, there has been a significant shift in the form of student aid, from grants to loans. Since 1990, the amount borrowed in Federal Family Education Loans and the number of borrowers have increased by 50 percent. Nor have states picked up the slack, particularly for poorer students. Nationwide, the share of need-based grants has fallen in proportion to all state grants.[24] Affirmative action in the legal realm is under fire from neoconservatives who now claim to champion need-based policies. But the supply-side policies and the attendant resource patterns of neoconservatives belie such a commitment. Regarding students as well as fields, supply-side policies concentrate wealth on the wealthy. Supply-side policies (and conceptions of education and of students) are evident not just in general federal economic and social policy but also in universities' own investment patterns. Universities, which are both cultural in their discursive effects and political-economic in their distributive effects, are inscribing themselves with the markers and practices of supply-side economics.

One of the more dramatic examples of such internal disciplining is to be found in the arts. Tom Moylan has graphically detailed one more recent example of such restructuring, in Canada's Banff Centre. Similarly, one of our students is now conducting a dissertation on restructuring fine arts departments in public research universities.[25] What she is finding is in some ways consistent with Moylan's analysis, but with a very significant variation. Like Moylan, she finds that one aspect of restructuring is relabeling and repackaging. Rooms and classes that were once labeled *studios* are now *labs*. Restructuring is also reallocating resources and restratifying fields. But this is not simply a matter of a "hostile take-over," in Moylan's words. It is a makeover, in the worst sense of the term. It is a gendered action, in which a field with relatively large numbers of women voluntarily inscribes itself with externally defined markers of desirability. It is a process of internally reshaping the field's essence, re-defining "centrality." Faculty, student, and financial/capital resources are shifted from some sites (for example, sculpture and painting) to others (such as graphic arts and design). This academic cosmetic surgery is more than superficial. It involves transforming, not just mortifying, the arts to increase efficiency, productivity, and thus attractiveness in the university.

This is but a small example of restructuring within the university. Public research universities dramatize the nature and workings of the changes. They demonstrate that restructuring processes are not simply the result of hostile external takeovers, of universities being dominated and driven by external, corporate patterns of resource flows. Restructuring is a matter of institutions internally reallocating their own resources.

As noted, public research universities have diversified their revenue portfolio, generally depending on state appropriations for less than 33 percent of their monies. Nevertheless, those state monies are a significant chunk of university budgets. They are based in considerable part on enrollments, particularly of undergraduates. States give public research universities monies to educate the state's students. But once universities receive those block grants of state appropriations, they reallocate them in ways that are not tightly linked to student numbers. In our university, not unlike many other public research universities, the biggest predictors of an academic unit's share of state appropriations are external grants and contracts. Large numbers of women faculty and students and large numbers of lower-division undergraduates are negatively correlated with shares, a finding that is consistent with national studies of faculty salaries (the salary effect of a field having relatively large numbers of women, holding constant productivity, is negative) and of departmental budgets. In another study, the factors most positively related to state appropriations are graduate hours (undergraduate hours have a slightly positive effect), with very strong "halo" effects for being a unit in engineering and natural sciences. In other words, independent of productivity measures (such as student credit hours or sponsored research), simply being a unit within engineering or natural science pays large dividends.[26]

Another dramatization of universities' reallocation of their monies internally is found in research expenditures. Nationally, instruction's share of institutional expenditures is down in every sector of higher education. Administration's share is up in every sector of higher education. In research universities, research's share of institutional expenditures is also up. Where does this money come from? The largest (share) increase in research expenditures over the past decade has been not from the federal government (that is down, from 69 percent in 1973 to 56 percent in 1993), not from the state and local government (that is down, from 10 percent in 1973 to 9 percent in 1993), not from the private sector (that is up, from 3 percent in 1973 to 7 percent in 1993), but from universities themselves (up, from 11 percent in 1973 to 20 percent in 1993). Universities are reinvesting their monies internally in administration and research.[27]

In the academy, Arthur Laffer (invest in the rich) has met Robert K. Merton (the Matthew Effect—the best get richer).[28] Sometimes the best and the rich fields match. Sometimes they do not. In 1992, in a study of restructuring, one of us was interviewing department heads in an East Coast research university that had nationally prominent departments in history, English, and some social sciences. Its science departments were not nearly so strong. One question heads were asked was, How do you think your department will fare in the restructuring process the university is undergoing? In response, the head of physics, who indicated that his unit was "second rate" in terms of academic standing, said that he was sure (and had been assured by central administration) that physics would do well. After all, "You can't have a first-class research university in the twenty-first century without a strong physics department." Heads in history, English, and sociology expressed no such confidence, despite the academic reputations of their units. Merit is no longer what matters most. The potential for wealth creation now dominates.

Subtexts

There are various disjunctures and ironies that underlie, but have not come close to undermining, the text outlined above. Cultural studies and women's studies are good examples of fields that hardly can be seen as favored by neoconservative discourse or supply-side policies. As noted earlier, women's studies continues to grow. So does cultural studies. Of course, such programs can be seen as constituting quite small, isolated, and neglected social spaces in higher education from which a few scholars launch cultural critiques of textual patterns and ideological agendas. Yet, as Moylan has suggested, to the extent that these programs become disconnected from larger social movements and critiques of the economic order, or to the extent they are unintelligible except to the initiated, these spaces may actually serve to reinforce the existing order and draw strength and resources away from other progressive programs and projects.

Amid a broad patriarchal text of downsizing and eliminating programs that have relatively large numbers of women, there is a feminist subtext of continued growth in women's studies, in faculty, students, and in legitimacy, as increased numbers of traditional, discipline-based departments incorporate women's studies and as increased numbers of distinct women's studies programs achieve departmental status. Yet such spaces of difference are struggled for and created not in vacuums but in situated professional and political contexts. The distinctiveness of such spaces can be mitigated and even diminished by the struggle to survive and by the context of what is privileged and why. Therein lies a central debate within women's studies about the academic elitism of the field.

Perhaps the greatest disjuncture in supply-side policies is between their claims and empirical outcomes in the distribution of resources. In the general economy, the three largest effects of Reaganomics in terms of wealth distribution are increased poverty levels, increased disparity in average household incomes, and increased public-sector debt. We can see similar developments in the higher education economy—increased disparity among fields and continued fiscal crisis.

Is it possible that supply-side-driven policymakers in higher education (as in the economy) are no better at identifying areas that have wealth-creation potential than labor economists are at predicting labor markets? Is wealth actually created by supply-side policies? Many of the commercially relevant fields in which universities continue to invest are quite expensive. Higher education managers may articulate corporate language, but they are generally horrible accountants. There is not a university president, provost, or vice president for research who has calculated out the investment side of the grants and contracts equation and who can provide an algorithm of the relationship between investment and yield. (And most would probably admit, in private, that most universities' entrepreneurial technology transfer efforts lose money in the short and medium term.) Moreover, most of the monies with which they are leveraging their entrepreneurial activities are public-sector monies. This marks a major disjuncture with the wealth-creation ideology of the productive marketplace—many of the fields in which universities invest are close not so much to the private marketplace as to the federal agency marketplace.

Alternatives

In many ways, if one returns to the theory, higher education is not following supply-side economics in investing (allocating) its monies internally. Ironically, an alternative to the current pattern would be to truly follow supply-side principles. For example, a supply-side portfolio strategy is to invest in small firms. Yet colleges and universities continue to invest most of their monies in large units. They also continue to merge units to achieve economies of scale, creating larger units rather than recognizing the value of small units. Moreover, it is not just small firms that should be invested in. Supply-side theorists call for investment in "low-capitalization" firms: "From 1963 through 1984, stock market performance was inversely related to capitalization." [29] *Capitalization* refers to the total capital funds of a corporation (stocks, bonds, profit, surplus, assets, or the total stated value of a corporation's stocks and bonds). In other words, translated into higher education, do not invest in capital-intensive, high-salary, expensive academic units. Yet those are precisely the kinds of units to which institutions are committing more and more resources.

Finally, to follow supply-side thinking, higher education executives should institute tax cuts and ensure not just low taxes but appropriate tax incentives. In higher education, there are at least three ways that institutions violate supply-side taxation policy. First, in the area of research, indirect cost recovery charges have increased over time, as have shares of central administration in allocating those monies. Such changes represent a disincentive for at least some sorts of activities in some units. What is valued are big-ticket, high-surcharge-paying grants—in other words, research grants in science, engineering, and social science from the federal government. Education and training grants yield lower overhead. More money goes straight to the student and the public, and less goes to university administration. In our current calculus and incentive structure, that is "inefficient." If universities really wish to diversify (and augment) their grants and contracts portfolio, they should reduce such charges, be more flexible in negotiating contracts, and provide more incentive for pursuing other sorts of grants and contracts. Second, many institutions have increasingly levied "taxes" on units, called administrative taxes. In the short term, such policies may raise more monies for the central administration, but supply-siders would argue that such policies take monies away from the wealth producers, thereby undermining the productivity of the units. Finally, there is currently too little incentive for academic units to recruit and teach undergraduates. In fact, there is a disincentive. In doctoral and research universities, monies are actually allocated away from units that produce large numbers of lower-division undergraduate credit hours. In a very real sense, all units are taxed in order to underwrite selective administrative, capital, and research investments. In a variety of ways, higher education managers are creating various taxes on units, on students (in the form of various fees), and on staff. At some point, supply-siders would caution, tax increases actually lead to decreased tax revenues (because disincentives lead to a decline in the taxed activity).

"True" supply-side policies are one possible alternative to the current pattern, though they fit within traditional categories. There is also an alternative, currently being realized in practice, which in some ways does not fit within our categories. Some of the units that are the biggest gainers in the current supply-side scenario are interdisciplinary centers, institutes, and committees, new organizational forms that draw on but go beyond traditional departmental structures. Such units are better resourced in the sciences and engineering than in the social sciences and humanities. That is predictable, given the supply-side focus on productivity and wealth creation: interdisciplinary units in sciences and engineering center on solving problems and creating commercial products that laypersons see as important; such units in the social sciences and humanities tend to turn problems into verbs (as in, "problematize"), identifying problems and generating textual products that are unrecognizable to laypersons. In our view, the production of graduate education and research in the sciences and engineering is taking place in these interdisciplinary units, relegating discipline-based departments to the task of educating undergraduates.

There are, of course, other alternative patterns. However, if much talk takes place of the "touch choices" that college and university leaders must make, there is, amid the neoconservative discourse of productivity and wealth creation, little discussion of alternative choices. The academy currently lacks a sustained debate about the economic interests that higher education should serve. It also lacks a sustained debate about the other interests it serves, its role in addressing the critical social, political, and cultural challenges of the day. The "tough choices" being made today are narrowly circumscribed by the material and ideological structures of supply-side policy.

In sum, we are unrepentant structuralists, whose terminology suggests that we see higher education as being shaped by significant and interrelated economic, political, and cultural/ideological structures. We live in a time of global, corporate hypercapitalism. The global market rules, privatizing even former centers of state socialism. In this context, how can one not address class-based and connected political-economic structures and ideologies?

As in the broader society, the consequences of capitalism in the academy are pervasive but do not fall equally across the system. Faculty (and students) are increasingly viewed in terms of their ability to generate revenue and commercial value and are differentially invested in accordingly. So academic capitalism plays out in restructuring colleges and universities and their professional workforce. Increased management (in terms of power and numbers of nonfaculty professionals) is pervasive, again not having equal effect across the system. Some faculty are more "managed" than others, in different directions, and with different levels of financial and nonfaculty support. Finally, the same is true with supply-side policies. The ideological underpinnings and material effects of policy have shifted from Keynesian to Malthusian principles, with Dickensian results. A policy of survival of the fittest versus full employment leads to reduced employment, increased poverty, and growing material disparity. Those conditions are accompanied by disdain for those less well off and by blaming victims for being unproductive, inverting them into victimizers and causes of their own and other social and economic problems.

The structural patterns we describe are not just inexorable external developments to which colleges and universities are subject and doomed. Higher education is not a "bit of excrement floating along on the tide of culture" (or of the economy).[30] The academy itself daily enacts and expresses social relations of capitalism and heightened managerial control grounded in a neoconservative discourse. And that enactment is characterized by all the attendant complexity, unpredictability, and variability that comes with negotiated social relations, offering us numerous examples of subtexts that break with the general pattern.

We have focused on three inversions. First, the public interest is best served not by separating public from private entities but by privatizing the public sphere, by connecting it to and sponsoring private gain. Second, the public interest is best served not by the unfettered exercise of expert, professional judgment but by the flexible exercise of managerial control of professionals. We believe those who speak of a postindustrial workplace in which information and expertise rule have it wrong. Increasingly in higher education, professional discretion is supplanted by managerial discretion. Third, the public interest is best served not by ensuring a safety net of support for fields that are a critical part of a liberal education and limiting disparities among fields but by transferring resources from such fields to those areas perceived as being close to corporate markets, thereby increasing resource disparities. That is, Robin Hood in reverse.

Where are these patterns leading? In higher education, as in society, supply-side policies have led to an increased bifurcation of work and working conditions. In the process, like the middle class, much of the traditional center of the university—letters, arts, and social sciences in particular—as well as many white-collar, middle-class, helping professions, are being squeezed. The connection is stronger than analogy. These academic fields are precisely the ones that have long prepared people for middle-class occupations. Indeed, these fields, at the turn of the last century, saw the emergence of a professional middle class that supported and legitimated, and yet mitigated, capitalism. The rising professions worked through the state, and they were independent of the laity. Now at the turn of the twentieth century we see some interesting changes and challenges. These same professions are increasingly being incorporated in and subordinated to the revenue, authority, and ideological structures of global monopoly capitalism.

In our view, a return to an imagined past of separate public and private spheres, of professional self-governance, and of state-stimulated demand is highly unlikely. Instead, professionals must work with their clients and with consumers in general to infuse the private sphere with public forms of economic, political, and normative control. Improbable? Perhaps. But consider recent developments in the health care system. There, the epitome of caring and elite professions are beginning to form common cause with consumers to leverage the incentive systems, authority structures, and policies of health maintenance corporations. Such (re)alignments may also be possible in the academy but will require new forms of organization and activity that bridge the disparate structures of profession and laity.

Notes

1 See Sheila Slaughter and Larry L. Leslie, *Academic Capitalism: Politics, Policies, and the Entrepreneurial University* (Baltimore: Johns Hopkins University Press, 1997); Gary Rhoades, *Managed Professionals: Unionized Faculty and Restructuring Academic Labor* (Albany: State University of New York Press, 1998); Sheila Slaughter and Gary Rhoades, "The Emergence of a Competitiveness Research and Development Policy Coalition and the Commercialization of Academic Science and Technology," *Science, Technology, and Human Values* 21, no. 3 (1996): 303–39; and Sheila Slaughter, "Who Gets What in Higher Education: Changing Patterns of Resource Allocation," Presidential Address, Association for the Study of Higher Education, Memphis, 1996.

2 See Committee A, "Academic Freedom and Tenure: Eastern Oregon State College," *Academe* 68 (May–June 1982): 1a–8a, and Sheila Slaughter, "Aca-

demic Freedom in the 1990s: The Politics of Retrenchment, Gender, and Professionalization," in *Higher Education in American Society*, 3d ed., ed. P. G. Altbach, R. O. Berdahl, and P. Gumport (Buffalo, N.Y.: Prometheus, 1994).

3 See Committee A, "Academic Freedom and Tenure: Sonoma State University (California)," *Academe* 69 (May–June 1983): 3–12.

4 This case is drawn from Slaughter and Leslie, *Academic Capitalism*.

5 Case drawn from Sheila Slaughter and Gary Rhoades, "Renorming the Social Relations of Academic Science: Technology Transfer," *Educational Policy* 4 (1990): 341–61.

6 See Gary Rhoades, "Managed Professionals: The Rise and Restratification of Professionals," paper presented at the Association for the Study of Higher Education, Memphis, 1996. See also the National Center for Education Statistics, *Faculty and Instructional Staff: Who Are They and What Do They Do?* a survey report of the 1993 National Study of Postsecondary Faculty (Washington, D.C.: U.S. Department of Education, 1994). And see Sheila Slaughter, "Retrenchment in the 1980s: The Politics and Prestige of Gender," *Journal of Higher Education* 64 (1993): 250–82.

7 See Stanley Aronowitz, "Toward Radicalism: The Death and Rebirth of the American Left," *Social Text*, no. 44 (fall/winter 1995): 73.

8 Figures related to the rise of academic capitalism are taken from Slaughter and Leslie, *Academic Capitalism*.

9 See Derek Bok, *Beyond the Ivory Tower: The Social Responsibilities of the Modern University* (Cambridge: Harvard University Press, 1982).

10 See Sheila Slaughter and Gary Rhoades, "Changes in Intellectual Property Statutes and Policies at a Public University: Revising the Terms of Professional Labor," *Higher Education* 26 (1993): 287–312, and "Emergence of a Competitiveness Research and Development Policy Coalition." On public universities and the public interest, see Gary Rhoades and Sheila Slaughter, "The Public Interest and Professional Labor: Research Universities," in *Culture and Ideology in Higher Education: Advancing a Critical Agenda*, ed. William G. Tierney (New York: Praeger, 1991). On the changing ideology underpinning professionals, see Rhoades and Slaughter, "Professors, Administrators, and Patents: The Negotiation of Technology Transfer," *Sociology of Education* 64 (1991): 65–77. On the shift from "social trustee" professionalism to the "technical" professionalism of the marketplace, see Steven Brint, *In an Age of Experts: The Changing Role of Professionals in Politics and Public Life* (Princeton: Princeton University Press, 1994).

11 On higher education's courtship of the private sector, see Sheila Slaughter,

Higher Learning and High Technology: Dynamics of Higher Education Policy Forma-tion (Albany: State University of New York Press, 1990). For data on private sector support of research, see National Science Foundation, *Science and Engineering Indicators* (Washington, D.C.: National Academy Press, 1993).

12 On international students and the trade balance, see Gary Rhoades and Don Smart, "The Political Economy of Entrepreneurial Culture: Policies toward Foreign Students in Australia and the United States," in *The Social Role of Higher Education: Comparative Perspectives*, ed. Ken Kempner and William G. Tierney (New York: Garland, 1996). If U.S. policymakers have not articu-lated the issue as clearly as have their counterparts in Australia, there are nevertheless so many international students coming into the United States that such students could be seen to counterbalance the trade deficit in the economy.

13 L. L. Leslie and P. T. Brinkman, *The Economic Value of Higher Education* (New York: Macmillan, 1988).

14 See Rhoades, "Managed Professionals."

15 On corporate alterations, see Patricia Gumport, "The Contested Terrain of Academic Program Reduction," *Journal of Higher Education* 64 (1993): 283–311. On retrenchment, see Gary Rhoades, "Retrenchment Clauses in Faculty Union Contracts: Faculty Rights and Administrative Discretion," *Journal of Higher Education* 64 (1993): 312–47. On tough choices, see the winter/spring 1995 issue of the *Journal for Higher Education Management*.

16 Keep in mind that one contract for the California State University system covers all the institutions in the system; so, too, with the State University of New York, the City University of New York, the Pennsylvania State University system, and other state systems. This Higher Education Contract Analysis System has been compiled by the National Education Association, in con-junction with John Lee of JBL Associates.

17 Slaughter and Rhoades, "Emergence of a Competitiveness Research and De-velopment Policy Coalition," table 3.

18 On the status of recent hires, see Jack Schuster, "The Academic Profession in the Twenty-First Century," paper presented at the Association for the Study of Higher Education, Memphis, 1996.

19 Many coalitions are possible, although at present they are neither emergent nor likely. For example, currently, graduate teaching assistants in the Uni-versity of California system are striking. Faculty in that system have voted against collective bargaining in the past, although the voting pattern sug-

gests considerable support for unionization in some fields and on some campuses. In any case, there is the opportunity for faculty to form common cause with their graduate students—of course, history gives us little optimism in this regard. A more likely coalition is among the various nonfaculty bargaining units on campus. The 1995 case of the strike at Yale University offers the potential of such cross-occupation coalitions. If faculty were not so profession-identified, they would see the potential advantages of joining forces with these groups too. Finally, there is the possibility of unions successfully organizing new managerial professions.

20 On "social movement unionism," see Paul Johnston, *Success while Others Fail: Social Movement Unionism and the Public Workplace* (Ithaca, N.Y.: ILR Press, 1994).

21 Slaughter, "Who Gets What."

22 On "illegitimate" change in liberal arts colleges, see Matthew S. Kraatz and Edward J. Zajac, "Exploring the Limits of the New Institutionalism: Causes and Consequences of Illegitimate Organizational Change," *American Sociological Review* 61 (1996): 812–36.

23 See Clifford Adelman, *The New College Course Map and Transcript Files: Changes in Course Taking and Achievement, 1972–1993* (Washington, D.C.: U.S. Department of Education, 1995).

24 On high tuition and high aid, see Larry L. Leslie, "What Drives Higher Education Management in the 1990s and Beyond? The New Era in Financial Support," *Journal for Higher Education Management* 10 (1995): 5–16. On patterns in student aid, see William Zumeta and John Fawcett-Long, "State Policy and Budget Developments," *The NEA 1996 Almanac of Higher Education* (Washington, D.C.: NEA, 1996).

25 See Tom Moylan, "People or Markets: Some Thoughts on Culture and Corporations in the University of the Twenty-First Century," *Social Text*, no. 44 (fall/winter 1995): 45–60. The doctoral student is Kimberly Lund.

26 See Cindy Volk, "Assessing Competing Models of Resource Allocation at a Public Research I University through Multivariate Analysis of State Financing," Ph.D. diss., University of Arizona, 1995. See also Marcia L. Bellas, "Comparable Worth in Academia: The Effects on Faculty Salaries of the Sex Composition and Labor Market Conditions of Academic Disciplines," *American Sociological Review* 59 (1994): 807–21. And see Slaughter, "Who Gets What."

27 On instructional and administrative shares, see Larry L. Leslie and Gary

Rhoades, "Rising Administrative Costs: Seeking Explanations," *Journal of Higher Education* 66 (1995): 187–212. On institutional investment in research, see National Science Foundation, *Science and Engineering Indicators.*

28 On the "Matthew Effect," see Robert K. Merton, "The Matthew Effect in Science," in *The Sociology of Science*, ed. Robert K. Merton (Chicago: University of Chicago Press, 1973). The Matthew Effect refers to a phenomenon of biblical origins and proportions—in the Gospel of Matthew, "to them that have shall be given."

29 See Victor A. Canto and Arthur B. Laffer, eds., *Supply-Side Portfolio Strategies* (Westport, Conn.: Quorum, 1988). In this book see also Truman A. Clark and Arthur B. Laffer, "Are Small Cap Stocks Still Alive?" 9–24.

30 These are the words used in an exam question posed by a sociology professor (an ethnomethodologist who vigorously rejected structuralist explanations) that one of the authors knew in graduate school.

Recapturing Academic Business

Christopher Newfield

Two Corporate Cultures

There has been much talk during the 1990s about the introduction of business practices to higher education. Critics suggest that the corporate model judges such complex activities as education, research, and community service in the one dimension of profit and loss. Admirers of business see a more corporate higher education as a more efficient higher education. Both positions view business management as a proxy for strict cost accounting.

But the meaning of business is more divided than it at first appears. The business world is at war with itself over what good business actually means. Hard-nosed finance remains the conventional wisdom, and it has enormous social and institutional power backing it up. But another business faction has more intellectual momentum at the moment, and probably larger numbers of adherents. This other faction traces value not to fiscal and labor discipline per se but to employee "empowerment" and human development.

The conflict between these positions is long-standing—management tries to reduce worker autonomy, and workers try to increase it. The modern form of the conflict continues the hundred-year-old battle between "scientific management" and the labor movement and the equally old battle between scientific and "human relations" management. The conflict has become even more acute in the last ten or fifteen years, as the boardroom has become more militant about shrinking labor costs and the cubicle has become more threatened. Efforts to improve profits by downsizing, outsourcing, temping, and otherwise liquefying labor co-exist with calls to rejuvenate American-style capitalism by making employees happier and more independent and thus smarter, more innovative, and more productive. The management world is divided on how to proceed—employee discipline or employee development? The speedup or the seminar? Mean business or self-management? Survival of the fittest or teach your neighbor to swim? Weird mixtures abound, as do erratic shifts from one strategy to the other.

The university would seem a natural habitat for the human development side. Because it is dedicated to education and research—developing minds, developing knowledge—we might assume that the university would be the place where empowerment and the "human relations" strain of management thinking would be most advanced and treasured. But this is not the case. Upper administrators at the large research university—my focus here—are as driven as any corporate boardroom by the prestige of financial discipline. Teaching and research cost money and threaten financial disruption and excess. University administrators appear no more interested than their corporate counterparts in putting human development ahead of financial accounting. The outcome seems familiar—"human relations" perspectives as the underdog.

I set out to investigate the forms this conflict between "downsizing" and "empowerment" takes in the university, where downsizing stands for a wide range of financial and labor discipline. What are the conflict's effects? What special resources do universities have that might move management away from downsizing? My own employer, the University of California (UC), provided the setting for my analysis.

Many shortages plague higher education, but a shortage of criticism isn't one of them. Excellent work has been done on the insularity and elitism of universities, on the snail's pace of racial integration and equity, on partisan politics corrupting trusteeship, on an excessive emphasis on "technoscientific" research and private investment, and on many other subjects. Most of these arguments see political and business forces violating the integrity of the university's educational setting.

Although I too dislike many of these interventions, I make a different argument. Rather than contrast educational and business cultures, we should increase the influence of education on business culture. The university is a major institution in a capitalist society. In that context, reorienting the university entails reorienting university business. We should not just critique but *redefine* academic business—that is, we should examine and revise the business model. This could lead to collaborations with management writers and trainers, people who surpass most academics in coping with managerial roadblocks and who could also learn from academic experience. We should go beyond critique to achieving real *managerial* power for the nonprofit approaches to human development that drew many of us into higher education in the first place.

The following sections offer a tour through some basic issues: the one-sided, disciplinary version of "business focus" at UC; the historical roots of financial control in universities; "human relations" management writers who oppose financial control in business; the inadequate version of human relations reflected in UC's faculty senate; and better human relations through a combination of senate and union perspectives.

The Power of Downsizing

Many members of UC's staff already have union representation. I went to the offices of the dean of sciences at UC Santa Barbara (UCSB) to talk with Martha Cody-Valdez, an administrative analyst who is an officer of one of these unions, the University Professional and Technical Employees (UPTE). This union, with seventeen hundred members systemwide, has bargaining authority for two employee groups—technicians and professional researchers. It is trying to organize the much larger pool of general administrative and professional staff, but the hodgepodge collection of job categories in this pool has not yet been sorted out into potential bargaining groups by California's Public Employment Relations Board.

I wanted to ask Cody-Valdez about her views on the interesting phenomenon of *professional* unions. Like many other people, I had been wondering whether white-collar employees will ease up on their traditional opposition to unions as they increasingly lose the workplace autonomy they thought came with professional status. In 1996, for example, faculty at the University of Minnesota voted to consider forming a union, thereby using Minnesota labor law to block changes in tenure regulations that were about to be imposed on them by the Board of Regents. I'm momentarily distracted by my discovery that Cody-Valdez is the daughter of the founders of Cody's Books in Berkeley, so before we could talk I had to reminisce about the mind-altering hours I spent there as a teenager and fight off an urge to ask for her autograph. When I finally asked about the issues her membership faced, I got a very good summary of what most people mean by "the corporate model" in the university.

"We're worried about the casualization or 'temping' of the workforce," Cody-Valdez said. "I think the university is trying to reduce the numbers of longtime staff and increase the numbers of casual employees. It'll then have more part-timers who can be brought in or dropped. The university is turning away from the model of having a stable, loyal, academic workforce. It's like it is saying, 'We want cheap people who are interchangeable.'"

"So it's the Silicon Valley strategy," I ask, "a two-tiered labor force, 'knowledge workers' and 'routine production workers,' working under very different conditions?"

"Sometimes it seems like that. The university is also trying to install market-based pay. They establish an 'average' set of pay rates in a campus's area. They then try to tie university wages to those of the local market, as they've defined it."

"What does that mean?" I asked.

"It allows them to lower wages for campuses in lower-wage areas, rather than having standard rates for each classification across the system. It isn't just for exerting downward pressure in lower-wage areas. It's for general downward pressure. I have yet to hear of them raising anyone's salary. 'O, gee, we're not paying you enough. Our mistake.'"

"Right," I laughed. " 'We hadn't checked your cost of living. We feel terrible.' "

" 'Yes, we're sorry. We owe you for years.' . . . I haven't heard them say that yet," Cody-Valdez continued. "Market-basing is a take-away plan. Libby Sayre, our executive vice president, told me about one university comparison study that came out high. Their analysts then threw in bank tellers, a notoriously underpaid group. So, surprise, surprise, after they factored them in, the average 'market' pay went down, and they said, 'Look, you're leading the market.' It's a way of keeping wages stagnant or actually reducing them."

"What else are you keeping your eye on?"

"We're concerned about performance pay. The university has been taking money out of pools allocated for regular merit raises or general pay adjustments and has been creating one-time bonus pools. The idea, they say, is to reward excellence, but it doesn't raise base pay. And its other effect is to increase the supervisor's discretion. The raises one used to get contractually are now in the hands of a manager who picks and chooses beneficiaries.

"The university has also been looking at outsourcing. A few years ago, there was a plan introduced at UCLA called UC 2000. It came right out and said we need to start contracting out a lot of these services, to cut costs, to get rid of all these employees with their big-ticket benefits. They put it out there and then the flak flew and they withdrew it, but you can see that these ideas are still part of their motivation. Some parts of the administration believe that even core functions could be handled by outside people—Manpower Temps for accounting. That's a big trend that worries a lot of us.

"The whole affirmative action fiasco is also troubling. The university is not a place where discrimination is unknown. In the tech contract the university wanted to weaken the affirmative action language, saying that they're just following the law. But weakening employee protections is the overall direction of the university's employee relations.

"Look at the new employment standards for staff that were initiated by the office of the president a few years ago. [This is called the Human Resources Management Initiative, or HRMI.] Take the new standards for performance appraisal. They've made it so vague and general that it's practically meaningless. The effect . . . is that if an employee feels that he or she got an unfair performance appraisal, and he or she goes to the manual to show that a supervisor violated the policy, they won't find anything. The new policy allows for almost anything. So it's taking away any rights you had under the old policy. The old policy was much more specific about what the university is supposed to do as well as what the employee is supposed to do. There's everything in the new policy about what the employee is supposed to do, but very little about what the university is supposed to do."

"I think you sense a pattern," I exclaimed.

Cody-Valdez smiled patiently. "We're also dealing with staff morale. One thing I've been hearing from staff is a general lack of acknowledgment and respect from faculty and students, especially faculty on campus. Like they're invisible."

"Does the staff feel more disrespected by faculty than by students or administrators?" I asked.

"Yes," she said. "The abusive incidents generally come from faculty."

In Cody-Valdez's description, UC's labor policy is a virtual checklist of the downsizing side of contemporary corporate strategy. Rather than increasing value through enhanced stability, morale, salaries, training, and the active encouragement of innovation and its inevitable mistakes, UC policy seems to emphasize improved numbers through improved discipline. Although Cody-Valdez didn't present her views as typical of "UC staff" and noted that personnel relations were better at UCSB than at many other UC campuses, my discussions with other UCSB staff showed mostly overlap with her descriptions of the employment atmosphere. They may have had less comprehensive and detailed views of the situation, but nearly everyone I asked about administrative "policy" described an overriding impression of containment and control.

Three Stages of Financial Control

Downsizing in the broadest sense is what most people expect from the "corporate model" in the university—even if you don't fire employees (and UCSB generally has not), you constantly squeeze them. Downsizing as the reduction of either workforce size or workforce costs continues two long-standing American business traditions: scientific management and antiunionism. The first increases external supervision of work, and the second decreases employee resistance to it. Scientific management successfully streamlined production, but it also reinforced a more general belief that labor efficiency required cutting labor freedom. Self-regulation meant waste.

From its inception, scientific management has been pummeled by critics both outside and inside business. But it has never been vanquished. This is true even in the professions or, more broadly, among "knowledge workers." Frederick Taylor, usually considered the father of scientific management in the factory, played a lesser-known role in sponsoring its application to the university around the turn of the century.

The historian Clyde W. Barrow has unearthed an interesting part of this story. In 1905, Massachusetts Institute of Technology president Henry S. Pritchett published an article called "Shall the University Become a Business Corporation?" Although he admitted that faculty-led European universities were actually more efficient than their more "business-minded" American counterparts, Pritchett argued that faculty management of large universities would be a setback for higher education. Businessmen, he claimed, were far superior to faculty as administrators, for "no type of man has been developed who is a wiser councilor than the businessman of large sympathy and of real interest in intellectual problems." A year later, prompted largely by Pritchett, Andrew Carnegie endowed the Carnegie Foundation for the Advancement of Teaching. The foundation's first president was Pritchett.

Pritchett wrote to Frederick Taylor in 1909 seeking advice on sponsoring "an economic study of education." Taylor suggested that the study be directed by a mechanical engineer named Morris L. Cooke. In his report, *Academic and Industrial Efficiency* (1910), Cooke held that

the problem of academic efficiency was in principle no different from that of industrial efficiency because "all large and continuing causes rest upon formal organization and upon some assured machinery of administration." Organization was primarily an engineering problem. Administering this organization was the function of management. . . . Organizational efficiency demanded that a worker not "produce any longer by his own initiative," but "executive punctili-

ously" the orders given by management, "down to their minutest details." . . .
Professors "must be governed and measured by the same general standards that
generally obtain in other occupations."

Cooke made a number of recommendations, including one to abolish
tenure on the grounds that it screened inefficient workers from management intervention.[1]

It turned out, of course, that management could give orders regulat-
ing the physical labor of manufacturing more easily than it could dictate
the motions and timing of office work. They gave it a good try, but the
more complex or conceptual the work became, the more difficult it was
to devise the single most efficient procedure or to know how to enforce
it. Some labor is more easily broken into minute component parts than
others, and the general category of "white-collar" work required more
subtle methods of orchestration. Direct, detailed supervision of teaching
and research did not generally take root. The more flexible idea of business management in universities did. The result of the first stage in the
development of the modern research university was to establish once and
for all that business as a form of practical reason is better at university
decision making than the thinking of faculty and staff. Scientific management did not become a set of regulative techniques in higher education so much as it served as the principle of objective efficiency by which
existing faculty and staff practices might be regularly judged.

A second stage involved developing the techniques whereby business
administration could be more directly installed within the university. Taylor applied the stopwatch to the arms and hands in motion on the shop
floor. Others learned how to apply the account ledger in the office. On its
face, financial accounting is simply a way to keep track of the firm's relationship with the outside world. What's coming in? What's going out?
What direction are sales going for a particular product? Accounting is
also widely used to identify strong and weak areas within the firm — costs
are high here, revenues are low there. But accounting can also be used
not simply as *one* type of information but as the most important kind.
Sociologist Neil Fligstein has shown how accounting had evolved by the
middle of the twentieth century into a "financial conception of control."
This conception "emphasizes control through the use of financial tools

which measure performance according to profit rates."[2] Financial measures dominate other estimates of a company's status—good community ties, a high-quality workforce, strong product development, a record of marketing innovation, and so on. During the last fifteen years, financial measures have further consolidated their position as the final judge in allocating power and resources within an organization. When they arrive on campus, they use instruments developed to calculate profit and loss to make policy in a nonprofit enterprise.

Financial accounting doesn't automatically lead to top-down governance. There are cases in which it democratizes an organization by giving managers and frontliners the same financial information, and I'll mention one example of this below. But accounting does support oligarchical control when financial information is closely guarded at the top or when it is used to manage units from outside and at a distance. Cooke made it very clear that the engineering of academic labor required not self-management but close supervision. Financial management inherited scientific management's insistence on external management by superiors. The numbers were used not for mutual consultation and collaborative planning but for justifying the override of the preferences of subordinates. They were used to decide from above which divisions or projects would be fed and which would starve, which would grow and which would wither, which would have a future and which would not. Finance assumed the same authority over the products of the knowledge worker that Taylor's assembly line had assumed over those of the manual worker.

Hostility to political and academic Taylorism was by no means limited to the New Left. Retired general and pro-business Republican president Dwight D. Eisenhower ended his second term by warning the country of the intrusive governing power of the "military-industrial complex." And centrist U C president Clark Kerr, appointed in 1958 and most famous for his backfiring efforts to clamp down on the Berkeley free-speech protests, warned that new financial powers had disrupted the research university.

Kerr noted in 1963 that the research university was attracting increasing national interest because of the American economy's dependence on the "knowledge industry" for continued world leadership. Contrary to impressions left by Robert Reich and *Wired*, this dependence is not new to the 1990s. Anticipating Daniel Bell and other observers, Kerr believed that the United States of 1960 was already becoming "postindustrial." "The basic reality, for the university," he wrote, "is the widespread recognition that new knowledge is the most important factor in economic and social growth. We are just now perceiving that the university's invisible product, knowledge, may be the most powerful single element in our culture, affecting the rise and fall of professions and even of social classes, of regions and even of nations." [3] The research "multiversity" was already in business big time by the end of the 1950s.

But Kerr was not most concerned about general business pressures on the university. He saw a more immediate danger in the partnership between the research university and the state. "Federal support of scientific research during World War II," he wrote, has had a greater impact on higher education than any event since the land-grant movement was enshrined in the Morrill Act of 1862.[4] Kerr detailed the ways in which an indirect form of "federal influence" operated through a nearly irresistible structure of financial opportunities to reduce "the authority of the department chairman, the dean, the president, [and] . . . faculty government." [5] The research institution had become a "federal grant university" in which direct state control is avoided in favor of a much more effective system of financial rewards and penalties that, for Kerr, amounted to a shadow government:

The university, as Allen Wallis, president of the University of Rochester, has remarked, becomes to an extent a "hotel." The [federal granting] agency becomes the new alma mater. The research entrepreneur becomes a euphoric schizophrenic. . . . There are . . . especially acute problems when the agency insists on the tie-in sale (if we do this for you, then you must do this for us) or when it requires frequent and detailed progress reports. Then the university really is less than a free agent. It all becomes a kind of "putting-out" system with the agency taking the place of the merchant-capitalist of old. Sweat shops have developed out of such a system in earlier times and in other industries.[6]

Kerr clearly feels that the loss of university self-management is very far along.

The second stage of the research university's modern history, then, curtails the university's self-governance through financial control. In a third stage, the federal role remains in place while commercial influence

comes to the fore. One example of this development is the increase in
UC partnerships with the private sector, which include not only patent
arrangements but also large-scale mergers, such as that between the
teaching hospitals of UC San Francisco and Stanford University. These
partnerships will undoubtedly multiply. *California State Budget Highlights,
1996–97*, prepared by the state's Department of Finance, underscores "an
increase of $5 million . . . for UC to work collaboratively with business
and industry to transfer academic research findings to the marketplace."
Public funds are to subsidize transfers of commercially valuable research
to the private sphere; returns to the university are somewhat less clear.

Kerr's analysis suggests a more important form of business influence.
For Kerr, the problem with federal grants was not their influence on research content but their influence on internal university governance. The
federal agency was able to shape hiring and firing decisions; the structure,
size, and budget of various departments; the allocation of physical space;
the construction of new buildings; the creation of "new classes of administrators"; and the expanding relative size of administration overall.[7]
Similarly, commercial influence doesn't stop with the university serving
as " 'bait' to be dangled in front of industry." [8] More fundamentally, it in-
ternalizes the standard of finance as the final judge of university affairs.

Today's sounds of scientific finance are not hard to hear. University
of California senior vice president for business and finance V. Wayne
Kennedy grounds the success of the university's public mission in strict
financial management:

Recognizing that faithful stewardship of the public's investment in the University of California is a top priority for our administration, the university is
strengthening its business focus and is now in the second year of an ambitious
program to overhaul and update its business practices with the expressed goal
of enhancing institutional accountability. We are strengthening our system of
controls as we continue to evaluate and redesign the university's fundamental
business processes. We are replacing outdated business systems and practices
with methods comparable to those utilized by the nation's leading corporations.[9]

Using a language that pervades Governor Pete Wilson's administration
and its legislative allies, Kennedy redefines the university's constitutional

status of "public trust" as a "public investment." The production of value depends on a "business focus." Business focus boils down to more economical forms of financial supervision. Although the "business" of the university is knowledge, the university's financial systems compete with research knowledge as the standard of reason.[10]

In the third stage, a private-sector model of financial control becomes the single most important form of "distance" governance through which complex institutions can be run from the top. It becomes the authorized language in which the university expresses its purpose to the major players of the outside world. Retaining scientific management's emphasis on external supervision, finance resists being contextualized as just one of a number of considerations in an intricate corporate culture. Finance must, of course, pay homage to "faculty consultation" and other complications, but it generally dominates the organization's "cultural" issues.

As such, financial accounting's tendencies are stark. It sees costs as negative, labeling them as investments only if they can be linked to a quantifiable expected return. If costs yield only nonquantifiable goods of the kind common in research and education—"critical thinking," writing skills, maps of housing segregation, a new scheme for proportional representation, a better understanding of the Boer War—it will be hard for finance to certify them as valuable investments. U C administrators show every sign of holding education and the liberal arts in high philosophical esteem. But it's hard for anyone to fight numbers with philosophy, especially under the usual kinds of political pressure. Nonquantifiable benefits almost always have less clout than quantifiable ones. Resources flow toward large revenue centers and away from nonfinancial activities; departments that attract outside funds—materials science, for example—have far greater influence than those defined by providing services and self-sponsored research (such as literature). Financial control tends to view labor as a cost, as a site of potential savings. From this perspective, better means cheaper, growth means restriction, productivity means discipline, knowledge means regulation.

It would be wrong to see the rule of financial control as the result of short-term crisis. Since the California "budget crisis" of 1991–94, the budget has reinstalled itself as a semipermanent straightjacket. The state's general fund contribution to the UC system was a little over $2 billion in 1996–97, about where it was in 1990–91 and still less than the 1991–92 figure. The budget crisis has changed UC's institutional culture. It has become increasingly difficult to believe that the system can continue to provide universal higher education, even in the three-tiered form that was established by the Master Plan for Higher Education in 1960. UC has shelved plans for at least two of the three campuses that were to have been added to its nine-campus system, which has not received augmentation in the same thirty-year period that saw the state's population double.

There's the additional problem of the governor's use of the budget for public discipline. UC's budget has always been a political football,[11] but this recent crisis was part of a continuing attack on UC administration (as overpaid) and faculty (as underworked) that symbolized the taming of the state's most independent knowledge workers. The university has emerged humbled and more dependent than ever on Wilson's good opinion, business's approval, and private fund-raising. Not so much business as "business focus" rules the knowledge roost, where medical and technological employees, properly disciplined, appeal to power brokers as eternal fountains of youth for a dubious economy.

There's been a subtle toll on the university community's expectations, one that has to be told in stories rather than numbers. From my vantage point, the most immediate casualties are dreams of the new—new programs, new disciplines, new combinations, new ideas given adequate institutional support. A few major initiatives struggle along on my campus, but without much hope of raising the kind of capital required for a near-term breakthrough. Such conditions favor the administrative rise to power of the relatively unambitious. They favor those who will not chafe against preestablished limits. Even the restive remainder rarely schemes against the administration's human bottlenecks, who not long ago would have seemed an affront to campus destiny. Few appeal the administrative refrain: "That's a good idea, but sorry, there's no money." Because serious new ventures will likely require outside investors, the university's control of its own research will continue to weaken.

In the 1990s, UC has become a showcase of a management technique that was developed during an early phase of the industrial corporation. Direct managerial supervision was replaced in a second stage with the financial incentives of federal grants, and these are in turn giving way to a more pervasive budget power modeled on—and linked to—the private sector. The boardroom wins and the cubicle loses—that is, of course, part of this story. But the other part is that budgeting becomes *the* fundamental governing principle of the university as a whole. It sits at the head of the table. Others may sit there too—faculty interests, student interests, staff interests. But finance controls the discussion, decides who is asking for too much, who is unreasonable, and when the discussion is over. Standard financial accounting manages university faculty and staff in the same way that it manages any other kind of workforce. Budget crisis becomes budget governance.

This version of the business model is both one-sided and ineffective, even on its own terms. The most direct way to confront it is through business's better half—"human relations" management theory and its substantial history of rejecting financial governance on both ethical and financial grounds.

Human Relations Management

The corporate world has seen a number of attempts to manage the financial managers. Some of the most interesting of these could be classed as part of an ongoing revival of the "humanistic" management that has tried to swamp scientific management more or less since its inception. This tradition sees organizations as a culture, a matrix of personal relations, a way of life. It traces productivity to relationships, collaboration, and creativity rather than to sheer efficiency and economy. As for the reverence for fiscal discipline that is on the rise in many universities, "human relations" theory considers it obsolete.

The current opportunity for human relations ideas is provided by the surprise identity crisis of capitalism itself. The year 1990 wasn't that long ago, but mainstream doubts about U.S.-style capitalism have mushroomed since then, and these are doubts coming from capitalism's friends. Who would have thought, at the beginning of this strange decade, that the *sans*-Soviet "triumph of capitalism" would lead to such widespread calls for capitalism's transformation *from within*? Even as free-market troubleshooters from major U.S. business schools parachuted into Warsaw and Prague, ardently pro-business economists and management thinkers behind the lines began to publish books called *Post-Capitalist Society* (1993), *Capitalism vs. Capitalism* (1993), and *The Seven Cultures of Capitalism* (1993).[12] These books all described capitalism as partially defunct, malignant, self-divided, and in need of drastic reforms. In the same vein, in his *Work of Nations* (1991) Robert Reich worried that American economic *success* would divide the national workforce into antagonistic cultures based on different levels of education, skill, and income. Many saw signs that, though we are not on the verge of being postcapitalist, we are becoming increasingly multicapitalist and perhaps postcorporate. And the strongest of these signs began to emerge not from Congress or from corporate boardrooms or, until very recently, from organized labor but from corporate cubicles — from the middle levels of the corporation or, more frequently, from the consultants who speak in their name.

The dean of management writers, Peter F. Drucker, recently summed up the situation like this:

Communism collapsed, but that does not mean that capitalism and democracy triumphed. . . . [N]ow that there is nothing to compare the democracies with, they have to prove themselves on their *own merits* — and they are at best getting a B-minus on that test. Above all, we are learning very fast that the belief that a free market is all it takes to have a functioning society — or even a functioning economy — is pure delusion. . . . For any [time period longer than] five years, a functioning civil society . . . is needed for the market to function in its economic role.[13]

Even for free-market advocates such as Drucker, the future of capitalism depends on the strength of civil society, on *cultural* forces that workforces and populations can shape. In the management of economies, *culture* has to share power with numbers, for numbers alone would make a mess of things.

Most progressives and radicals saw global capitalism as the end of revolution, but many business writers saw it as a revolution just begun. "We are at that very point in time," one observer said, "when a 400-year-old age is dying and another is struggling to be born. . . . Ahead, the possibility of the regeneration of individuality, liberty, community, and ethics such as the world has never known, and a harmony with nature, with one another, and with the divine intelligence such as the world has never dreamed." The speaker is not a grassroots idealist but the major architect and former chief executive officer (C E O) of Visa International, Dee Hock. His New Age follows from his experience with new wave corporate forms. He describes Visa International, for example, as a synthesis of "Jeffersonian democracy . . . the free market . . . [and] government franchising," which adds up to a "self-organizing" system in which "authority, initiative, decision making, wealth — everything possible is pushed out to the periphery of the organization, to its members." [14] The new corporation, for these writers, doesn't extend the authoritarian order of industrial capitalism into the high-tech, service-based future but shatters that order in a fusion of anarchy, creative chaos, and flexible organization.

This sounds wrong enough about corporate reality to be read as another managerial smokescreen, one meant to conceal the logic of capitalism as applied to a workforce whose expectant middle and upper reaches are more overworked and insecure than ever. But capitalism's friends and enemies have generally agreed that it is revolutionary, whether this feature is expressed as Shumpeter's praise of "creative destruction" or Marx's comment that "all that is solid melts into air." And these days, many capitalists sound oddly serious about a version of workplace democracy.

Since the 1920s, human relations management writing has contrasted itself with scientific management by teaching the dependence of real business success on respected and fulfilled (rather than strictly regulated) employees. As I mentioned at the start, the most recent incarnation of this consultant wisdom centers on employee empowerment. Empowerment has more species than the toad, but a few common features remain steady across the broad and complex human relations management literature.

The first is a boosted kind of *individualism*. The new wave employee should be a rugged corporate individualist, continuously innovative and actively creative. Every idea is valued, and every real idea yields a company payoff. This payoff cannot be separated from the individual employee's personal growth. "Traditionally," Peter Senge writes, "organizations have supported people's development instrumentally — if people grew and developed, then the organization would be more effective. [Hanover Insurance C E O William] O'Brien goes one step further: 'In the type of organization we seek to build, the fullest development of people is on an equal plane with financial success.' "[15]

The second feature of empowerment is the necessity of *horizontal* structure. Human development depends on opposing management tyrants who kill creativity and change. Tyrants may live in the boardroom or two desks over, but real development requires flattened layers. *Equality* gets rediscovered in less political terminology; hierarchy gets reduced enough to allow the turbo-individualist to raise hell and push the outside of the envelope. The employee is responsible for his or her own performance, but the flip side is that the New Age manager gets the bureaucracy off the employee's back.

A number of management writers are incensed by the idea that the most draconian downsizers have become venerated individualists of contemporary business. Drucker says, "What is new and by no means desirable is the way in which [downsizing is] being carried out. This is what bothers me. A lot of top managers enjoy cruelty. There's no doubt that we are in a period in which you are a hero if you are cruel. In addition, what's absolutely unforgivable is the financial benefit top management people get for laying off people. There's no excuse for it. No justification. No explanation. This is morally and socially unforgivable, and we'll pay a very nasty price." [16] Much downsizing expresses a simple kind of exploitation that makes real individualism impossible.

Third, the employee needs a *supportive and anticonformist group life*. A few years ago, McKinsey and Company's organization-performance group issued a "ten-point blueprint for a horizontal company," and most of these points center on the elimination of the kind of competition and inhibition that can ruin groups even in the absence of an oppressive manager. The demand to perform must be accompanied by systems of support—continuous education, a culture that reveres (rather than contains) innovation, team-based pooling of expertise, and lots of resources for processing tension and conflict. The concept of the "team" figures prominently, conjuring images of following orders and marching in step, but this is exactly what the successful group avoids.

In its best moments, the new human relations is trying to figure out how to enable people to bring their eccentric individuality to the group without fearing discipline. The individual who doesn't fear punishment for nonconformity will be less defensive and more cooperative. The result is supposed to be, in Reich's phrase, a "web of enterprise," a new stage of "alliance capitalism," or a "virtual corporation" in which relationships are so egalitarian, fluid, supportive, and intimate that maximum freedom and group welfare can go hand in hand.

Although it contradicts most known experience of the capitalist corporation, such a specter of employee power shouldn't be rejected out of hand. What if something happened *inside* that we couldn't predict? What if the *culture* of corporations weren't fully determined by their financial structure? What if the kind of egalitarian group relations we associate with worker cooperatives began to take over the cells of the top-down corporation? What if personal ties and information were failing to follow the regular channels of the hierarchical maze with no immediate surface change?

Human relations writers do not picture looming revolution. Some of the most thoughtful corporate trainers I've talked with measure change in units of twenty to fifty years. But they are working with what they see as a contradiction between the old partners of profit and top-down control. Their substitute is a delicate and perhaps equally contradictory pairing of profit and empowerment. New wave capitalism depends on new forms of autonomous, cooperative, and otherwise empowered labor. But how much empowerment can capitalism take before it changes into something else?

The Insufficient Senate

Well, empowerment is a nice idea all right, but what influence can it have on the executive suite? It is true that Bill Clinton sought a private audience with self-esteem guru Tony Robbins, but that's not exactly progress.[17] It actually implies regression—an indifference to the *structural* sources of concentrated wealth and economic power that have successfully presented themselves as unopposable forces of nature.

The future of employee control ultimately lies in the sum of the attempts of millions of employees to put their ideas into practice. But the research university offers a particularly good test case of how various empowerment concepts might successfully resist the downsizing that is supported by some of the most powerful actors in U.S. society.

The university has a long tradition of nurturing an empowered work-force, known as the tenured faculty, which has generally had near-absolute immunity from the threat of job loss and much customary input into governance. The university has also been a prototype of the "high-tech" workplace, where knowledge workers successfully demand good care and feeding and where traditional management pressures routinely backfire against productivity—where an overmanaged knowledge worker can go on a silent creativity strike, and only love and money can restore her special magic to the organization's brainware. At least that's the theory. The university has also pioneered the containment of knowledge workers, and its workers have lots of experience trying to deal with this.

But one of the interesting things about UC's recent history is that what looks like a strongly "human relations" workplace has not produced any strong human relations objections to the university's retro version of "business focus." There has, of course, been a persistent, low-voltage attempt to remind business-minded administrators of the educational mission, but for reasons I'll mention shortly, these have not been effective. The more important omission has been any serious contestation of the meaning of business itself. Rejection of UC's rhetoric of scientific management has fallen largely on the shoulders of (usually pro-union) staff: Cody-Valdez, for example, wrote a critical review of the Human Resources Management Initiative for a UCSB staff and faculty newspaper. Faculty have been mostly silent.[18] Virtually no one has pointed out that, on the capitalist terrain of UC as a multidivisional corporation, recapturing the university begins with redefining university business.

An obvious first step for faculty who want to take a stronger role is thus to oppose systematically the application of rearguard management theories to *any* university workers. Evidence suggests that a business focus that boils down to labor discipline weakens an organization in the long run; reengineering that emphasizes squeezing labor costs hurts rather than helps innovation;[19] destabilizing long-term employees has only a short-term payoff; tightening supervision neither saves much money nor improves operations; and keeping a lock on everyone's budget discourages creativity while neither increasing revenues nor improving services.

UC employees have plenty of their own evidence to support these findings. As the language of financial control has waxed, actual finances have waned. Nongrant revenues, research support, salaries, and enrollments have been flat or falling, and services to students have fallen. The only things going up are student fees, which have more than doubled since 1990, and administrative expenses, which by one count increased 16.3 percent in 1995–96.[20] Some of this is obviously outside their control, but were the administrators who apply "private sector" methods actually judged by them, we would have had some administrative shrinkage after all.

One of the major obstacles to recapturing academic business is what we might call the "graven image." Human relations approaches get derailed more often by paltry imitations of their methods than by outright opposition. Every manager in America has learned to speak the language of empowerment, delayering, and team-based process redesign, while playing politics as usual with money and promotions. Most companies have established procedures that *appear* to honor employee participation and limited self-rule.

At UC, administrators perform mandatory bows to the value of "faculty consultation" and to "shared governance." As far as I can tell, this homage is usually sincere. Shared governance refers to the partnership between UC administration and the academic senate, whose membership is generally limited to "ladder-rank" (tenured and tenurable) faculty and which has a separate division on each of the system's nine campuses. Tenured faculty are not only the university's most powerful and protected group but are widely regarded as having significant control in all relevant areas of UC policy. But does the senate model of participation really bring employees on-line? Or does the success of its imitation of participation block the real thing?

UC's academic senate was always structured for *selective* participation. According to historian John A. Douglass, the senate's modern functions were gradually established by President Benjamin Ide Wheeler, who after his appointment in 1899 tried to "bring faculty into the management of university affairs." Wheeler was a kind of anti-Taylor. He "convinced the Regents that faculty were not simply employees of the state, but members of an academic community engaged in a free-market of teaching and research." As a professional community, faculty should have some powers of self-management. First in 1885 and again in 1920, the regents agreed that the faculty senate "was to determine the conditions for admissions, certificates, and degrees," subject to their approval. The senate was routinely "to advise the president on all 'appointments, promotions, demotions, and dismissals' of professors; advise the president regarding 'changes in the educational policy of the university'; and advise the President regarding budget issues." The senate could organize itself as it pleased. "Though this structure had antecedents in British universities," Douglass concludes, "California was the first to formalize it in the United States and took it to its greatest point of development." [21] At least in theory, "shared-governance" means some self-governance.

How much is some? The senate's powers were limited by the language of their establishment. Strictly speaking, the faculty's role is advisory. This means that in routine cases, it tends to be reactive rather than proactive. As Kerr put it, the faculty "is more likely to accept or reject or comment, than to devise and propose." [22] It means that in crisis situations, administrators and regents can ignore faculty with relative impunity.

The most famous recent case involved Regent Ward Connerly's successful attempt in July 1995 to eliminate the use of race, ethnicity, and gender as factors in admissions, hiring, and contracting at UC. The academic senate asked that Connerly delay his proposals so that faculty could either participate in their development or at least be formally consulted. Backed by Governor Wilson, Connerly refused, correctly observing that final authority over all UC policy belongs to the regents. When President Richard Atkinson later attempted to delay implementation of the regents' actions in admissions, he was forced to recant publicly and to acknowledge the regents as a higher power. [23] When the American Association of University Professors found that the manner in which the regents proceeded in eliminating race and gender criteria did indeed violate norms of shared governance, the regents either denounced or ignored the report. When the senate argued that the regents' Standing Orders of 1920 delegated authority to the senate to "determine the conditions for admission," the president, backed by university lawyers, argued that this did *not* mean that the senate had the authority to challenge Connerly's unilateral proposals about admissions criteria beyond minimum "conditions." The Standing

Orders meant that faculty set "minimum academic qualifications" for admission—grade-point averages, standardized test requirements, and high school course distributions. But the phrase *conditions for admission* did not refer to "other admissions criteria," the president wrote. These, "and the selection from among the students who meet those criteria, are the responsibility of the regents and the administration."[24] This distinction between setting basic standards (faculty) and the actual power of selection (administration) rests on the refusal to grant *executive* authority to faculty, whose role is that of technical consultant. Faculty have advisory input but no policy-making agency.

Conflicts like that around admissions also show that there are limits to the domain in which the senate can effectively operate. The senate's base has always been educational policy—the hiring, firing, and evaluation of academic personnel, admissions, curricular revisions, degree requirements, and so on. The most effective faculty protest I've witnessed at UCSB was based on the faculty right to review educational policy. In 1990–91, President David Gardner announced, after consulting the chancellor of the Santa Barbara campus, that some officials in the Education Abroad Program (EAP) had persuaded him to move the UC headquarters of the EAP to Oakland. The EAP had been offered to the new Santa Barbara campus thirty years before and had been developed by Santa Barbara personnel into one of the best education abroad programs in the country. The office of the president's explanation for the move was almost exclusively budgetary—it offered administrative savings in the long run.[25]

UCSB's academic senate strongly objected on the principal grounds that EAP was an academic program long nurtured by Santa Barbara faculty and that its departure would have an educational impact about which both the president and the UCSB administration had failed to consult the appropriate senate bodies. The senate raised the political costs of Gardner's decision with a well-planned emergency resolution that denounced this decision as an abrogation of the senate's rights of consultation. There were suggestions of a no-confidence vote in Santa Barbara's chancellor, who had known about the plan for months but had failed to notify the senate. These moves raised the costs high enough that Gardner tabled the idea. I watched in surprise as a series of faculty—especially faculty near retirement age—stood up in that meeting and declared, "My rights as a citizen of this university have been violated." I half expected some-one to pull out a flag reading "don't tread on me."

Another fact about this event was also important. The office of the president did not formally concede to the senate any right to share in the decision about the move. Gardner passed the issue on to his successor, Jack Peltason, who, under continuing pressure from Santa Barbara, re-jected the idea. Their silent dictum: we admit nothing. They especially didn't admit any formal senate authority over the budgeting process. Most budgetary issues large and small have academic implications—a million bucks for a new radio system for facilities management could be seen as affecting the funds available for new faculty hires, biology tutors, and so on, and discussions of radios could lead to phone calls to the bud-get office.

This is precisely where the plug gets pulled. Money matters evoke a sharp bifurcation between administration and senate. The baseline as-sumption is that the administration controls the budget process and budget information. The information is officially public, and faculty are an official part of the process, but reality is differently dictated by a gen-eral practice of divided sovereignty. Faculty can seek budget information, as they did during the financially scariest months of early 1993, and their direct questions will receive narrow answers. But they will exhaust them-selves in unsuccessful efforts to get the big picture. Just as important, they will have little voice in policy solutions.

At one meeting in 1993, I watched a distressing sequence. A staff mem-ber stood to ask the budgeteers on stage why "contract and grant" money couldn't be used to make up some of the shortfall in the instructional budget, which depended heavily on the state's general fund. An admin-istrator said it's illegal to shift funds like that. Someone else in the audi-ence rose to give an example of how such shifts are made routinely in his department. An administrator said well, yes, it is done sometimes. A third person raised her hand and asked why we wouldn't therefore make some transfers from contract and grant money in this emergency case? An administrator said it's really not that easy to do. A fourth rose to give another example of its ease. An administrator said yes, it is sometimes possible. A fifth asked, so why don't we? An administrator said the money is restricted. And so it went. Faculty and staff had "input," but the budget process was not visibly affected. Long-time senate participant-observer Dick Flacks put it to me this way: "The senate long ago got a strong voice in hiring and other educational issues. Budget policy remains an area of struggle." Or as Avery Gordon said, "We don't need more input without impact."

The psychological effects of this system on faculty are a sadly neglected area of real importance, and I'll just make one general comment here. The advisory role—which gets smaller as the issue gets bigger—means that faculty become accustomed to lots of work with little power. A large percentage of faculty administration goes into labor-intensive forms of self-policing where the final decision still belongs to someone else. This comes to seem normal, even convenient. We become fond of our permanent training wheels.

For example, the "step system" of faculty advancement and promotion means that each fall quarter about a third of a department's faculty must have the research and teaching of several years reviewed by the other two-thirds of their department. Most step increases amount to about 3 percent of base salary, averaged over a time-in-step of anywhere from two to five years. Thus, in my department of thirty-five faculty, careful reviews require fifteen to thirty faculty to spend about five hours apiece (counting file reading) deciding whether the candidate should receive a 1 percent annualized raise; furthermore, they would still only be *advising* a whole train of faculty and administrative bodies, at the front of which is an engineer—always an administrator—who makes the official decision. And this is the area of academic personnel, UC faculty's zone of power.

Most departments devise shortcuts, such as delegating the most routine cases to a small personnel committee. But the point remains the same: the more fully democratic the participation, the more trivial it seems; oligarchy then feels like a godsend of liberated time. Under the circumstances, it's hard to imagine *more* empowerment on personnel, which would mean more personnel work in departments in exchange for more final authority. This is indeed the classic position of labor in our economic system. It is labor in exchange for a wage, influence over workmates, and no steady, systematic comanagement.

The outcome has been well summarized in a recent piece by Linda Ray

Pratt, the chair of the English Department at the University of Nebraska at Lincoln:

The clear trend in administration is to encourage more participation at lower levels, such as the college, but to invest greater authority for final decisions at the higher levels of provosts and presidents. At the upper levels of administration, decisions about budget priorities are often openly political and designed to appease or inspire state, federal, and business interests. Whether the faculty and the administration can forge effective alliances at the college level to promote the academic agenda at the upper levels of administration is not yet clear.[26]

Current difficulties, however, are crystal clear. And so is a partial cause. Academic senates on the UC model are more an expression of than an obstacle to the two-tiered system Pratt laments. They are advisory rather than legislative; they assume bifurcation between educational and financial issues; and they accept separations, much like those of the traditional corporate pyramid, between frontliners and the boardroom. Shared governance is split governance. More accurately, it is split management. Such a system, without modification, cannot usher in the ideals of a more open collaboration envisioned by human relations theory. But this system can divert us.

Senate and Union

As a way of creating a dynamic UC culture, the split governance of senate and administration is very unevolved. It also forgoes the benefits of collaboration. Of course, there's some negative incentive to improve staff and faculty collaboration (students, a third major partner, are beyond my present scope). Business people have rarely paused to parse the differences between "staff" and "faculty" — they're just variations on "employee." This was true of Cooke's plan for faculty supervision. It was true during UC's loyalty oath controversy in 1950, when the university held that academic freedom did not pose an exception to regental authority and thirty-two faculty were fired for refusing to sign. It was true of Ward Connerly's plan for eliminating race and gender factors in UC admissions and hiring, when, hearing that some faculty thought he had violated their consultational rights, he invited them to "go back to the classroom." [27] The era of top-down management is not over, and senates do not offer faculty special immunity.

Under these circumstances, academic senates will have a better chance of making universities into exemplary creative cultures by synthesizing their perspectives with those of academic unions. I offer three examples of these combinations, which both follow and extend the three features of human relations thinking that I described above. I apologize in advance for the stereotyping to come.

1. Senate members are especially good at seeking *autonomy without management*. Unions are better at knowing that *autonomy requires defense against management*.

Most faculty I know view meetings and memos as a distraction from their real work of research and teaching. They understand the tremendous inspiration, pleasure, and productivity that arise from the nearly entirely self-managed task. Many of us have great freedom in designing and teaching our courses. Many have the same or greater freedom in designing our own research. Collaboration is almost entirely voluntary and self-directed. Complicated institutions like UC, of course, develop complicated bureaucracies as their basic metabolism. But within these places, senates can defend the kind of direct and unmediated self-management that most faculty experience at least some of the time. Senate members have continuous experience with the value of hands-on, autonomous work, and they should celebrate it every chance they get as a pillar of creativity.

Senates, however, are not as good about seeing the limits of accommodation and consensus. They tend to be deference cultures. Their membership often shows an aversion to the conflict on which self-management depends. Faculty who don't show this aversion tend to be marginal in senates. Union members, on the other hand, have a more acute sense that they must *oppose* administrators when they horde power, withhold information, fake consultation, waste money, defer to the strong, squeeze the weak, and favor the mediocre.

Here's a longish example of a kind of thinking that in my experience appears in unions far more regularly than in senates. Jay Stemmle, one of the leaders of the graduate student union movement at UCSB, was telling me about administrative opposition to a graduate union. "There's this idea of university exceptionalism. This is not a workplace at all, it says. It's a culture, a community. There's a cultural argument, a community argument against labor organizing on this campus."

"Why," I asked, "don't they see 'union' as compatible with 'community' "?

"We had a meeting with the American Federation of State, County, and Municipal Employees [A F S C M E], which represents various types of maintenance and clerical workers. And some of the A F S C M E people think the administration consists largely of control freaks who assume a system like this is much better run in a top-down fashion, that this is efficient and they're disturbed by any kind of democratizing impulse. With the grad students, the administrators say they're afraid of disruptions in mentorship. They're afraid of a fair grievance procedure because they feel that student employees should not be filing grievances at all. It's about giving up authority. They have a desire to see themselves as benign despots. It's important. They know they have more power but they're also invested in feeling that they know what's right. That they have the big picture. That they dispense justice.

"I'll give you an example," Stemmle continued. "At the very beginning of the legal case involving UC San Diego, the United Auto Workers' students were trying to argue that readers, tutors, and teaching associates should have collective-bargaining rights under the Higher Education Employer-Employee Relations Act. The act was a liberal compromise between labor and management, and it says that the three systems of California higher education [U C, California State University, and the community college system] have to negotiate with unions, but that once negotiations have begun the unions can't strike. U C's latest court initiative is to say that the act doesn't apply to them at all. The law only applies to these three educational systems, and one of them is trying to say that it doesn't apply to them at all.

"Well, the argument U C made in this case was that we should think about the television show *Star Trek*. The Public Employment Relations Board—which is the governing body for labor in public education in California—should be like the *Starship Enterprise*. It should follow the prime directive, which is not to interfere with what is going on on Planet U C.

We're paying these people a lot of money to make these kinds of arguments."

The union leaders with whom I spoke were all quite aware that the wish for unilateral control is common in management. They were equally aware that the preconditions of workplace autonomy—grievance procedures, for example—required a systematic confrontation with management. In the wake of the academic senate's relative weakness on the budget process, admissions, and suspended wages, the senate should consider the need for confrontation with the administration in specific areas where genuinely shared governance is not yet in sight.

2. Senates are good at *handling hierarchy with "guild" conservatism*. Unions are better at *handling hierarchy by seeking financial control*.

As the Education Abroad uprising suggested, UC's academic senates excel at raising the cost of change. They drag their feet, assert reviewing privileges, force the convening of new committees, and make life tiresome for administrators who, often being faculty, are disrupted by opposition. Kerr again puts the point nicely: "There is a kind of 'guild mentality' in the academic profession. . . . The guild was isolationist toward society, devoted to producer against consumer sovereignty, and committed more to guild rules than to quick adaptation to popular demand. . . . The guild view stands for self-determination, and for resistance against the administration and the trustees. . . . The guild view is elitist toward the external environment, conservative toward internal change, conformist in relation to the opinion of colleagues."[28] This is the best kind of conservatism—it puts tradition before authority. It is not an unthinking rejection of the new but a simple refusal to favor the ways of others over one's own simply because the others' ways have clout. This is the way faculty most easily stand their ground.

Faculty have been less good at getting control over the numbers. Given the financial nature of contemporary corporate power, it's hard to have any real footing without it. Human relations theorists have been trying out the idea of democratizing finance, though they would never call it that. They call it "open-book management." Management writer Jim Kouzes told me a story about one famous case.

"Take the Springfield Remanufacturing Corporation, in Springfield, Missouri, run by a right-wing Republican by the name of Jack Stack. And

Jack is a free enterprise capitalist—he's as Adam Smith as you can get. But he faced a crisis in 1983 when he managed the plant. He was ordered by International Harvester to sell the factory or shut it down. So he got a group of people of average education or below to get together with him and buy the company and turn it around.

"The problem was that Stack had the highest leveraged buyout in corporate history. He raised $100,000 from employees and borrowed $8.9 million. He had eighty-nine parts debt to one part equity. As it turned out, it's a tremendous success story. They went from a loss to making a profit within four years of the buyout. They've had an increase of 23,000 percent in corporate stock values. They went from about 190 to 800 employees. They've had sales growth exceeding 30 percent a year.

"Stack started by saying to himself, 'The only way I'm going to make this happen is if I give these employees the skills, tools, and capability to do this. We need to give everybody in the company a voice in running the company and a stake in the financial outcome.' He taught everyone, including people who sweep the floor, how to read a balance sheet, how to read an income statement, how to read a financial statement. Weekly he gives them a report on how well they are doing in their area. It's called 'open-book management.' It's been one of the revolutions in business. The whole assumption that underlies open-book management is that the skills of finance, which we think only somebody with an M BA can manage to comprehend, are skills that everyone can learn."

Stack wrote a book—*The Great Game of Business* (1992)—in which he stresses the simultaneous financial and personal benefits of opening the books. "The more people know about a company, the better that company will perform. This is an iron-clad rule. You will *always* be more successful in business by sharing information with the people you work with than by keeping them in the dark." He adds a bit later, "Numbers can give meaning to your job, show you exactly where you fit in, why you're important." [29]

I don't need to belabor the radical change this practice would mean for universities. Think of the secrecy around budgeting; of the discretionary funds and the side deals and private arrangements; of the numbered photocopies of partial budgets that are passed out at administrator's meetings with senate representatives and collected at the end; of the public university library where the most recent budget available is 1986–87. Think of the absence of general justification and debate about the priorities behind the resource allocation that shapes the university for decades to come. Think of the sheer financial inefficiency of such restricted financial inputs—of so many wasted ideas, missing feedback, and neglected enthusiasms.

Open-book management is not only a management idea; it traces its lineage to the union movement and to workplace democracy initiatives after World War II. It also plays a role in increasingly popular employee stock ownership plans, and in the growing influence in the boardroom of union pension funds. For example, U P T E is affiliated with the Communication Workers of America, which is trying to unionize the higher education workforce as "the higher education union for the information age." The first issue of its paper, the *Campus Voice*, carried an article by Mark Blum called "Preparing to Fight over Institutional Finances," in which he tries to demystify budgeting so that employees can try to influence the process. "The budget is only a plan," Blum writes. "It is a statement of the priorities of the people who made it up." [30] The union recommends developing the kinds of continuing discussions about financial management that senates should do much more to support.

3. Senate members cherish job security, that is, their *tenure*, and would be good at explaining *why tenure is so great*. Unions are good at linking job security to all kinds of labor and showing why *general tenure is a general benefit*.

The senate's conservatism overlaps with human relations radicalism on the benefits of stable employment. Rather than defending tenure as the right of their members' unique achievements, senates could defend it as a major pillar of everyone's creativity. Kerr argues that the basis of faculty "inventiveness" is "the protection and solidity of the surrounding institutional structure":

The university . . . needs to create an environment that gives to its faculty members:

a sense of stability—they should not fear constant change that distracts them from their work;

a sense of security—they should not need to worry about the attacks against them from outside the gate;

a sense of continuity—they should not be concerned that their work and the structure of their lives will be greatly disrupted;

a sense of equity—they should not be suspicious that others are being treated better than they are.[31]

This vision could lose its paternalism while retaining its conviction that brilliance does not flow primarily from the fear and competition of the marketplace. Senate conservatism is sometimes senate anticapitalism. It reflects local knowledge that empowerment rather than profit or downsizing is the basis of great research and teaching.

It's union thinking, however, that argues that some version of tenure would enhance every kind of labor. Faculty tend to think of tenure as the earned privilege of their exceptional talent, merit, and past achievement. Unions see it as the privilege of productive work. Stemmle had a good way of saying it:

The university is sounding more and more like Borders Books. They're now using exactly the same arguments. "It's not that we're anti-union. It's that unions are inimical to Borders' culture." The university pushes the same idea really hard. "We're special." They don't use a language of the family. It's that there's something so delicate about academic work. Something so delicate about producing new knowledge. New knowledge, the university says, is produced with genius or native intelligence, instead of with work that's done by all kinds of different people in all kinds of different roles.

We've tried hoarding tenure as a special grace distinguishing the best. Not many are impressed. Why not try spreading tenure around? Show that it's something that all kinds of laborers earn. Show that academic work requires all kinds of people—it's a public and a social activity as well as a hermetic and spooky one. Show that the world of work actually *is* inside, and not just outside, the university, that all sorts of people are partners together. Ask managers to be smart enough actually to orchestrate the efforts of their employees instead of simply controlling or terminating them. We'd have better work, better political alliances, and more energy and pleasure running through the institution were faculty and unions together working toward tenure for all.

Faculty and staff have the resources to use human relations approaches to fight off scientific management. They can improve human relations approaches in the process. The composite portraits I just offered are sketchy, and I've only hinted at the momentum behind employee empowerment in some major sectors of the corporate world. I'm convinced that university culture will stay stuck in a downsizing managerial past unless faculty and staff can pool their strengths as complementary varieties of academic labor. And the potential benefits are enormous: Establishing the knowledge worker democracy in governance that's already crucial to knowledge work itself; employing it as genuine shared governance in budgeting, the firm's basic operating code; building a secure framework for the kinds of transforming collaborations that, in our ongoing Taylorist twilight, we are only beginning to imagine.

Notes

I want to thank Randy Martin, Monica Marciczkiewicz, and Bruce Robbins for their patience and editorial suggestions. I'm especially grateful to Avery Gordon for her typically tireless and invaluable conversation.

1 Clyde W. Barrow, *Universities and the Capitalist State: Corporate Liberalism and the Reconstruction of American Higher Education, 1894–1928* (Madison: University of Wisconsin Press, 1990), 61–71.

2 Neil Fligstein, *The Transformation of Corporate Control* (Cambridge: Harvard University Press, 1990), 15.

3 Clark Kerr, *The Uses of the University* (Cambridge: Harvard University Press, 1964), v–vi.

4 Ibid., 48.

5 Ibid., 58.

6 Ibid., 59–60.

7 Ibid., 67.

8 Ibid., 89.

9 V. Wayne Kennedy, "Message from the Senior Vice President—Business and Finance," "Annual Financial Report, 1995–1996," http://www.ucop.edu/ ucophome/eao/reports/mesbf.html.

10 Financial authority was, of course, abetted by "big-machine" scientific research during and after World War II, when research and accounting became increasingly interdependent. For parts of the story see Richard Rhodes, *The Making of the Atomic Bomb* (New York: Simon and Schuster, 1986), and Stanley Aronowitz and William DiFazio, *The Jobless Future: Sci-Tech and the Dogma of Work* (Minneapolis: University of Minnesota Press, 1994).

11 Kerr notes that federal programs have generally "operated fully within academic traditions." "By way of contrast, state control of state universities has been a real problem" (*Uses of the University*, 57).

12 Peter F. Drucker, *Post-Capitalist Society* (New York: HarperCollins, 1993); Michel Albert, *Capitalism vs. Capitalism*, trans. Paul Haviland, intro. Felix G. Rohatyn (New York: Four Walls Eight Windows, 1993); Charles Hampden-Turner and Alfons Trompenaars, *The Seven Cultures of Capitalism* (New York: Currency-Doubleday, 1993).

13 Peter F. Drucker, "The Relentless Contrarian," interview by Peter Schwartz and Kevin Kelly, *Wired*, August 1996, 184.

14 M. Mitchell Waldrop, "The Trillion-Dollar Vision of Dee Hock," *Fast Company*, October/November 1996, 75, 77.

15 Peter M. Senge, *The Fifth Discipline: The Art and Practice of the Learning Organization* (New York: Currency-Doubleday, 1990), 143.

16 Drucker, "Relentless Contrarian," 119–20.

17 John Micklethwait and Adrian Wooldridge, *The Witch Doctors: Making Sense of the Management Gurus* (New York: Times-Random House, 1996), 9.

18 Martha Cody-Valdez mentions one example of faculty involvement. "A Berkeley Academic Senate report on HMRI pointed out that while the theory that incentive pay works 'may be popular in management literature . . . it is not clear there is empirical evidence that this works better than a merit system that keeps salaries even with inflation and builds a retirement base' " ("HRMI Negatives Outweigh Positives," 93106, January 8, 1996, 2).

19 D. Dougherty and E. H. Bowman, "The Effects of Organizational Downsizing on Product Development," *California Management Review* 37, no. 4 (1995): 28–44.

20 Charles Schwartz, "Looking into the UC Budget — Report #19" (unpublished manuscript).

21 John A. Douglass, "Shared Governance: Shaped by Conflict and by Agreement," *Notice* 20 (November 1995): 4–5.

22 Kerr, *Uses of the University*, 100.

23 The regents were divided about Connerly's proposals (the votes on two re-

lated resolutions were 14-10 and 15-10 in favor of banning race, gender, and ethnicity as selection factors). The regents were more unanimous about the question of their own sovereignty.

24 "What Admissions Authority Does the UC Faculty Have?" *Notice* 20 (June 1996): 4–5. "According to one U C Deputy General Counsel Gary Morrison, a condition is 'a characteristic that is required, not that is desirable.' 'It is something that must be met to get over the bar.' It follows from this, he says, that the regents have charged the senate only with determining minimal standards for admission. Meanwhile, he says, the administration's authority over admissions derives from the broad authority the regents have granted to the president and chancellors. As Standing Order 100.6 notes, campus chancellors are to be 'the executive head of all activities on that campus, except as herein otherwise provided. . . .' Thus, in the General Counsel's view, what has not been delegated to the faculty has been delegated to the administration and what *has* been delegated to the faculty concerns only basic entrance requirements."

25 According to one knowledgeable faculty observer, one of Gardner's financial vice presidents offered a savings figure of $175,000, which critics pointed out would be negated in the long run by higher Oakland salaries, moving costs, and so on.

26 Linda Ray Pratt, "Negotiating Agendas? Academic Management for Quality and Control," *Profession 1996*: 42.

27 *Sacramento Bee,* August 17, 1995, A1.

28 Kerr, *Uses of the University,* 99.

29 Jack Stack, with Bo Burlingham, *The Great Game of Business* (New York: Currency-Doubleday, 1992), 71, 74.

30 Mark Blum, "Preparing to Fight over Institutional Finances," *CWA Campus Voice* (summer 1996): 3.

31 Kerr, *Uses of the University,* 95.

The Stratification of the Academy

Zelda F. Gamson

Higher education is a mammoth industry. There are more than thirty-six hundred colleges and universities in this country with one million faculty members and fifteen million students. The property owned by colleges and universities has been estimated to be worth over $200 billion, total expenditures to be $175 billion, and annual university research and development expenditures to be about $20 billion.

This overall picture includes an enormous variety of institutions. Among four-year institutions, only 8 percent of private colleges and universities and 3 percent of public universities are very selective. All the rest, both public and private, are less selective or totally unselective, with the largest percentage concentrated at the bottom.

There are tremendous inequalities in the academy on almost any measure we might want to use. For example, the average family income of students in the very selective schools is *three to four times* that of students in the least selective schools. Faculty salaries do not show as extreme a ratio, but the differences are quite consistent: faculty in private research universities earn almost twice as much as faculty in liberal arts colleges. When we factor in total income—which includes consulting income, royalties, and other institutional income—faculty in private research universities are by far the highest paid, earning two and one-half times more than liberal arts college faculty. Average instructional and student services expenditures per student, a figure that is imperfect but the best measure of institutional resources available for educational (as opposed to research) purposes, declines markedly across the spectrum. Expenditures per student in private universities are more than twice those in liberal arts colleges and more than three times those in community colleges.

The Power of the Research Culture in the Expansionary Period

The academy is clearly at the end of the expansionary period that began after World War II and reached its pinnacle in the 1960s and 1970s. When Christopher Jencks and David Riesman published *The Academic Revolution* in 1968, the research university was at its height. The victory of the "academic revolution," as they called it, had been a genteel and well-funded affair underwritten by enormous amounts of federal support for higher education: government support in 1950 was *3 percent* of what it was in 1980.[1]

Universities hired staffs of academics whose main work was doing research rather than teaching. If they did occasionally teach, these researchers were to be found in the graduate seminar, not the undergraduate lecture hall. The bargaining power of the faculty was heightened considerably during the early 1960s, especially in the research universities, when there were not enough college professors to teach the advance guard of the baby boom generation, which was beginning its march through higher education. College faculty began to be recruited nationally according to their scholarly research rather than their teaching ability. Faculty who never again did any scholarly work after their Ph.D. dissertations (and many did not) thought of themselves primarily as members of their disciplines—biologists, sociologists—not as educators.

In a general trend away from localism and single purposes, denominational colleges became more secular, single-sex colleges went coed, and teachers' colleges and other specialized institutions broadened their curricula. The exhilaration of expansion during this period propelled colleges across the country to broaden their missions and curricula. But in the process, older sources of legitimacy, such as commitment to a religious order or a particular population, became less serviceable, and the transformed institutions sought new markers of identity. The situation was ripe for what Paul DiMaggio and Walter Powell term "mimetic isomorphism," the imitation of apparently successful organizations by less successful ones.[2] Imitation is likely when organizations have ambiguous purposes or face uncertainty about their future. Many colleges and universities during the 1960s and 1970s allowed themselves to be pulled toward what appeared to be the only worthwhile model to emulate: the research culture.

The research culture draws its essential character from graduate faculty in research universities. It has three main elements: First, it is based on national rather than local allegiances. Second, it values research over teaching and service. Third, it prizes pure over applied research activities.[3] Through the socialization of new generations of faculty, through invisible colleges of scholars across the country working in similar subdisciplines, and through the peer review of grant applications and publications, these graduate faculty define the content, methods, and research problems addressed in funded projects, journals, and professional associations.[4]

The preeminence of the research culture is underscored by almost a century's worth of institutional ranking schemes. These ranking systems not only ensure visibility to those at the top but also legitimate an institutional hierarchy based on measures that are closely related to the research culture.[5] To some extent, this can be said of the category system invented by the Carnegie Foundation for the Advancement of Teaching and widely used by researchers and granting agencies. These categories have spurred many a doctorate-granting university to be reclassified as "research university," and "research university II" to be classified as "research university I." This giant classification sweepstakes can be seen as a kind of race whose winners are Harvard, the University of California at Berkeley, and Stanford.

By these means, a kind of invisible hand has guided the competition for faculty reputation, power, and prestige and, by extension, institutional prestige. In his study of the career mobility of faculty in a highly ranked department in a research university, Darwin Sawyer noted that "the professional status of an individual is as much an organizational resource in the institutional career of the department(s) which employ him/her as the institutional status of the department is a personal resource in the organizational careers of its members."[6] Prestige is a resource that enables universities to garner more tangible resources. An institution can offer its prestige by extension to its other constituents who, in return, place additional resources at its disposal. The greater the prestige generated by the institution, the more advantages it has in the competition for research funds, graduate students, and undergraduate enrollments.

It is no wonder that many formerly specialized colleges and universities aped the overwhelmingly successful culture of the research university. This mimicry became especially strong during the 1970s, when the scramble for resources became intense and administrators sought new ways to sustain the level of security and growth of the 1960s. The buyer's market of the 1970s allowed many institutions to hire faculty with more prestigious pedigrees than they had previously attracted.[7] This new breed of faculty brought a commitment to scholarly work that corresponded to administrators' desire for institutional prestige.

Faculty in liberal arts colleges, state colleges, and universities—places noted for their commitment to teaching and students—talked about needing more time for research. Faculty teaching loads declined everywhere but in community colleges, where the research culture never took hold. This correspondence of interests led relatively quickly to the inclusion of new criteria for hiring, promotion, and tenure that emphasized scholarly standards.[8] In other words, faculty who published a lot were favored with pay increases, leaves, sabbaticals, and release time. This shift toward a research culture is demonstrated by the change in faculty responses to a survey taken by the Carnegie Foundation. The survey, first taken in 1969, asked faculty to respond to the following statement: "It is difficult for a person to receive tenure if he/she does not publish." In 1969, 19 percent of the faculty in master's-level institutions agreed with this statement. Twenty years later, 65 percent agreed. In liberal arts colleges the change is not as dramatic but nevertheless striking for teaching institutions: 18 percent agreed in 1969, and 39 percent agreed in 1989.[9]

The march of the research culture throughout higher education was uneven, to be sure, but it took hold and delivered the goods—at least during the expansionary period—from donors and state budgets, if not from federal research programs, whose grants and contracts overwhelmingly went to research universities. As with the general economy in the postwar era, a rising tide raised all boats. All of higher education benefited from the expansion of the system, and the research culture legitimated that system. But while all the boats were rising, not all were rising at the same rate. The luxury liners—research universities, and the leading private ones in particular—led the way, followed by a variety of small yachts, sailboats, and tugboats.

The Tide Turns

As the expansionary period peaked and then declined, the research culture began to lose its power. There are demographic, economic, and political reasons for this. Declines in the traditional college-going age group, whose impact has been greatest in the unselective colleges and universities, especially private ones, have led to great competition for a smaller pool of students in the last few years. The decrease in the eighteen- to twenty-two-year-old, college-going population was balanced to some extent by increases in the attendance of older students overall, but not necessarily in the schools that have experienced the greatest enrollment stress—less selective private colleges with small endowments. Many of these colleges are barely surviving today, and some have gone under. It does not help them to know that the tide is shifting in the other direction, as the children of the baby boomers hit the campuses in full force.

College and university tuitions have been rising. In the thirteen years between 1976 and 1989, tuition and fees in public four-year colleges and universities almost tripled; in private institutions, they increased three and one-third times. Job insecurity, falling wages, and economic uncertainty have led students and their families to find paying for a college education, even in the public sector, a major hardship. Indeed, surveys show that one of the greatest concerns of the general public is the costs of higher education. This concern has found its way into public policy and the media. Higher education has increasingly been treated as just another entitlement burden on taxpayers; decreasing support for higher education can be used to offset state deficits and as a trade-off with claims from other constituencies.

A series of reports and books attacking higher education have appeared in rapid fire from the mid-1980s through the 1990s: in the mid-1980s, we had *Involvement in Learning*, a higher education sequel to the U.S. Department of Education's *A Nation at Risk*, which focused on schools; *To Reclaim a Legacy* under the leadership of William Bennett when he headed the National Endowment for the Humanities; and *Integrity in the College Curriculum*, issued by the Association of American Colleges. A critique by insiders and liberal reformers took shape in hundreds of reports from state and federal agencies and from higher education associations, which argued that undergraduate education was in serious trouble and that faculty seemed unable or unwilling to do anything about it. More recently, Bruce Wilshire in *The Moral Collapse of the University* and Page Smith in *Killing the Spirit* offered explanations about why this was so, and those explanations rested squarely in a critique of the research culture.[10]

These critiques did not reach the general public. A campaign by conservatives, with a well-funded media program backed by right-wing foundations and think tanks, took higher education to the streets. First there was Allan Bloom's *Closing of the American Mind*, then in rapid fire Charles Sykes's *Profscam*, Dinesh D'Souza's *Illiberal Education*, Martin Anderson's *Imposters in the Temple*, and Roger Kimball's *Tenured Radicals*.[11] These books attacked the faculty for "political correctness" and 1960s radicalism; the curriculum for faddishness and neglect of the canon; and administrators for lack of leadership. In less than ten years the sanctity of the academy was in serious jeopardy. State and federal governments have been taking more control over university budgets, admissions criteria, financial aid, outcomes, research conditions—and most recently faculty workloads. The story line from the states and Washington goes something like this: Colleges and universities are irresponsible and arrogant. They cannot explain what they do. They charge high tuition and misuse money. Faculty have lifetime employment and long vacations and do anything they want.

What they want to do is research, not teach. Their research is silly and useless. (Remember Senator Proxmire's Golden Fleece Awards?) They need to be brought into line.

Tenure and promotion committees and college presidents playing the Carnegie sweepstakes may not know it yet, but the research culture is losing its currency. The gains brought by the research culture are beginning to erode: research grants are harder to get, overhead is down, and the cost to institutions of carrying out research is up. Declines in tuition dollars because of lower enrollment or large amounts of student aid lead to questions about faculty productivity and teaching loads. Assistant professors, those indentured for years before winning tenure, are gasping for air from the stratospheric publication requirements to which they are being held. They have been evincing surprising support for the abolition of tenure. Like other industries, universities are hiring casual labor. So-called part-time or non-tenure-track faculty have been a growing part of the faculty labor force outside of the top tier.

Attacks on the research culture have not seriously affected the schools in which that culture was created. In the leading research universities, faculty continue to reap the fruits of the research culture in low teaching loads, time and resources for research, and tenure. Despite efforts to spread their largess more widely than in the past, federal agencies, private foundations, and major donors still disproportionately fund a tiny group of leading research universities. Faculty salaries in most colleges and universities have been stagnant, whereas salaries in leading private research universities have been marching upward at a faster rate than those at equally eminent public research universities.

The stratification system in the academy is stronger than ever. The gulf is widening between a small number of affluent and highly selective institutions—where competition for admission is fierce and mostly privileges the wealthy—and hard-pressed public and private institutions. Low-income students are increasingly concentrated in community colleges. This divide mirrors the growing income inequality in the society as a whole.

What will replace the research culture in the majority of colleges and universities is still unclear, but we have glimmers of the future. Some colleges—women's colleges, sectarian colleges—are refocusing on the particular constituencies they had abandoned twenty or thirty years ago. Regional colleges and universities are rebuilding ties to regional and local organizations through service learning and mission-oriented research and professional expertise. There is much talk about recalibrating the faculty reward structure toward more recognition of teaching and service. Others are turning back to community as a way of enhancing their appeal to students and of recapturing faculty commitment to their institutions. It will be interesting for all of us to watch — better yet, to participate in — the process of finding new purpose in a world that has changed around us.

Notes

This essay was presented at the 1996 Annual Meeting of the American Sociological Association.

1 See table 95 in American Council on Higher Education, *1989–90 Fact Book on Higher Education* (New York: Macmillan, 1989).

2 Paul J. DiMaggio and Walter W. Powell, "The Iron Cage Revisited: Institutional Isomorphism and Collective Rationality in Organizational Fields," *American Sociological Review* 48 (April 1983): 147–60.

3 See Dorothy E. Finnegan and Zelda F. Gamson, "Disciplinary Adaptations to Research Culture in Comprehensive Institutions," *Review of Higher Education* 19 (winter 1996): 141–77, for a fuller discussion of the research culture and its implications.

4 Tony Becher, *Academic Tribes and Territories: Intellectual Enquiry and the Culture of Disciplines* (Milton Keynes, England: Open University Press, 1989).

5 See David Webster, *Quality Rankings* (Springfield, Ill.: Thomas Crown, 1986), for a detailed analysis of the use of rankings in higher education.

6 Darwin O. Sawyer, "Institutional Stratification and Career Mobility in Academic Markets," *Sociology of Education* 54 (April 1981): 86.

7 A recent study of how this happened in "comprehensive" universities — institutions with both arts and sciences as well as professional degrees at the bachelor's and master's levels — is reported in Dorothy E. Finnegan, "Segmentation in the Academic Labor Market: Hiring Cohorts in Comprehensive Universities," *Journal of Higher Education* 64 (November/December 1993): 621–56.

8 Françoise A. Queval, "The Evolution toward Research Orientation and Capa-

bility in Comprehensive Universities: The California State System," Ph.D. diss., University of California at Los Angeles, 1990.

9 Carnegie Foundation for the Advancement of Teaching, *National Survey of Faculty* (Princeton, N.J.: Carnegie Foundation, 1989).

10 Study Group on the Conditions of Excellence in American Higher Education, *Involvement in Learning: Realizing the Potential of American Higher Education* (Washington, D.C.: U.S. Department of Education, 1984); National Commission on Excellence in Education, *A Nation at Risk: The Imperative for Educational Reform* (Washington, D.C.: U.S. Government Printing Office, 1983); National Endowment for the Humanities, *To Reclaim a Legacy: A Report on the Humanities in Higher Education* (Washington, D.C.: U.S. Government Printing Office, 1984); Association of American Colleges, *Integrity in the College Curriculum: A Report to the Academic Community* (Washington, D.C.: Author, 1985); Bruce Wilshire, *The Moral Collapse of the University: Professionalism, Purity, and Alienation* (Albany: State University of New York Press, 1990); Page Smith, *Killing the Spirit: Higher Education in America* (New York: Penguin, 1991).

11 Allan Bloom, *The Closing of the American Mind: How Higher Education Has Failed Democracy and Impoverished the Souls of Today's Students* (New York: Simon and Schuster, 1987); Charles Sykes, *Profscam: Professors and the Demise of Higher Education* (Washington, D.C.: Regnery Gateway, 1988); Dinesh D'Souza, *Illiberal Education: The Politics of Race and Sex on Campus* (New York: Random House, 1992); Martin Anderson, *Imposters in the Temple: American Intellectuals Are Destroying Our Universities and Cheating Our Students of Their Future* (New York: Simon and Schuster, 1992); Roger Kimball, *Tenured Radicals: How Politics Has Corrupted Our Higher Education* (New York: Harper Perennial, 1991).

The Ascent toward Corporate Managerialism in American and Australian Universities

Jan Currie and Lesley Vidovich

A shift from collegial to managerial forms of university governance has been widely observed as a "global" trend,[1] and the strengths and weaknesses of collegial versus managerial approaches have been debated at some length in more recent literature. Contrasting these styles as binary opposites, however, masks their complexities and ignores the possibility of multiple and often hybrid "models" of decision making. Our primary intention here is to investigate some of the dynamics and tensions inherent in the way different decision-making styles are currently played out in universities. We draw on interviews with academics in six universities in Australia and the United States to identify some of the "messy realities" of university governance, including unintended effects of the predominant "top-down" approaches, as perceived by our respondents.[2]

The choice of countries was not accidental. They both have adopted New Right practices and the rhetoric of globalization as an ideology that assumes the dominance of market forces. A number of commentators in Australia have described changes in Australian universities as representing an Americanization of higher education, and thus case studies of universities in both countries allow us to examine this phenomenon. Such comparisons also enable American educators to contrast their own experiences with change processes in a more centralized system.

In the concluding discussion, we propose that the first step in dislodging the hegemony of corporate managerial discourse would be to preserve and extend the remnants of genuinely consultative and participative decision making that are still evident (albeit in fragments) in some of the universities studied. Next, the advantages embedded in alternative modes of decision making could be legitimated in recognizing multiple styles, the particular combination of which would vary across and within universities, as well as over time. Then, more careful consideration must be given to the way in which "top-down" and "bottom-up" styles articulate.

Conceptual Tools

Three particular terms—"collegiality," "bureaucracy," and "managerialism" (including "corporate" managerialism)—were used frequently by interview respondents to describe both the existing and the changing nature of decision making in their universities. It is important to emphasize that these are not unproblematic "pure types" about which there is common understanding, and thus we will begin by describing their features in order then to critique them and later use them as analytic tools to examine our interview data. Although bureaucratic and managerial styles have been clearly distinguished as "ideal types" in the literature, respondents often used them interchangeably, especially when referring to top-down modes of decision making. Collegiality was usually juxtaposed against these other forms.

In its ideal type, collegiality is characterized by shared decision making, along with trust, openness, concern, and cooperation.[3] It is associated with the exercise of individual autonomy within the "umbrella" of collective action, so that leadership functions can be extended through many levels of the organization from senior to junior staff.[4] Although this type is usually linked with traditional-style universities, in reality dissatisfaction with control by "god-professors"[5] and claims that traditional university governance was authoritarian, undemocratic, hierarchical, and characterized by poor communication channels[6] have been common. Even if some form of collegiality did exist in the past, it has come under pressure as the market mentality dominates and there is a push for rapid responses to changing external circumstances, thus rendering the time-consuming consultative processes too slow.[7]

Bureaucracy (the second ideal type referred to by respondents) features highly centralized decision making with control through close supervision and an emphasis on standard operating procedures to produce uniformity across the organization. In Australia, the former colleges of advanced education were characterized by bureaucratic structures/processes to a greater extent than were the traditional universities.[8] In the United States community colleges have been known to be more bureaucratic than research universities. When S. Lawton outlined a critique of bureaucracies on philosophical, technological, social, and practical grounds, he identified the practical problems of inefficiencies and inability to attain specified purposes as the primary concerns.[9] Such difficulties were exacerbated by the growing volume of information required to make appropriate decisions. Furthermore public service bureaucracies were seen to benefit their own members more than the public they were supposed to serve.

In more recent times, the ideal type of managerialism has been heralded as a panacea for the inefficiencies of unwieldy and self-serving bureaucracies and for the even slower pace of democratic decision making, with its proliferation of representative committees. Hence, efficiency (minimizing costs) and effectiveness (maximizing outcomes) are emphasized as the key features of managerialism.[10] Managerialism is commonly perceived as the administrative form associated with the prevailing ideology of neoliberalism, the New Right, or, as it is more commonly known in Australia, economic rationalism.[11] It simultaneously features the contradictory directions of centralization and decentralization (or devolution) of decision making.[12] A managerial elite at the top sets the goals, and then a line management system is established (from the vice chancellor or president through to heads of departments) in which each subordinate is accountable to a superior for his or her performance.[13] Budgetary responsibility is devolved through this route. Managerialism has been described as a mechanism for "tight-loose" coupling with central control over goals or "ends" but flexibility over the procedures or "means."[14]

Criticism of managerialism is extensive in the current literature, given its prominent position in public sector restructuring, including universities. The claimed enhanced efficiency and effectiveness as the primary advantage of managerialism has been challenged on various grounds, especially by academics. G. Treuren maintains that little evidence exists that line management has led to greater productivity or efficiency.[15] Instead, there have been assertions that both efficiency and effectiveness have suffered because managerialism has impacted on staff to increase alienation and decrease morale so that commitment to work toward management-prescribed goals is reduced.[16] There is also the argument that the increasing percentages of staff and of budgets spent on "administration" is both inefficient and ineffective as it diverts resources away from the core productive activities of teaching and research.[17] The Solomons describe some of the effects of adopting the corporate metaphor that tends to shift resources of the university "upstairs": "Administrators come to think of themselves as the university, just as corporate management has come to think of itself as the corporation."[18] Others argue that devolution of some of the administrative tasks to those who are still trying to teach and research is likely to be done only badly as academics have not been trained in management skills.[19] Moreover, the system of accountability required to monitor the performance of academic staff necessitates much documentation—form filling and report writing—so that the amount of time lower-level line managers can spend on their own area of expertise is then restricted.[20]

The rhetoric of devolution promises professional autonomy, but critics argue that the power relationships are obscured and, in particular, that questions exist over whether it is responsibility, without power, which is devolved. A number of commentators draw on Foucault's notions of disciplinary power and surveillance to describe the new forms of govern-mentality by institutional managers.[21]

Performance management (inherent in the system of accountability associated with managerialism) has been criticized for distorting and narrowing the work of academics in favor of the most readily docu-mented and measured activities and therefore ignoring issues such as quality, potential, and reflective practice, such that in the end academic work will be "transformed into something not recognizable as academic work."[22] The role of managerialism in distorting the university "enter-prise" toward economic priorities, ignoring social and cultural dimen-sions, has been a major concern about the reforms to university manage-ment.[23]

The various critiques of managerialism might be drawn together by pointing to its overemphasis on processes or "means" and its concomi-tant narrowing of the goals or "ends" that are deemed to be legitimate outcomes. Thus, while bureaucracies (as large organizations with both ends and means predetermined) epitomized modernism, the rhetoric of managerial culture (with flexibility created through local discretion over the means) appears to be more consistent with a postmodern approach to organizations. Arguably though, managerialism may represent a more subtle control mechanism capable of bringing surveillance closer to the "workface" through more sophisticated accountability procedures—and thus we would argue a case for heightened modernity.

When a governance style is described as managerial, the adjective "cor-porate" is often used, signifying that business/industry has been the source of the model. With stronger links being forged between the cor-porate sector and universities, the cross-fertilization of cultures (theo-retically two-way) is likely to be enhanced. In Australia, a number of com-mentators have argued that the ideologues promulgating this "corporate" managerial approach to public sector reform have come from the govern-ment rather than the corporate sector.[24] This observation is consistent with the notion that the state has been redefined as a mechanism for steering market forces.[25] A. Yeatman situates the reconfiguration of the state in a global context: "This has indeed meant—at least in the Anglo-American liberal democracies—a rolling back of the *welfare* state."[26] It has not meant a rolling back of the state as such. Instead, the direction of the state's interventions and commitments have changed. Cerny summarizes this change as one from the welfare state to the competition state.[27]

Regardless of which agent has forged the changes, the suitability of directly importing corporate models for university governance has been questioned extensively.[28] It is ironic that businesses, which supposedly provided the model for more efficient and effective higher education institutions, are moving to flatten management hierarchies, at a time when universities are still initiating moves to build them, particularly by strengthening middle management in the form of executive deans.[29] This is very well captured in a quote from one of our respondents describing the decision-making structure at Florida State University: "Outside, they are cutting down middle-management and doing more and more team decision making and more collegial decision making. We are going more toward top-down hierarchical decision making in universities" (FSU572).

The Australian Context

In Australia, while legislation for education remains a state responsibility, the federal government, largely through its control of income tax since World War II, has the "power of the purse." Thus, during the latter half of this century the federal government's role in determining education policy directions has escalated significantly. In the higher education arena, a key turning point for federal government control occurred in 1974 when the Whitlam Labor Government at the federal level abolished university fees and took full financial responsibility for the sector. Despite the fact that governments had been the almost exclusive providers of higher education in Australia, universities had enjoyed relative autonomy in determining their own directions. This tradition was largely maintained until the 1980s when the Hawke Labor Government at the federal level set in motion a "revolution" designed to increase the federal government's control over universities in order to harness them to serve the national interest.[30]

Under Minister Dawkins (1987–91), the entire education "industry" was to be restructured to improve its efficiency and effectiveness, consistent with reforms across the public sector in Australia.[31] Education would no longer have its own portfolio but would be driven by economic parameters, as reflected in the new title of the Department of Employment, Education and Training (DEET). The large, independent education commissions, which offered expert advice to the minister, would be replaced by the smaller and underresourced National Board of Employment, Education and Training, giving tighter control to the minister.

Minister Dawkins released a Green (discussion) Paper on higher education reforms in 1987 and then the White (policy) Paper in 1988, with the latter showing few changes from the former (despite extensive submissions from interested parties), suggesting that the government's agenda was already firmly set.[32] The essence of the White Paper was to bring together "old" and "new" (former colleges of advanced education) universities to graduate more students at a faster rate from a smaller number of institutions (reduced to thirty-seven universities through amalgamations). Institutions would negotiate their profiles for teaching and research with the federal government, taking national priorities such as science, technology, and business into account. Both competition and attraction of nongovernment funds would be encouraged, especially in the research area. In terms of university management, the minister's intention to streamline decision making along corporate lines was clear:

The governing body will only operate more effectively where the number of members is substantially lower. . . . An appropriate guide to size and composition can be drawn from boards of large private sector organizations. . . . The Government expects governing bodies to delegate clear responsibility and authority to their Chief Executive Officers. . . . It will assist institutions in undertaking reviews of their internal management structures. . . . [T]he reviews will be designed to help institutions achieve

—strong managerial modes of operation; . . .

—adequate levels of consultation with, and accountability to, government, employers, employees, students and the community;

—streamlined decision-making processes; and

—maximum flexibility in the capacity of an institution to implement new policies, with minimal time lag between making and implementing decisions.[33]

In general, the White Paper reforms were noted for the speed and success of their implementation, with almost all in place by the end of the first triennium of operation of the new Unified National System of higher education in 1991. Policies on university management styles, however, were slower than most others to be implemented. Arguably, the momentum for reform of university management was maintained by the federal government with its program of quality reviews between 1993 and 1995 and the review of university management conducted by a banker, David Hoare, in 1995, just before the Labor government was voted out of office in 1996. The subsequent coalition (conservative) government instituted severe cutbacks to higher education in its 1996 budget (total cuts for 1997–2000 of 6 percent to operating grants, as well as no supplementation for salary increases, which totaled another 12 percent), forcing institutions to restructure further with sizable redundancies of staff. The overall effect of the government-driven reforms has been privatization and corporatization of Australian higher education, so that according to many commentators it increasingly resembles an American-style market system.[34]

The American Context

In contrast to the more centralized control of higher education in Australia, where change can be rapid and systematic, higher education in the United States is decentralized, and largely controlled by state legislatures rather than the federal government, so the changes tend to be more incremental and not evenly applied across the nation. As described by A. C. J. McGuinness, "American higher education remains perhaps the most diverse, decentralized, private, market-driven system in the world."[35] At the same time, he noted that higher education (with approximately thirty-five hundred institutions) is moving toward a more public system, with 80 percent of enrollments in public institutions.

As has occurred in Australia, American universities have been affected by fiscal constraints, especially the public institutions. As many writers have noted, American public higher education in the 1990s is undergoing a period of financial cutbacks more severe than any since World War II.[36] The reduced funding by states for higher education began in the early 1970s during the Nixon administration when the idea of market forces in higher education was introduced.[37] In the Reagan years of the 1980s, greater competitiveness entered the system through the formation of such groups as the Business-Higher Education Forum and through congressional legislation that translated competitiveness policies into law.[38] These laws allowed universities to participate in profit taking and develop business arms and links with corporations. Slaughter points out that these laws encouraged deregulation, privatization, and commercialization of university activities, breaking down the relatively rigid organizational boundaries that had previously guarded universities' autonomy. She describes these moves as a shift toward "academic capitalism," especially in the fields of science and engineering where universities were rewarded by the federal government for pursuing commercial initiatives.[39]

A. Zusman has noted that one of the impacts of the budget cuts and the need to privatize and commercialize the university is a greater centralization of authority within the university. Slaughter also concluded that retrenchments "generally undermine faculty participation in governance and faculty authority over the direction of the curriculum."[40] Concurrently, there has been a shift to adopt business language and practices. As early as 1983 George Keller wrote about the management revolution in American higher education, and his book soon became the bible of the current crop of university administrators. E. H. Berman comments on this in "The Entrepreneurial University":

By the 1980s "strategic planning" had become fashionable on many American campuses. And so it was at my institution, the University of Louisville. One of the new president's early efforts was the development of a strategic plan to better position the university for its redefined mission within the state system. This plan led to a significant institutional reorganization. This reorganizational phase was marked by presidential demands for greater "accountability," especially from the faculty; an emphasis on increased faculty productivity; new budgeting techniques and lines of reporting; and the addition of numerous well-compensated administrators. Faculty and staff salaries and increments from now on would reflect "performance-based" measures, standards from which high-ranking administrators and the president himself were exempted.[41]

Berman's description of key changes in his university is often reflected in the critiques of reforms in Australian universities, which suggests that the ascent of managerialism in universities has occurred in both countries, despite their different historical contexts. A better idea of the extent of convergence is revealed by our data.

The Study

We report here part of a larger study in which we analyze the changing nature of academic work. During interviews with academics at six Australian and American universities, we asked respondents about perceived changes in decision-making styles in their universities. We wanted to explore if and then how managerialism was moving into these universities and why there was such a tendency to accept the shift to greater control by managers in both countries. At the same time, we wanted to examine whether there were different ways of expressing these changes and whether the language used was indicative of different responses to managerialism.

The Australian universities chosen for this study represent a range of different contexts evident in the higher education sector (enrollments given are approximate sizes):

—University of Sydney (SU)—a large, "old," traditional university established in 1850, with an enrollment of thirty thousand

—Murdoch University (MU)—a small, "alternative" university established in 1975, with an enrollment of eight thousand

—Edith Cowan University (ECU)—a "new" university that began as a postsecondary college in 1902 and after a series of amalgamations became a university in 1991, with an enrollment of seventeen thousand

The institutions from the United States represent state universities in different geographic locations (although all were located in the southern states, which tend to be more "antiunion"), as well as being of different standing within the ranking of what has been termed the one hundred "research" universities:

—University of Arizona (AU)—in the first third of research rankings, established in 1885, with an enrollment of thirty-four thousand

—Florida State University (FSU)—in the top part of the second tier of research rankings, with an enrollment of thirty thousand

—University of Louisville (LU)—in the lowest part of the second tier of research rankings, established in 1798, with an enrollment of twenty-two thousand

There were 153 respondents at the Australian universities and 100 at the American universities. Respondents represented a range of discipline areas across education, social sciences, and the sciences, as well as a range of academic ranks from professor to assistant professor/associate lecturer. Approximately one-third of both samples were female academic staff. Interviews, which were semi-structured and of approximately forty-five minutes duration, were recorded on audiotapes and later fully transcribed. These transcribed interviews were then entered into the NUD.IST software program to facilitate analysis of responses. In reporting the findings, extensive use is made of direct quotes to allow the voices of academics at the grassroots to be heard. The coded number after each quote is included to show that the views of different individuals from different institutions have been presented.

Findings

When the responses about decision making from academics were quantified, the overwhelming majority (73 percent) in the United States and a majority in Australia (59 percent) indicated that decision making had become more top-down, bureaucratic, centralized, autocratic, and managerial. Some (19 percent in the United States and 17 percent in Australia) said that there was a combination of decision-making styles operating in their universities, depending on the level. They often identified more democratic decision-making practices at the departmental or faculty level and more bureaucratic and corporate managerial procedures at the overall institutional level. Murdoch, Sydney, and Florida State respondents were more likely to describe a combination of top-down and bottom-up decision making (27 percent for Murdoch, 25 percent for Sydney, and 23 percent for Florida State) than were those at the other universities, for which we recorded less than 15 percent in this category. A minority in both countries (6 percent in the United States and 18 percent in Australia) said that decision making was still collegial and faculty were participating in decisions. A handful (4 percent in each country) said that they did not know enough about how decisions were made to comment. In the following sections, we will give you a flavor of their comments, which detail some of the consequences of the movement away from collegial decision making toward changing decision-making styles. Variable and often contradictory perceptions point to the messy realities of university decision making.

Corporate Managerialism

Corporate managerialism as noted above refers to a number of ideas, centralizing as well as decentralizing and streamlining decision making in universities and inclining them toward the market. A business ethos is applied not only to the generation of knowledge but to the whole way in which universities are run, as suggested by this University of Louisville academic:

The central administration is seeing the university as if it were a business,[42] cost efficiency kinds of considerations—Fordism—which is not just an economist's assembly line model but also this idea of a productivity model—judging the quality of what goes on in the university not in terms of what goes on in the classroom but how many students are processed, at what rate, and how efficient the system is. The intensity of that has grown as well as the sense that the central administration has to control the faculty. (LU425)

This respondent was not the only one to describe the university in this manner. Here are two others from American universities who observed a similar phenomenon:

I see corporate managerialism as trying to run the university more like a business, more like a company, and taking more of the decision making out of the hands of faculty and putting more of it into the hands of corporate managers—you have a string of vice presidents in charge of all different developments. You have the emergence of corporate-university links and technology parks. The notion that a business model can be superimposed on universities is a very popular notion and is always being asserted. I see governing boards and legislators in controlling public sector institutions as seeing it as desirable to emphasize corporate models of accountability, especially for fiscal resources and accountability for defining the product of our work. (FSU542)

I would say the university is bureaucratic moving towards corporate managerial. The new president believes in TQM. He views the running of the institution in the way that you would run, I don't know, a manufacturing plant. Almost nothing comes as an issue from below and works its way up. The department heads are appointed from above. They serve at the desire of the administration. The faculty are like obedient slaves in a way. (AU694)

These descriptions, as noted by the first respondent, seem to suggest that universities are not moving toward post-Fordist work relations that are based on high trust and collective participation.[43] Rather, they have adopted work relations based on Fordist (low trust and divisions between managers and workers) or neo-Fordist (low trust and managerial prerogative) work relations. This is revealed below in quotes describing the lack of trust and the gap emerging between managers and academics.

Australian academics identified a "managerial" ethos more than a "business" ethos pervading their universities, perhaps because of the strong emphasis on public sector management reforms in Australia (although the intermingling of these is seen in the term "corporate managerialism," used by some respondents, such as those at the University of Arizona and Florida State University quoted above).

It is more managerial. It is less democratic as a result. Any sense of a coherent university has been lost by the production of fiefdoms, where the different faculties are run by robber barons who call themselves pro-vice-chancellors and who get motorcars and so on. They are called senior management. It came with the previous vice-chancellor and the appointment of the Boston Consulting Group and the throwing of at least a million dollars at them to produce a bunch of flow charts. . . . It had almost no beneficial impact, but it gave the green light to restructure or managerialize. (SU741)

There is a feeling that we are overmanaged and underled, that the *management* somehow or other simply regard themselves as the most important component of the university and the academics and students as just the workers or the products. And [this] creates, I feel, a managerial style that *alienates* members of the staff quite easily. The notion of collegiality, decision making by consent and consultation, all of these things have been fairly seriously eroded. I think increasingly, under the current vice-chancellor, there has been lack of consultation, communication, input from the staff as a whole. (SU708)

The alienation that results from the imposition of corporate managerial processes is also seen in the following quotes:

Because of the disenfranchisement that occurred, there is a *lack of trust* between administration and faculty, a lack of shared understanding of what we're trying to do, what we'd like this institution to become. After a while, you just say, "to hell with that." I don't identify with the college, I don't identify with the administration, and I'm going to back away from the whole process. (LU427)

It's close to corporate managerial, and it's moving down to the level of the deans, who used to be much more collegial. The idea that one can manage a university in terms of accountability and productivity is a carryover from the corporate world of the 1980s. I don't think it can work, and it only *alienates* the faculty from the administration. (FSU512)

The only strong feeling that I can identify is rage, absolute, *unadulterated rage.* The sense of community has entirely disappeared, and that's not entirely accidental. The only thing that produces today a sense of community is a common sense of outrage against the central administration. (LU413)

Along with this sense of rage, for some, there is also a sense of powerlessness and of turning away from the university. This was expressed especially at the University of Louisville, where academics felt that they could not change the plans that were being imposed by the Board of Trustees and accepted by the president: "We feel so powerless. They're going to implement their plan whether we like it or not. The entire faculty voted against this plan. But they're putting it through anyway. So it does feel kind of yucky!" (LU424). During the time of the interviews at both Florida State and Louisville, there was outrage over the process of choosing the provost, a process that was a change from the past. At Louisville, the president named himself chair of the Provost Search Committee and declared that he was not going to be bound by the Search Committee's decision. As one professor declared, "In short, he could go to someone never considered by the committee, if he so desired, and name that person provost. . . . [T]hat's about as authoritarian as you can get" (LU413).

At Florida State, in 1994 the president rejected the two finalists that the Provost Search Committee gave him and appointed another internal candidate instead. The person selected had been rejected by his peers, which rankled some faculty members. In fact, one faculty member moved a motion at the Faculty Senate that the provost decline to accept the post and support a national search. The Faculty Senate voted reluctantly to accept the appointment, noting their disappointment and "giving the President one more opportunity to back us in a shared governance."[44] The excuse the president gave for making the appointment and not having a second national search was the need to move quickly on the decision and position the university for the next legislative session.

In the United States, the boards of regents/trustees are the intermediaries between the state legislatures and the universities. Members are appointed by the state legislatures and most often come from business and law backgrounds and only occasionally from a background in higher education.[45] Therefore the chancellor and the boards are very much identified with doing the business of the legislature. This, along with the co-option of the administration in this process, was expressed by a Florida State professor quite aptly:

The administration seems to be going along with the attack on the tenure system; the chancellor has gone along with it; the people who should be our front line of defense are going along with it. The administration virtually runs the show. Faculty do not seem to have much of a say in things that really matter. The administration is dancing between the faculty below and those above them, the regents and the chancellor; when their interests conflict, *they do the bidding of the regents*. The alternative would be that they could be the spearhead of our resistance; it's been more a matter of being in cahoots with the regents. (FSU598)

A faculty member at the University of Arizona expressed similar sentiments: "We are being told by the administration that pressure from these two issues [core curriculum reform and the length of time it takes students to graduate] is coming from the *state legislature*, and I feel our highly paid administrators have really bungled the job of explaining to the public why the university needs more resources" (AU670).

Besides the sense of powerlessness and betrayal by university administrators experienced by some respondents, others talked in general about the replacement of collegiality with line management in their universities: "It certainly isn't collegial any more, there's a line management structure that the [vice-chancellor] has put in place that has killed collegiality and that caused a lot of upset. We've moved from being a university to being the faculty of science. We almost don't see management outside the faculty of science any longer. We've become a small university within the university" (SU738).

Thus it appeared that managerial structures were killing off any collegiality that might have been there. A University of Louisville academic said that "we have much lower expectations about our role in faculty governance than we did five, ten, or fifteen years ago. So in that sense the administrators have been successful" (LU407). In Australia, a similar feeling is emerging that through a particular form of managerial devolution, administrators (more often referred to as managers) are becoming equally "successful" in altering the shape of universities.

Devolution

Devolution is a common feature of corporate managerialism, as outlined in the discussion of conceptual tools. It is being instituted in universities across Australia in strikingly similar forms, and we report here on how our Australian respondents saw devolution occurring. What we found surprising is that, even though it is clear that in American universities many responsibilities have been devolved to faculties and departments, not one of our American respondents used the words "devolved" or "devolution" to describe this process. In reflecting on that fact, an American colleague noted that it was probably because it had all happened incrementally and not in one fell swoop, as it had in many Australian universities. And it may also be reflective of the different national characteristics whereby the American universities start from a more decentralized base within state systems and the Australian universities are affected by centralized federal agendas so that the rhetoric of managerialism spreads more quickly.

It appeared in some Australian universities that the rationale for devolution was to allow for rapid adaptation to the changing external climate. This is described well by a Sydney academic: "The oligarchic model was unable to adapt quickly enough to the requirements that were really corporate requirements. You could no longer run the place keeping it all in your head, what you promised here, what you would do there. So the [vice-chancellor] ultimately realized that the place would have to be devolved into more manageable units, and so in that sense the oligarchic model was wiped out" (SU726). One Murdoch academic who linked devolution with the rise in managerialism seemed to identify the links between the manager as monitor and the use of a devolved structure by the managers at the center, highlighting the contradictory nature of managerialism:

It's an interesting combination of things, [be]cause if you have devolution of budgeting and decision making and you have a climate in which it seemed that a notion of the manager is appropriate for the university, then you can see the two coming together. And if you have other things pounding in there like emphasis on quality—well, how do you judge quality? . . . [Y]ou have to have indicators. Who's going to do the monitoring? . . . [T]he manager's going to do the monitoring. (MU025)

In describing devolution in the three Australian universities, the majority of respondents saw the process of devolution as holding out false promises and creating more negative than positive impacts. Nevertheless, there were a few who saw, within the context of their previously very autocratic university, a chance for devolution to increase democratic processes within departments. When asked about what had changed in decision making in their universities, about a third of the Australian respondents spoke about devolution in one way or another.

Positive View of Devolution

The only respondents who mentioned a positive view of devolution came from Edith Cowan University, which had recently converted from being a college of advanced education and was previously an amalgamation of teachers' colleges. This clearly had an effect on this university, which was described by many respondents as bureaucratic or autocratic in the past and moving toward corporate managerialism. For them, devolution allowed academics to become more involved in decision making. They also moved from having a vice-chancellor who was a former teachers' college director to one who came from a traditional university and who believed in establishing a sense of trust in the university and building up collegial decision making.

There is a genuine endeavor, I believe, by people at the deans' level and down to encourage collaborative devolved decision making, and with the structure that was being put in place over the last few years, there has been an increased degree of autonomy for departments to make decisions. It has meant that staff members feel . . . that they are more involved in making certain types of decisions than they have been in the past, but it's not all decisions. (ECU134)

We have had more responsibilities devolved to us, and we had to make more decisions ourselves. But we wanted that, and it's good for staff morale. (ECU160)

It appears that at Edith Cowan a form of relatively more "democratic devolution" may have emerged. An alternative reading might be that this was just the first flush of having more participation in decision making, which may have masked the underlying, more managerial forms of devolution present in their system. (Some of our follow-up interviews in 1997 suggest this to be the case.) The form that most universities are experiencing could be termed "managerial devolution," which has the effect of decreasing collegial decision making and leaving only the trivial kinds of decisions for academics to make at the lower levels.

Negative Effects of Devolution

By far, the majority of those who commented about devolution saw the negative consequences. Deans were more stressed about their responsibilities, and academics felt it led to bad relationships, fragmentation, the passing down of more administrative work and reinforcement of top-down decision making through clearer line management, and the development of smaller management groups. Most of the academics interviewed were fairly insightful about the consequences of devolution and could see that, as described by one Murdoch academic, "devolution has happened not at a time of growth in the budget. They wouldn't dream of devolving when there was money there, but now that there are hard decisions to be made, they are being passed down" (MU075). They could also detect where the real power lies within an institution, and that is where the budget decisions are made: "There is a devolution of decision making occurring from the dean downward to the faculties, if you like, but still, if you take the guideline [of] who controls the purse, can control the decisions, then still decisions are made beyond the department level in my school" (ECU175).

The other major change has been increased administrative responsibilities for deans, heads of departments, and academics. This change has happened with the same amount of money going to schools and faculties, as one Murdoch academic queried, "So what's happening with the devolution of budgets, the administration doesn't seem to be getting any smaller" (MU082). And a Sydney academic bluntly identified the effect of devolution on those below: "Everything has been devolved at this university. What the center has done is they've, pardon the expression, . . . *devolved all the shit work* down to these five super faculty type things, and they won't do anything at the central level, so there's nobody out there that has a grand vision about how Sydney University should run" (SU729). Perhaps the more serious repercussions are in the divisiveness, the fragmentation, and the bad relationships caused by decisions made closer to the departments, as expressed by one respondent: "The school is going to be making the really tough decisions. Like Economics had to do [retrench staff] and that really poisons relations" (MU075).

Much dissatisfaction existed at Sydney University, where the vice-chancellor hired the Boston Consultancy Group to develop a new structure for the university. A major restructuring occurred in 1992, which devolved authority down to different levels, but few academics felt it achieved its goals of improving administration in the university. One Sydney academic complained that "the human dimensions of this university, which were very strong, have largely disappeared" (SU715). Others from Sydney pointed to further negative effects of devolution:

The effect of the Boston changes, if you like to call them that, has been to fragment. The notion that devolution has delivered vastly enhanced efficiency and effectiveness . . . is not supported by any figures I've seen. (SU708)

It really was not a very good restructuring. It was an ill-conceived one because it was a far more complicated system that was introduced. Where the university set out to have a flatter administration, which was supposed to be more responsive, what we got, in fact, was a more hilly one, if you like, *another layer was added in between senior management and faculties so the potential for things to go wrong was increased*. Our administration, it turns out, after the great upheaval, is, I believe, *costing more than it did before*. Now we've got fewer administrators, but we've got many more who are on attractive salary packages at a higher level. (SU707)

When we searched the transcripts for other words that might give us an indication of whether the American academics used different words to describe the same process, we found that some academics talked about decentralization in a manner similar to how Australian academics spoke of devolution. It appeared that the moves to decentralize were occurring incrementally and that some American administrators had already devolved power to colleges/faculties and were in the early stages of devolving power to even lower levels and appointing not only deans but chairs of departments so that the line management was well entrenched to the lower levels. According to one Louisville respondent: "The dean is talking about decentralizing power to the level of the chairs and then giving the chairs more discretion. One of the things that they want to do is to *appoint chairs rather than elect them*" (LU423). It was clear from one of the respondents that this proposal to appoint department chairs had come from the Board of Trustees as part of a range of changes they wanted to impose on the university. This development was identified by one respondent as "dramatically changing where authority is and how much more centralized administration is occurring" (LU420).

There was only one Florida State academic who talked about decentralization within the rhetoric of corporate managerialism in much the same way as Australian academics saw devolution as a false promise. "This university is supposed to be democratic and is supposed to have faculty governance and is supposed to be participative and decentralized. I think that ethos is still in there, but we may be in an *early version of corporate managerialism*. All the other stuff is basically a cover up" (FSU094).

Our American respondents described the process of managerialism more in terms of the "central administration" and "administrators" gaining more power, whereas Australians referred to the process of "managers" gaining power and a growing sense of "corporate managerialism" invading their universities. Janice Newson, an observer of the Canadian higher education scene, suggests that when one uses the term "administration," it refers to a more passive approach to implementing policy, and when one uses the term "management," it refers to a more active role in formulating policies.[46] One of our coresearchers from an American university said that most American academics saw their universities in "functionalist" terms and were not used to engaging in the more critical analysis that many Australians employ to describe their universities.[47] It may also be a result of the stronger role of the union movement in Australia and its development of a critique of managerialism in its publications and the more uniform sweep of managerial reform in Australia as mentioned above.

E. H. Berman, another of our American coresearchers, identified the faculty as part of the problem in his university (Louisville), which was not unionized, and noted that "in the aggregate they are without a basic understanding of the requisites of democratic decision making which should transpire in a university."[48] Another respondent, Basile, noted that even though his university (Florida State) was unionized, the union had little say in administrative policies (unions dealt mainly with salary issues and individual grievances).[49] Berman and Basile both felt that academics were being disenfranchised and there was no notion of the "collective" force of the faculty successfully standing up to administration (despite faculty meetings opposing certain university policies). There may be a difference in the strength of unions between northern and southern universities that would require further investigation. From these case studies, it appeared that there was limited involvement by faculty in making crucial financial decisions within their universities and little success by faculty in opposing decisions that the state legislature, boards of regents/trustees, or the university presidents wanted to impose on faculty.

Despite the differences in rhetoric and the differential strength of opposition by faculty (including the differences between unionized and nonunionized faculty), there was a growing sense of managerialism emerging on both sides of the Pacific. In addition, academics perceived that a cultural gap was developing between administrators and academics that was not helped by the differences in their salaries, as expressed in this quote: "The university administration is approaching corporate managerialism. If you look at the salaries of administrators, they're paid enormous salaries comparatively speaking; they're in the top 10 percent, and the faculty is in the bottom 25 percent nationally. There is a lot more of the administrative fiat being passed down to faculty" (FSU510).

Others talked about not only the gap in salaries but also the gap in attitude; one definitely senses that in the past, when the gulf was not so wide, relations between administrators and academics were better and the workplace was a happier one, as the following quote indicates: "Another thing is that the whole university has changed from being a very collegial one to a much more managerial type of institution. And whereas once academics and administrators worked very happily together, now a gulf has been created between administrators and academics, and I think this has created a lot of problems" (SU715).

Other Top-Down Forms (Bureaucratic and Autocratic)

Many of the respondents described top-down forms that they did not label as managerial. In particular, "bureaucratic" and "autocratic" were frequent descriptors of decision-making styles. Further, a number of respondents conflated bureaucratic and managerial practices. Here are two samples of the general description of top-down decision making: "I think our president is a pretty top-down administrator" (LU405); and "Top-down to me, the Faculty Senate is a joke. Decisions get made at the steering committee level, and those people are quasi administrators and they work very closely with the provost and the top guns. We have pseudo-faculty governance" (FSU553).

Others identified autocratic styles as the dominant mode in their universities: "At the point of central administration, it's as autocratic as is possible for the central administration to make it" (LU413); "A lot of lip service is paid to shared decision making, but when it comes right down to the tough decisions, I see that it is mostly autocratic or decisions made by a few insiders" (AU610); "It's autocratic. There are various autocracies within the university" (FSU549).

In these next quotes respondents talk about the university as "bureaucratic," with the following University of Louisville quote representing a common theme: "Oh, it's almost clearly bureaucratic. I don't see any evidence of anything other than bureaucratic, and I think that's true both in the school and the university as a whole. I think that it's increasingly bureaucratic in the department as well" (LU403). And these sentiments were echoed at the University of Arizona and at Florida State University: "It's not collegial—it struck me that it's more driven bureaucratically or in a corporate way, filtering from the legislature" (AU691); "This place is very bureaucratic; most decisions are made by administrators" (FSU545); "It's very bureaucratic. The Board of Regents treats us like another state agency, and we start responding that way" (FSU547); "It's a state bureaucracy" (FSU573); "I get the sense that we're pretty bureaucratic in a lot of ways. There is this collegial overlay with the Faculty Senate" (FSU563).

Some voices from Australia resonated with the same concerns—that the system is becoming more hierarchical and more bureaucratic. A Sydney academic said, "It's becoming more bureaucratic. Corporate managerial dignifies it too much!" (SU726). And other respondents noted:

It is bureaucratic, but it is also a finely tuned hierarchical string, so if you want to get something done, I would not proceed as I may have ten years ago by getting my colleagues to agree with me. The first thing I would do is to grab the dean and ask him if he wanted to go for a beer. Once I have the dean on my side, I wouldn't care because I know then that he would do it. So the dean has more authority. (MU037)

The first thing I would say is that Edith Cowan University is a microcosm of the State Ministry of Education; it was run along highly centralized, bureaucratized lines. There has been a strong ethic of no administrator worth his salt would ever trust a staff member further down the line. So effectively decision making was very bad. (ECU176)

Fragments of Collegiality Remain

There is no doubt that the push toward managerialism and often increasing bureaucracy is changing the way universities are run. In most cases, however, academics reported positive feelings about the way their departments or sections operated. Here there was more of a feeling of collegial (or democratic) decision making in both American and Australian universities. Some academics even perceived that there was some collegiality operating in their whole university. A Florida State academic described it this way: "I would say collegial is pretty close to it. The Faculty Senate here is really quite powerful; at least there is a pretty strong appearance that it has a lot of power. I would say that it is probably as collegial as you would find at any major university" (FSU543).

Yet it was much more common for respondents to identify collegial decision making at the lower levels within their universities, particularly at the departmental level. "Our department is pretty collegial; almost everything is open to all faculty, and all major decisions are voted on by all the faculty" (AU639). Other respondents noted similar sentiments:

In the department, it is still collegial, very democratic. (LU413)

The closer you get to your own workplace, the more impact you can have and the more difference you think you can make. Decisions taken at the school level are most democratic. But the School Board still only advises the head of school, and it is not mandatory for the head to take that advice. The major impediment is that there's no way of enforcing the decisions made by School Board. The School Board is democratic, it's everyone, part-time, Level As, even if you are a woman! [Laughter.] Everyone can have input, you don't feel constrained by rank or gender or anything else. It's still up to the head of School to implement decisions; at the same time, I can't recall an incident where the head has demurred and said that I don't choose to accept that advice. (SU071)

Despite the differences in terminology used, our interviews with American and Australian academics between 1994 and 1996 suggest that an ascendance of corporate managerialism (albeit at different rates) has been occurring across the six institutions studied. This is consistent with the hegemonic position of the managerial discourse reported in the literature.[50] However, hegemony is never complete, and our data exposes differences between and within universities in the extent to which the managerial ethos has been adopted. Further, our data reveal numerous sites of struggle operating against the imposition of a homogeneous managerial culture. In fact, a growing cultural gap between management and academics was perceived by numerous respondents, who also suggested that tensions coalesce around the position of deans because they are increasingly appointed by management rather than elected by colleagues. But our interviews reveal that attitudes by "grassroots" academics to the changing nature of decision making vary considerably, and therefore we must not ascribe to them a consensus negative response. As J. Newson points out, the recent emphasis on corporate needs and procedures in universities has occurred with the active support of many academics, especially those whose area of expertise is closer to the market, strategically placing them in a position of advantage.[51]

Although hegemony is not complete, the corporate managerial style was certainly prevalent in the universities studied, with many academics seeing it as a threat to collegiality and professional autonomy. Yet D. Meadmore et al. maintain that the repressive effect of management should not be overemphasized.[52] They draw on Foucault's thesis that power can also be productive, and as it is both exercised and resisted at all levels, all participants are able to mediate the power and produce alternative discourses. Thus there will be multiple sites for the emergence of counterhegemonic discourses. S. Grundy has argued the need to produce such counterhegemonic discourses that take account of the unpredictabilities and uncertainties involved in desirable educational practice. She maintains that as the ideology of managerialism is about installing processes to enhance the predictability of outcomes, to challenge managerialism involves accepting the risk that unintended outcomes may result, as "the elimination of risk is only possible if human action is transformed into technical production."[53] A. Hargreaves, too, believes in the value of risk for fostering learning, adaptability, and improvement in postmodern educational institutions and therefore the need to embrace risk rather than avoid it.[54] Trust is risky, but according to Hargreaves, building desirable collaboration and collegiality requires both interpersonal trust and, more important, trust in expertise and processes that help postmodern organizations adapt to a continually changing environment. Sadly, declining trust between management and academics was often reported by our respondents.

Our data provide evidence of the retention of significant collegial fragments in these six universities, especially at the lower levels and sometimes within Faculty Senates/Academic Boards, where alternatives to the hegemony of managerial discourse may be more readily constructed. A number of respondents made the point that academic issues are more likely to be decided by collegial processes, and administrative and budgetary issues, by managerial or bureaucratic processes. This finding is consistent with that of H. de Boer and L. Goedegebuure in their study of universities in seven European countries, and it begins to suggest that different decision-making styles may not be totally incompatible.[55] L. Angus argues that not only can participative and managerial forms be compatible but also together they may well result in both better decisions and a greater commitment to them.[56]

There is sufficient historical evidence of the existence of organizations with hybrid decision-making styles that allow for a relatively high degree of self-government where there is a majority of professionals.[57] In particular, I. Moses cited Mintzberg's work on "professional bureaucracies" as a useful way to examine the possibilities for university management styles.[58] R. Middlehurst and L. Elton also describe a scenario in which different decision-making types can operate at the same time in different sectors of a university: "a bureaucratic model in areas of administration; a market model for certain internal and external services; a collegial model of a consensus-seeking community of scholars, which might be applicable to a course team; and a political model, which may dominate the actions of a vice-chancellor who tries to reconcile conflicting interests."[59]

Similarly, Hargreaves emphasized the need for "menus," which offer choices among multiple models, to prevail over "mandates" or single models.[60] Thus, decision-making styles would be in a state of flux, and leadership could be exercised by different participants on different occasions. Inevitably there would be tensions between the different styles, but if we return to political models of decision making, such as discussed in the seminal work of Victor Baldridge, we may be tempted to consider the productive effects of conflicts, such that the negotiations, bargaining, and compromises result in a stronger commitment to better decisions.[61] A political framework for decision making will cater for change (a key element of "healthy" organizations) more readily than collegial, bureaucratic, or managerial "pure types." A political framework, within which struggles for domination are played out among groups that are all seen to have a legitimate stake in the decision making, is more likely to produce the unpredictability of outcomes and adaptability that were identified earlier as highly desirable for educational organizations.[62] In particular, the contestations characteristic of political decision making may open up discussions about organizational goals, broadening the agenda from the narrow, economically defined "ends" for which the managerial model has been criticized. M. B. Ginsburg argues for a democratic political model for educators as they engage with their communities, emphasizing a "power-with" rather than a "power-over" approach so that decisions are achieved through open dialogue and negotiation among equally situated participants. He draws on Giddens's notion of "democratic dialogic spaces" that can invoke active trust based on "open and uncoerced discussion." [63]

While political models also have their weaknesses, such as conflict and instability, R. Birnbaum argues that they are relevant in academic institutions, because educational goals and outcomes are difficult to define and measure:

The idea that political processes in academic institutions are somehow "dirty" reflects the misunderstanding that if people would only act in the best interests of the institution, they would agree on what to do. It assumes that the institution's best interests are either known or knowable, rather than different people, especially committed to what they believe to be the institution's welfare, can, in good faith, have completely different ideas of what that means and how it should be accomplished. . . . A major advantage of political systems, therefore, is that they permit decisions to be made even in the absence of clear goals.[64]

We conclude by supporting a multifaceted paradigm of university governance, predicated on dislodging the current hegemony of managerial discourse. This involves legitimizing different forms of decision making and giving careful consideration to the ways in which they articulate (an area for further research). Thus, instead of viewing decision making in terms of mutually exclusive "ideal types," we might achieve greater analytic scope by conceiving a series of overlapping spheres (illustrated by Venn diagrams) representing collegial, bureaucratic, and managerial styles. The spheres need not be restricted to these three types, and flexibility would be obtained by changing the size of the spheres (to represent relative dominance) and the degree of overlap of the spheres (to represent the emergence of hybrid forms of decision making). Size and overlap would vary between and within institutions, depending on the particular locus and time. Then it would be important to lay over the top of this diagram a political framework that would enable discussion of the political strategies that various stakeholders use to make their particular style of operating more dominant.

A multiplicity of models is consistent with the future of academic work predicted by J. McCollow and B. Lingard, who argue that fragmentation within institutions and across the system will see multiple and overlapping models of the academic as sui generis, as state professional, as market professional, as corporate professional, and as worker. They suggest that there would be "radical discontinuities" among these types, and therefore universities would defy systematic or enduring categorization.[65] In terms of university governance styles, we also envisage discontinuities; further, we maintain that universities and their "stakeholders" may best be served by mixed modes of decision making in which the dominant model will vary according to locus in the university and will change with the issue and the time.

Notes

Note that citation abbreviations such as "FSU572" refer to the interview numbering codes.

This research study has been funded by grants from the Australian Research Council and Murdoch University. We thank them and the 253 respondents who were interviewed and gave us insights into their lives as academics. In addition, we thank the three universities in the United States (Louisville, Arizona, and Florida State) that provided Jan Currie with assistance during study leave, and colleagues in each of these universities:

Edward Berman, Sheila Slaughter, and Steve Klees. The research team in Australia also included Anthony Welch (University of Sydney) and Harriett Pears (Murdoch University).

1 A. Yeatman, "Corporate Managerialism and the Shift from the Welfare to the Competitive State," *Discourse* 18, no. 2 (1993): 3–9; P. G. Altbach, "Problems and Possibilities: The American Academic Profession," in *Higher Education in American Society*, ed. P. G. Altbach, R. O. Berdahl, and P. J. Gumport (Amherst, N.Y.: Prometheus Books, 1994).

2 S. J. Ball, *Education Reform: A Critical and Post-structural Approach* (Buckingham: Open University Press, 1994).

3 E. Miller and M. Findlay, *Australian Thesaurus of Educational Descriptors* (Melbourne: Australian Council for Educational Research, 1996).

4 R. Middlehurst and L. Elton, "Leadership and Management in Higher Education," *Studies in Higher Education* 17, no. 3 (1992): 251–64.

5 I. Moses, "Tensions and Tendencies in the Management of Quality and Autonomy in Australian Higher Education," *Australian Universities' Review* 38, no. 1 (1995): 11–15.

6 G. Moodie, "The Professionalisation of Australian Academic Administration," *Australian Universities' Review* 38, no. 1 (1995): 21–23.

7 B. Bessant, "Corporate Management and Its Penetration of the University Administration and Government," *Australian Universities' Review* 38, no. 1 (1995): 59–62.

8 Department of Employment Education and Training, *National Report on Australia's Higher Education Sector* (Canberra: Australian Government Publishing Service, 1993); J. McCollow and B. Lingard, "Changing Discourses and Practices of Academic Work," *Australian Universities' Review* 39, no. 2 (1996): 11–19.

9 S. Lawton, "Why Restructure? An International Survey of the Roots of Reform," *Journal of Education Policy* 7, no. 2 (1992): 139–54.

10 L. Angus, "Educational Organisation: Technical/Managerial and Participative/Professional Perspectives," *Discourse* 14, no. 2 (1994): 30–44; J. Marceau, "Management of Higher Education Policy," in *The Human Costs of Managerialism*, ed. S. Rees and G. Rodley (Leichhardt: Pluto Press, 1995).

11 Simon Marginson, *Education and Public Policy in Australia* (Melbourne: Cambridge University Press, 1993); M. Pussey, *Economic Rationalism in Canberra* (Melbourne: Cambridge University Press, 1991).

12 Angus, "Educational Organisation"; A. Zusman, "Current and Emerging Issues Facing Higher Education in the United States," in *Higher Education in American Society*, ed. Altbach, Berdahl, and Gumport, 335–64.

13 P. Watkins, "The Transformation of Educational Administration: The Hegemony of Consent and the Hegemony of Coercion," *Australian Journal of Education* 36, no. 3 (1992): 237–59.

14 Angus, "Educational Organisation"; Ball, *Education Reform*; Lawton, "Why Restructure?"

15 G. Treuren, "The Changing State-University Relationship: State Involvement in Academic Industrial Relations since the Murray Report," *Australian Universities' Review* 39, no. 1 (1996): 51–58.

16 Altbach, "Problems and Possibilities"; Bessant, "Corporate Management"; Moses, "Tensions and Tendencies."

17 R. Solomon and J. Solomon, *Up the University: Re-creating Higher Education in America* (Reading, Mass.: Addison-Wesley Publishing, 1993); R. Welch, "Rise of the Managerial Cadre," *The Times Higher*, June 16, 1995, 12.

18 Solomon and Solomon, *Up the University*, 33.

19 Welch, "Managerial Cadre."

20 L. Hort, "Managing Academics' Work: Future Performance in Higher Education," *Australian Universities' Review* 39, no. 2 (1996): 3–5; D. Meadmore, B. Limerick, P. Thomas, and H. Lucas, "Devolving Practices: Managing the Managers," *Journal of Education Policy* 10, no. 4 (1995): 399–411; Yeatman, "Corporate Managerialism."

21 S. J. Ball, "Management as Moral Technology," in *Foucault and Education*, ed. S. J. Ball (London: Routledge, 1990); Ball, *Education Reform*; P. Fitzsimmons, "The Management of Tertiary Educational Institutions in New Zealand," *Journal of Education Policy* 10, no. 2 (1995): 173–87; Meadmore et al., "Devolving Practices."

22 Hort, "Managing Academics' Work," 5.

23 Marceau, "Management of Higher Education Policy"; R. Bates, "The Educational Costs of Managerialism," paper presented at the Joint Conference of the Educational Research Association and the Australian Association for Research in Education, Singapore, 1996.

24 Pussey, *Economic Rationalism*; Marginson, *Education and Public Policy*; Bessant, "Corporate Management"; C. Symes, "Selling Futures: A New Image for Australian Universities?" *Studies in Higher Education* 21, no. 2 (1996): 133–47.

25 Bates, *Educational Costs*; B. Lingard, "Review Essay: Educational Policy Making in a Postmodern State: On Stephen J. Ball's Education Reform: A Critical and Post-structural Approach," *Australian Educational Researcher* 23, no. 1 (1996): 65–91.

26 Yeatman, "Corporate Managerialism," 3.

27 P. Cerny, *The Changing Architecture of Politics: Structure, Agency, and the Future of the State* (London: Sage, 1990).

28 P. Coaldrake, "Implications for Higher Education of the Public Sector Reform Agenda," *Australian Universities' Review* 38, no. 1 (1995): 38–40; E. H. Berman, "The Entrepreneurial University: Macro and Micro Perspectives from the United States," in *Universities and Globalization: Critical Perspectives*, ed. Jan Currie and J. Newson (Thousand Oaks: Sage, in press); S. Marginson, "Remaking the National Higher Education System for an Era of Globalization: The Case of Australia," in *Universities and Globalization*.

29 Middlehurst and Elton, "Leadership."

30 P. Karmel, "Reflections on a Revolution: Australian Higher Education in 1989," in *Higher Education in the Late Twentieth Century*, ed. I. Moses (St. Lucia: University of Queensland, 1990), 24–47.

31 J. Halligan, *Political Management in the 1990s* (Melbourne: Oxford University Press, 1992).

32 J. Dudley and L. Vidovich, *The Politics of Education: Commonwealth Schools Policy, 1973–1995* (Melbourne: Australian Council for Educational Research, 1995).

33 J. Dawkins, *Higher Education: A Policy Statement* (Canberra: Australian Government Publishing Service, 1988), 103.

34 McCollow and Lingard, "Changing Discourses"; G. McCulloch and K. Lewis, "Can We All Survive in the Market?" *NTEU Advocate*, May 2, 1997, 2.

35 A. C. J. McGuinness, "The States and Higher Education," in *Higher Education in American Society*, ed. Altbach, Berdahl, and Gumport, 158.

36 Sheila Slaughter, "Introduction to Special Issue on Retrenchment," *Journal of Higher Education* 64, no. 3 (May/June 1993): 247–49; Solomon and Solomon, *Up the University*; Altbach, "Problems and Possibilities"; Zusman, "Current and Emerging Issues."

37 Committee on Economic Development, 1993.

38 Sheila Slaughter and Gary Rhoades, "The Emergence of a Competitiveness Research and Development Policy Coalition and the Commercialization of Academic Science and Technology," *Science, Technology, and Human Values* 21, no. 3 (summer 1996): 303–39.

39 Sheila Slaughter, "National Higher Education Policies in a Global Economy," in *Universities and Globalization*, ed. Currie and Newson.

40 Zusman, "Current and Emerging Issues," 276.

41 Berman, "The Entrepreneurial University," 7–8.

42 Emphasis added is indicated by italicized type in this quote and in all the quotes that follow.

43 P. Brown and H. Lauder, "Education, Globalization, and Economic Development," *Journal of Education Policy* 11, no. 1 (1996).

44 G. Fineout, 1994. "Faculty Assembly Spurns Governance Compromise," *The Louisville Cardinal* 67, no. 2 (September): 1.

45 Solomon and Solomon, *Up the University.*

46 Janice Newson, "The Decline of Faculty Influence: Confronting the Effects of the Corporate Agenda," in *Fragile Truths: 25 Years of Sociology and Anthropology in Canada*, ed. W. Carroll, L. Christiansen-Rufman, R. Currie, and D. Harrison (Ottawa: Carleton University Press, 1992), 227–46.

47 Klees, personal communication, June 17, 1997.

48 Berman, personal communication.

49 Basile, personal communication.

50 Angus, "Educational Organisation"; S. Grundy, "Beyond Guaranteed Outcomes: Creating a Discourse for Educational Praxis," *Australian Journal of Education* 36, no. 2 (1992): 157–69; Watkins, "Transformation of Educational Administration."

51 Newson, "Decline of Faculty Influence."

52 Meadmore et al., "Devolving Practices."

53 Grundy, "Beyond Guaranteed Outcomes," 167.

54 A. Hargreaves, "Restructuring Restructuring: Postmodernity and the Prospects for Educational Change," *Journal of Education Policy* 9, no. 1 (1994): 47–65.

55 H. de Boer and L. Goedegebuure, "Decision-Making in Higher Education: A Comparative Perspective," *Australian Universities' Review* 38, no. 1 (1995): 41–47.

56 Angus, "Educational Organisation."

57 C. Handy, "Education for Management Outside Business," in *Education of the Professions*, ed. S. Goodlad (Guildford: Society for Research into Higher Education and N F E R-Nelson, 1984); T. Schuller, *Democracy at Work* (Oxford: Oxford University Press, 1985).

58 I. Moses, "Is Performance 'Management' Appropriate in a Learning Institution?" *Journal of Tertiary Educational Administration* 11, no. 2 (1989): 127–41.

59 Middlehurst and Elton, "Leadership," 254.

60 Hargreaves, "Restructuring Restructuring."

61 Victor Baldridge, *Power and Conflict in the University* (New York: John Wiley and Sons, 1971).

62 Grundy, "Beyond Guaranteed Outcomes"; Hargreaves, "Restructuring Restructuring."

63 M. B. Ginsburg, "Professionalism or Politics as a Model for Educators' Engagement with/in Communities," *Journal of Education Policy* (Yearbook 1996): 5–12.

64 R. Birnbaum, *How Colleges Work: The Cybernetics of Academic Organization and Leadership* (San Francisco: Jossey-Bass, 1991).

65 McCollow and Lingard, "Changing Discourses."

II

The Academy's Labor

Education for Public Life

David Montgomery

The crisis we are dealing with is not confined just to the academic world. If we are going to think about where we are and what our futures are to be, we must keep two things in mind. First, our futures will involve us in a type of economic life very, very different from that which we experienced in the thirty to forty years or so after World War II. Second, the emerging economy is also producing a new kind of social, cultural, and intellectual life among the American people, which is attempting to wrestle with this world and create some kind of alternative to the free-market mania that now dominates the public discourse of our life. The 1996 teach-in at Columbia and the struggle at Yale reveal this development. I think it is precisely for that reason we find ourselves here right now.

In one sense, crisis is nothing new. It is the basic nature of the economic system in which we live to destroy old social formations, create new ones, and then destroy those new ones in turn. It has done so for at least three to four hundred years now. I was reminded of that coming down to New York on the train from New Haven, first passing through Bridgeport, Connecticut, and seeing the gigantic industrial complexes that once had hired workers in the tens of thousands, now completely shuttered up, performing no work whatsoever. Most of the activity in this vicinity is found in parking lots. Going to the next stop, Stamford, Connecticut, I remembered that in the days of my youth, this was the scene of one of America's greatest general strikes. In 1946, when the workers at Yale and Towne were out on strike and were beaten up by the local police, everybody else went out on strike to their assistance. Anyone looking around that city now would say, "Where is a single one of the factories that were involved in that struggle in 1946?" They are gone, but what is there instead? Shining, new corporate headquarters that have to draw in their workers from New York.

Not long ago those Stamford businesses were complaining that there was no place in the vicinity where people who did the service work could even live, because the rents were so high. The people who once did the manufacturing work in Stamford and waged that historic strike can no longer live there or carry on such occupations. But one thing exists there in even greater quantities than ever before: wealth.

If we are living in a period of competitiveness, stringency, and downsizing, we are also living in a period when important numbers of Americans have incomes like they have never dreamed of before. What has been happening to most of us has to be put in context: wealth has not disappeared. There has been no plague that suddenly took all the money off the face of the United States of America. The question is, Who has it, and how is it being used? What is the purpose to which this wealth is being put? And, indeed, part of the new formation of wealth comes out of the extraordinary generation of money out of money.

An economist colleague of mine recently calculated that of the global transactions in the hundreds of billions of dollars that float around the world every twenty-four hours, hardly 10 percent represent the actual exchange of goods. The rest is money making money. What we see in my university, Yale, is an endowment that just spirals upward, yielding a 27 percent per year return. Where does all that surplus come from? How is this generation of untold wealth happening at the same time as the casualization of work and similar job prospects that all of us face? This, I think, is the central question that we find ourselves dealing with today.

Half a century ago, the men and women who had endured the Great Depression and fought World War II insisted that they would never again live through the economic misery that they had experienced. They dreamed that they would rid themselves of the racism, the segregation, the routine lynching that was part of our lives through the 1930s and the 1940s, that they would not have to endure the kind of war to which so many of us, in that age, were called away, wiping some forty million people off the face of the earth. They wanted some kind of a life fit for human consumption, in a world where no one lorded it over others. My generation, we saw all these hopes snuffed out by a cold war. It did more than simply wipe out alternative social, political, and ideological futures for America that were sacrificed to the Eisenhowerism that we came to know too well. It also generated a kind of sustained prosperity built around military budgets, the suburbanization of everyday life, and, in large part, the development of an educational system bigger than this country had ever before imagined.

Educational credentials came to be required in virtually any kind of occupation. Research and development activity received money funded from the state on a scale unprecedented in our history. In *The Cold War and the University*, Noam Chomsky et al. present a series of reflections by people in a variety of disciplines on what the cold war meant to their studies.[1] These essays illuminate the way in which our paradigms, our research, our thinking, and even the subjects that we taught were shaped by the particular needs of the state in this cold war setting, while previously unheard-of sums of money came pouring in. Think of something like the National Defense Education Act of 1958 and the sort of fellowships that it made available. Consider the way in which the people who were starting so many of our ethnic studies programs received their training. In area studies programs the funding came from the National Defense Education Act, and many of the scholars now admit, "Oooh, we never had such fellowships as this before!" There are ways some deeds come back to haunt their initiators. Yes, indeed.

This growth of academic life in financial terms placed colleges and universities among the key mass economic enterprises of our society today.

But that era of steady growth has come to an end. It was clear by the end of the 1960s and the beginning of the 1970s that the postwar nexus of economic activity was no longer returning the rates of profit and the rates of growth it had generated during the previous quarter of a century. Business embarked on a quest for new openings for investment that would begin to raise the level of return. *Business Week* and other magazines summoned the nation's leaders to undertake one of the most difficult selling jobs in modern history: convincing Americans of the idea of doing with less so that big business could have more.[2] Only by following that path could the accumulation of capital and wealth resume the upward spiral that it had enjoyed under that cold war complex earlier on. So the catchwords became "competitiveness," "globalization," "privatization," "making money out of money." Now what has this meant for us in the academic world?

It has meant, it seems to me, that we have found ourselves in the public sector faced with a frontal assault on the public sector per se. Nothing more systematic has reshaped government policy and the molding of public power since Margaret Thatcher showed how it was done in England, which Reagan then picked up — Reagan was still a piker by comparison with Thatcher, never quite having the chutzpah to go all the way down the line that she had, but we are now catching up.

With everything becoming privatized, watch out for the bipartisan commissions that will be created in the coming months to figure out how to dismantle more of the public sector in the United States, and above all else, watch out for what happens to the juiciest slush fund of all, social security. Think of what could happen if private banks gain control of those billions of social security tax dollars that by law must now be invested in treasury bonds and are really the backbone of how the public debt is funded in the United States. And this is what they're telling us: "We want to take it over. Why, government bonds can earn only 7 percent! We can get 27 percent at Yale. Think of what we can do with this loot!"

Here is the offensive, then, that we find ourselves facing today, and it is coming at full tilt. Scholarly commissions will, with bipartisan support, determine ways in which more and more of government activity can be privatized. But in the academic world, the battle cry is for budget cuts in the state sector, in public institutions: "We can't afford any more." The cutbacks must come, and have already been coming, hand over first during the course of the last decade, along with promises, of course, that the taxes of every individual are going to be reduced. All this adds up to a new American dream that everybody's taxes will be cut to the bone and every human being will be given her or his own private gun.

The public universities have faced the cutback on that level. The private ones have had a different setting, facing the extraordinary paradox of actually spiraling income—especially in the elite institutions, where it is known that as jobs become increasingly harder to get, the competition to obtain the sort of credentials that may open doors to those positions in which earnings still rise becomes even more intense. So the Ivy League can continue to raise tuitions all they want. Somebody will pay them so as to attain those jobs. At the same time, the returns on investment of endowments escalate beyond all prior expectations. Moreover, the shrinking of economic prospects for most people opens up an opportunity for university management to attack costs wholesale. And these attacks are publicly justified, as they say to the public, "Look, everybody else is taking it in the neck, why should you guys get off easy?" And indeed, a great many people think just that way: "I'm suffering, it's your turn now."

The management of my university and of many others sees here an opportunity to slash costs to the bone, first and foremost through casualization. Casualization means a variety of things to us. It means, on the one hand, that a core of workers will be maintained, and maintained fairly well, with some security. There especially has to be a core of administrators—we couldn't think of getting rid of them—but also a core of superstar faculty. They will pay enormous salaries for a handful of people on the faculty and make up the difference by using adjuncts, having the teaching done at public institutions primarily by adjunct professors and at private institutions primarily by teaching assistants (TAs). Wherever possible, both are employed. The result is that a graduate student having gone through years of miserable pay as a TA faces the prospect of even lower pay as a adjunct professor—two thousand dollars per course.

Consider the November 1996 issue of the *Organization of American Historians Newsletter* on the cutbacks in universities and the struggles being waged against such cutbacks. Even the tenured people are facing an attack on tenure itself, led by the University of Minnesota. Regents there had developed a plan in effect to eliminate tenure so that faculty can be dismissed, must be reviewed for renewal every few years, and can be subjected to a pay cut or a dismissal if the administration is not satisfied with that person's work or (in a lovely phrase) if that person does not have a cooperative attitude.

This situation led, of course, to the very rapid development of organizing efforts at the University of Minnesota. But it has also meant ever-increasing casualization for the nonteaching staff of the universities; for example, Yale's Law School has seen its dining room staff cut from fourteen workers to four, plus people sent in by subcontractors. Cooking is done by national chains, which put out what you can get elsewhere. And, indeed, Yale's management now has a fascination with national chains. They want to get them all up and down Broadway; the newest plan is to eliminate the Co-op and put in Barnes and Noble. Everything will have a national name, and every student can eat Taco Bell!

This notion of bringing in the subcontracting chain has been combined with another managerial dictum that cannot be ignored: the big money lies in health care. In your universities, watch the plans for the medical schools and the health plans, because these are the moneymakers. These are the schools which decision-makers are linking up with the cost-cutting health maintenance organizations.

This phenomenon is not peculiar to the United States. In November 1996 there was a strike in England of its entire education system. What is noteworthy about this strike—a strike against a 40 percent increase in students, with a 30 percent decrease in available budget and no increases in salary for anybody—is that university professors voted 85 percent in favor of the strike; science and finance researchers, 70 percent in favor; lecturers, 52 percent; the amalgamated engineering and electrical union, 73 percent; transport, 87 percent. In other words, from the maintenance to housekeeping to teaching staff, all voted in favor of the strike (and 85 percent of the student union voted to go out with them).

It is crucial to be aware that the crisis hits everyone in the academic system at once. It's crucial to us, I think, because we find ourselves facing the urgent necessity to defend our own conditions of work. Are we academic laborers? If not, what else are we? We are people involved in intellectual and cultural work. We are trying to create new ways of thinking about the world, new ways of imagining society. We are trying to create links between the academic world and the nonacademic through our teaching, our speaking, our writing, whatever it may be. And if that's not work, I don't know what is! Furthermore, it is what we get paid for.

The question in this kind of production of research and of new human beings with new ideas is to guarantee some kind of security and stability for the conditions in which we do it. In a larger sense, that quest means also that we must join ourselves together, to wrest control of our society from this great lust for private ownership. The most dangerous myth of our times is the myth that nothing can be done well if it is done publicly—that the only efficient way to do anything is to turn it over to somebody to make money out of it. We have long known that the most valuable things in life simply cannot be bought and sold in the marketplace, that they must be organized by public activity. This defense of the public sector must be central to all the struggles in which we engage. Finally, we must all remain aware that in the development and use of whatever particular personal talents, ambitions, and prospects that any of us may have, we are engaged together in attempting to create a new kind of cultural and social formation that will challenge this lust for privatization and private profit, and to teach America again what a real public life means for our country and our world.

Notes

1 Noam Chomsky, R. C. Lewontin, Ira Katznelson, Laura Nader, David Montgomery, and Immanuel Wallerstein, *The Cold War and the University: Toward an Intellectual History of the Postwar Years* (New York: New Press, 1997).
2 John Carsen-Parker, "The Options Ahead for the Debt Economy," *Business Week*, October 12, 1974, 120–21.

Doing Academic Work

Stefano Harney and Frederick Moten

The Academic Worker

When professors get together outside the university they talk about that thing which dominates them, their work. This conversation may take the form of discussing a product of that work—a lecture in class, a research paper, committee deliberations—but most often it seems to be about conditions of work. One hears talk about course load, the trials of tenure and promotion, salaries and compensation, and of course the quality of the students on which some of academic labor is supposed to fall. In themselves, these conversations are not surprising. Mail carriers have very similar conversations, as do primary school teachers, subway drivers, and millions of other working people in the United States when they come together with those who share their position in the production process. But what is interesting among academic workers is the simultaneous disavowal of the very social conditions of work about which they speak. Mail carriers may not develop sufficient solidarity for effective political action for many reasons having to do both with their workplace and with life beyond their workplace, but they are unlikely to deny that the mail does not move unless they all work together. Nor are they likely to doubt that their product results from common effort.

But the academic worker often disavows both this mutual interdependence and the sociality of her or his product. This omission is perhaps most telling in the attitude displayed toward students but is present as well in the way academic workers see each other, see race, see the university as a site of work, and at bottom see themselves. For us, this disavowal is both a theoretical and political problem. Our position in this paper is that most professors in the United States are part of the service sector proletariat in this country. There is thus no need to romanticize the relationship between professors and other working people, no need to agonize over the right channel for some connection to labor in other forms. The connection is material. Professors as teachers, writers, and researchers work for someone else producing what is explicitly a commodity as part of a system of industrial capitalism that relies on their surplus labor just as much as it does on the surplus labor of mail carriers, computer technicians, maintenance staff, or marketing specialists. But the subjectivity currently produced by academic labor warrants investigation—for clearly, most professors would not see themselves as described in these opening statements.

An investigation of academic labor subjectivity is both fraught with difficulty and urgent. Any attempt to think one's own position bears risks of myopia, particularly when that position is itself disintegrating, revealing more starkly the contradictions of this mode of producing academic knowledge. Moreover, because we regard this investigation also as a political project, we will be making some overgeneralizations as a step toward trying to imagine academic labor in general. The diversity of academic workplaces from community colleges to multiversities presents variations we can only acknowledge, not explore, at this stage. So too, the wage contracts for academic workers resist too much generalization. What truly does the adjunct finishing a doctorate at CUNY and teaching at Borough of Manhattan Community College have in common with an adjunct named David Dinkins teaching one course at Columbia or one named Jacques Derrida putting in the same number of hours in the same city at NYU, both for more money than a full-time assistant professor's salary? Our answer is that they share something nonetheless in the nature and conditions of knowledge production in institutional higher education. It is this nature and condition of knowledge production in the colleges and universities that we want to explore. We want to situate the academic worker in that work. Much has been written situating the academic worker within wider social contexts and locating the social position of intellectuals generally. But subjectivity comes also from doing work, not just being a type of worker. And if we are going to explore how professors are invited to see themselves in highly individuated ways, we should start by looking at academic workers producing in the colleges and universities.[1]

Let us start by noting that as workers, the economic fate of most professors in this country is tied most closely with the other people who work in their workplace as part of production relations as a whole, and not to their individual talents as teachers or scholars. In other words, it is tied to the fate of the industry and social relations in that industry. It would seem to follow that a political dialogue and action between professors and other workers in the same place of production would be on the agenda. It is not. It would also seem to follow that a political dialogue would be on the agenda between academic workers across the industry. It is not. Such a dialogue would obviate the need to think about the basis for communication between professors and other laborers that would be unmediated by class ideology. Any self-critical dialogue would have to admit that a common point of reference and common reason for wanting to cooperate is already in place.

Political dialogue and action across the industry is admittedly more difficult strategically than one constructed narrowly along occupational lines. But the discussion founders on conceptual grounds before it can address the strategic issue. For although academics can conceive of themselves socially in their common conditions of work, they cannot, for the most part, conceive of themselves socially in their actual production. They may have to put up with similar constraints, such as crowded offices, broken copiers, and low salaries, but these are regarded too often as relations to things and not to another person. Politically we could hope that this initial sense of common conditions could lead to a deeper sense of participation in a common production process, one that they themselves give its particular social nature, as bearers of definite social relations. But neither the recognized conditions around work nor the unrecognized conditions of a common production process have been enough for the subjectivity of academic workers to break into a collective agency. In fact, the subjectivity produced by this particular production process cries out for investigation.

We argue that the very way in which academics think of themselves as workers interferes with effective political agency predicated on collective self-recognition and representation. While this is a problem for all wage labor, knowledge production generates a version of interference that is particularly acute. This is so because academic workers, as makers of worldly representations, also produce themselves as a productive force that is "usable in common" only in that the discourse of disciplinary knowledge is truly a social product. But typically that product appears under the sign of an individual author, craftsperson, or scientist who believes she controls her tools and product. It is as if knowledge and the discursive instruments that create it could be held in the academic's hand, as so many objects. While this may be a nostalgic and historically inaccurate view of craftwork held by the academic, the image of solitary self-possession remains potent. The absence of immediate supervision; the luster of authorial imprimatur; the seemingly discrete sites of production; and, most important, what at first sight appears as the disarticulation of knowledge production from its circulation and consumption—all reinforce this view.

But no worker subjectivity in capitalism is ever more than contingent. In this article, we want to push at this subjectivity, finding the weak points that open onto new agency. What we can say already is that it would appear to be not (or not just) the social position of the academic worker in society that complicates the project of collective agency. Certainly all of us have encountered the disjunction between the social tastes of academics and their ability to consume at that level. And certainly all of us have encountered and perhaps used the social capital of the professoriat to assert authority or privilege where our claims to power are otherwise materially weak. For a few of us this may even mean material changes in our circumstances that authorize our social distinctions. But too much concentration on the social position of intellectuals risks not only a flirtation with functionalism and tax brackets but also a sharp distinction between the social relations of production and the social relations in production. Michael Burawoy gives us the idea of "relations in production," and we want to use the idea as a corrective and as an opening into a new line of inquiry. Burawoy uses this term instead of the more commonly used "forces of production" to denote the political, ideological, and material conjunction of subjectivity formation in the workplace. For Burawoy, this is a prime site of contingency, and for us, the investigation of academic relations in production is a place to start to push at the subjectivity of the academic worker.[2] It is a way of getting away from the question of what it means to be an academic worker, a question that seems to lead to social positioning, and to ask finally what is means to do academic labor.[3]

Academic Work

How is academic work done? What are our actual conditions under which this work is done? What are our practical relations to one another in that work as full-time academic workers? (We will address part-time workers subsequently.) Let us see how far a description of those conditions and relations will take us. Even a cold description of working conditions has little explanatory power in itself, but it is a necessary first step.

As C. L. R. James once reminded us about a whaling ship, a factory has no look, only relations. Most of us working in academia are familiar with the trinity of tasks common to our job descriptions. We teach, we publish, and we sit on committees. Under what conditions do we perform those tasks? We participate in decision making about the fate of our fellow academic workers and sometimes about other workers, such as student aides and secretaries. We participate in deciding on the value of the knowledge product, on curriculum or editorial committees. Some of us participate in criticism of our workplace and its relations. This participation itself has constraints. Whatever their specific configuration, such constraints stem, as they do for all wageworkers, from our compulsion to produce surplus value, our lack of access to the means of production, and, perhaps most important our total dependence on a production process in general and in history that is capitalism.

The majority of academic workers in this country cannot stop work in protest of conditions. Moreover, at many work sites the power of management exercises both real and perceived constraints over even the limited freedoms enjoyed by most workers. For those able to secure tenure-bearing appointments, the first six years of academic work are almost without any of the limited freedoms outlined above because of impending tenure decisions. This period of insecurity is far longer than for most workers in other unionized fields of production. If it corresponds to the kind of apprenticeship once characteristic of some skilled trades, it also enforces a social distance between full-time and part-time workers, as if to say there is a seven-year difference in skill between those working in part-time and non-tenure-track positions and those tenured faculty members who shepherd the apprentices.[4] Contrast the recent ability of full-time and part-time United Parcel Service workers to see each other in the other's place, where any worker believed she or he could be forced to lift 150-pound packages alone, on the one hand, or suffer the loss of benefits, on the other.[5] After this lengthy apprenticeship, promotion decisions controlled in part by management continue to exercise censure over the freedoms in the workplace outlined above. Again, in other unionized fields of production, workers have in place more defined and legally circumscribed systems of seniority and promotion. In fact, the involvement of academic workers in the system of seniority in the academic workplace, called promotion and tenure, is more directly parallel to current trends of managed employee involvement, often in nonunion settings. Tenure committees most closely approximate the managerialist concept of teams, in which workers are encouraged to judge the quality of one another's work while the ultimate decision making remains lodged with management. Management thus achieves a worker-against-worker surveillance in the name of the common goal of quality and flexibility—in the academic workplace, what we would call academic standards and collegiality. Tenure committee members thereby often reproduce workplace fear and hierarchy while also projecting the partly false image of worker control. The same accusation of bad faith pervades labor union critiques of the team concept.[6] What makes academic worker teams more threatening to efforts at the liberation of academic work is that unlike with a Saturn car team, academic workers also reinforce the notion of individuality in these standards and collegial behaviors. The Saturn team at least recognizes in each car the social basis for judgments of quality and flexibility, even if those workers do not always recognize that the quantification of that quality and flexibility is derived from their collective labor power. Academic laborers fail to recognize both the sociality that makes this self-surveillance necessary and the self-surveillance itself.

Despite self-policed efforts at productivity, the elimination of departments, like product lines or public services, proceeds apace, affording fewer protections for displaced workers (tenured professors) than many unions have negotiated on behalf of their skilled manual and service workers. The insecurity of the academic worker and the looming threat of losing or never finding another good job are certainly shared by many other wageworkers. All such workers must necessarily feel confused when they not only have been hired by things, by machines, money, products, but now have also been fired by those things with the collapse of stable capitalist accumulation in the last thirty years. Though working for things is hard enough for the wageworker, being fired by them is certainly harder and cause for self-reflection. Of course, that self-reflection must contend also with ideology in the media, in politics, and in education that speaks of the world as if objects were subjects, "erecting them into autonomous power over against him," as Marx says.[7] And for the academic worker that self-reflection might be all the more acute if he saw the product of his work as a description (and even a condition?) of this predicament. But although the circumstances of their industry would call for it as much as it would for hospital or sanitation workers, academic workers have not produced these kinds of reflections on their own obsolescence.

Like the overwhelming number of workers who are wageworkers in the United States, the producers of knowledge working in universities rarely own any part of this means of production. The few who have access to some means of production through such patterns of ownership and control as patents, intellectual property, and biotechnological apparatus appear to have this access exactly at the point where the academic workplace articulates with other private and public sector workplaces and production processes. Few whose whole production process is based in the university have this option of ownership and control. Moreover, at the level of ownership, not access, the "worker shares" or "employee stock options," for instance, exist for some in the service sector and for some blue-collar, unionized workers but not for professors as a class.

Other constraints on workplace decision making and freedom are better acknowledged, but these constraints have rarely become the object of concerted action by the workers so constrained. Moreover, the boundaries of these constraints have often been drawn too narrowly, occluding many parts and products of the university workplace. For instance, the most commonly investigated constraint on knowledge workers has been the source and availability of capital reinvestment. Rivaling capital reinvestment as a constraint on the power of workers to produce knowledge freely and cooperatively is the area of production orders. The first area is commonly thought to be a matter of state funding or private philanthropy, whereas the second area is associated with private firms, especially weapons manufacturers, biotechnology, and legal-managerial consultancies. Investigations have concentrated on the source of these orders and reinvestment and who controls them. In practice, not only are the state, private patrons, and private firms permanently entwined but so too are orders and reinvestment. Although private philanthropy can extricate itself, it rarely does, and even more rarely does it set up an alternative set of social relations.

State and private firm orders and reinvestments always run together. The nature of knowledge production requires frequent changes and upgrading in fixed capital, of course—new labs, new computers, and new business school buildings. But it also requires investment in new ways of thinking about how knowledge can be produced and new ways, that is, new forms of industrial design, of arranging workers as they make this product. Such new ways might include the creation of centers, journals, seminars, and conferences. These new forms of design have the added benefit of taylorizing academic workers by allowing management to learn about how the academic knowledge process works and can be improved. Academic workers can participate in the redesign of their own work, in the separation of their tasks from their purposes. On the other hand, perhaps, as Christopher Newfield seems to suggest in his essay in this volume, these moments can be moments of resistance. Reorganization, rationalization, and various kinds of corporatization illuminate in the act the question of a rationality that must contend with not only all the attendant problems of social production and private accumulation but particularly the rational limits of knowledge production, where, as we shall see, the process of production itself appears to contain elements of circulation and the realization of value. We will return to this possibility later in the argument. But for now it is enough to mark the other side—the danger such reorganization presents to academic workers who have a special facility to be complicit in their own disciplining.

Beyond the commonly leveled criticism of this further corporatization of the university (a corporatization of a corporation?) being a reorganization in service to private firms, there are troubling but unexamined reorganizations of production that are tied to wider social relations of production and not to the narrow orders and invoices of firms and states. Here we can consider again the nature of knowledge production and knowledge products. Two kinds of products leave the university: knowledge sold directly as know-how, enlightenment, and entertainment, and knowledge embodied in the student-product. Each has an exchange value, but the first product is most easily traced to the orders and invoices of firms and states, by which we mean its value is realized and measured more easily.

The second product is tied to the ideological state apparatus where the difficulty of realizing its value in fact propels it. The social imaginary acts on knowledge production just as the state and the private firm, which are, after all, only part of that social. The state and the private firm are impulses within that social imaginary but are not exhaustive of it. The social imaginary produces the notion of job readiness, of relevance, of political correctness, of critical thinking, of higher education. Orders are made and invoices sent for writing for business classes, interdisciplinary approaches to science teaching, arts administration, and filmmaking. Of course, the university as a site of production is within this imaginary and acts on it, its products appearing as strange orders returning to it. The professor who so much regarded herself as a craftsworker, as an author of a work, sees around her knowledge without signature, orders and invoices without origin coming not to her but to her workplace, returning unfamiliar. In this she shares a discomfort with the university workplace as a whole, which struggles "to measure its outcomes" as a way to insist that some value from the knowledge product has indeed been realized in and through the student.

One remarked-on indication of the tenuous control professors have over their own workplace is the growth in casualized labor. Private firms offering temp pools of lecturers are now widely used in Great Britain, for instance. A growing surplus labor pool produced by the industry itself, just as other industries have always produced their own surplus labor pools, is now set up in classic opposition to the permanent workers. The brotherhood and sisterhood of academic discourse and the search for a "noncommodified" way of speaking to each other does not extend to this pool and in fact is set up in opposition to it, contributing to a certain kind of subjectivity of the privileged worker. The risk is that full-time academic workers will regard themselves as the fullest and most complete examples of academic subjectivity. Cary Nelson's call for reducing the number of Ph.D.'s awarded, for instance, sounds like nothing so much as a return of an older craft union rhetoric that confined itself to controlling who could enter the labor market.[8]

The adjunct pool Nelson wants to reduce resembles surplus labor pool populations in other respects too. It takes advantage of sexism and racism and concentrates women and people of color in its ranks. All the discrimination dynamics evident in the construction trades are present in the North American academic labor force and especially in the pool of surplus labor. Thus the presence of women and people of color in the surplus pool is used as evidence of their unsuitability for permanent work, and their absence from permanent work positions is used to represent their scarcity for such positions. Who has not heard a chair of a department say "if only there were a fully qualified minority applicant," thus bringing both contradictory moves into play. Within this discursive formation, affirmative action enters as an artificial manipulation of real labor market conditions, rather than action against manipulated labor market conditions. And this move is only one in the discursive struggle over affirmative action. We will return to another later.

With Nelson, then, we have an extension of the team concept beyond the responsibilities of promotion and tenure and onward to the control and conditioning of the academic labor pool as a whole. Nelson's call for academic workers to take the lead in policing their own levels of employment fits with the manipulation of academic workers by university administrations, states, and private firms encouraging professors to guard standards—that is, levels of production—and collegiality—that is, flexibility and docility on the job—among their colleagues through teams of promotion and tenure. It would be interesting to see in this context who would discipline academic workers attempting a slowdown to protest conditions. Would it be their colleagues? Would the adjunct labor pool be called into service? That such potential complicity among colleagues in the policing of work conditions is not regarded as such by most academic workers is part of our present mystery.

Academic Labor Speedups

The surplus pool is already used to discipline permanent professors, of course, and especially professors in the first seven years of full-time work. It is especially useful against politically active new faculty, but it has a still more basic function in the university. More and more teaching universities and colleges are demanding and getting more surplus labor from their professors as a result of this pool. In the majority of North American universities up through the 1970s, tenure and promotion were possible with little research or publication as long as teaching and service were adequate. But more and more universities are making appeals to this surplus labor pool to squeeze more surplus value from their permanent professors. This happens in both direct and indirect ways. Younger professors in small colleges, technical colleges, and teaching colleges are told directly that if they do not produce, in ways their senior colleagues often did not, the university can go back to the labor market for someone who will accept these conditions of work. Meanwhile, both older and younger professors alike are threatened indirectly by new questions of the cost of tenure and the very survival of the university as private firm or public concern. The argument runs this way: if we do not begin to improve in the ratings of our research, we may not remain solvent; departments may be eliminated and positions cut. In most cases, the university administrations propose to replace costly departments and tenured faculty with cheaper programs using casual labor, writing programs instead of English departments, for instance—unless tenured faculty speed up production, unless they submit to a speedup of the line.

That so many senior faculty, not to speak of junior faculty, have responded to this management ploy by producing more articles and more books and more grant applications allows us to reflect on a classical question of the two sides of increased productivity and consequently enables us, at least for a moment, to situate academic labor very squarely in the category of mass production. What are the benefits of an increasingly powerful and increasingly socialized process of knowledge production? If it is true that this productivity does not necessarily create academic jobs, what does it create for a society of producers? The question seems both easy and difficult. More knowledge would always seem to be a good thing, presuming we are speaking of a self-critical knowledge. Fields such as cultural studies and physics appear to be models for this kind of increased productivity of self-critical knowledge. Yet beyond the boundaries of intellectual property, who really owns this knowledge, and especially, who controls its growing surplus? Is there a kind of disarticulation of ownership that complicates our understanding of the benefits of increased productivity? If we have difficulty in tracing the ownership, do we not also have difficulty in imagining the realization of surplus value? Where, after all, does this product give up all this new value, and to whom?

What we do know is that the increased rate of production of knowledge has not slowed management's pursuit of surplus value through cutting labor costs while gratefully accepting labor gains in productivity. Thus universities continue to eliminate departments, postpone and cancel new full-time lines, and expand casual employment despite the proliferation of journals, conferences, and book series. Interestingly, those attempts at resistance to this regime come through the knowledge production itself. Here the confusion between the in-fact-social nature of academic production and the presumed-individual nature of that production by the professor undermines attempts to resist or reverse this management ploy. Believing that knowledge production is an individual enterprise in which the worker controls her means of production, the professor mistakes access to the tools needed for her product for the whole means of production. She believes that if her product is unsuitable for the regime that she can resist that regime. (Or if her product is very suitable she will be inevitably rewarded.) But an individual cannot redirect much less desocialize production at this level of complexity and sophistication in industrial production. The collective knowledge product remains. Within the regime of increased production, newly produced knowledge contributes to the force of production.

Resiting the Line

What, then, has this description of conditions yielded? Have we "sited" an academic production line that reveals the social production of knowledge? Both the industrialization of academic labor in the post–WWII years and its selective deindustrialization, casualization, and new taylorization evoke images of academic workers on an assembly line. The imagery of the line is bound to disturb the subjectivity of the academic worker. The line invokes the solidarity of the industrial worker, the interdependencies of task, the place of the academic worker in the society of producers. The image of the line can no doubt help us think about academic work. But why is that image so rarely provoked by conditions? What happens during academic work that leads away from consideration of sociality? What happens to the academic worker as she acts out the contradiction of selling her labor power so as to appear to possess it or, as Michael Brown says, as we observe his "labor power's self-referring inconsistency with itself"?[9]

Class Struggle

There is always something dissatisfying about the line as place to understand class consciousness. Consider members of the League of Revolutionary Black Workers in Detroit in the late sixties, for instance. Their action against the line and its brutality had as much to do with their understanding of the attempted separation—both by police and by Dodge foremen—of immediate action from larger purposes in the African American community. But the self-referring, practical inconsistency of academic labor power goes beyond even this conjuncture of lines. Making knowledge and making cars is finally different. With cars, production, circulation, and consumption are separate. Sometimes the articulation that is supposed to exist here is not present, and the disarticulation of consumption, for instance, can plunge an industry and its workers into a crisis. With knowledge, this disarticulation appears to vie with articulation all the time. The production of knowledge seems to have elements of disarticulation right inside it. Consider the following questions: Where is the site of production in the classroom? What is produced? Who produces, who consumes, who circulates? Any answer appears to confuse not only the point of production but also the bearers of labor power by generalizing production through consumption and circulation. The professor produces the lecture but tries to realize its value in the quality of the questions he receives after. The students consume the lecture but generate questions. The professor circulates already produced knowledge that he has consumed for his lecture notes. The students produce knowledge on exams and circulate the knowledge of the professor through these exams. The professor consumes the knowledge of the student on the midterm exam in order to produce a new exam at year's end. At no point is any producer not simultaneously a consumer, and at no point is production not subject to the immediacy of circulation. Most important, if value is being realized in any of this circulation, then it is being realized in all of this circulation. The argument could thus be made that both professor and student (not to mention the absent labor of the graduate tutor) are coworkers in the production of knowledge, and that all are involved realizing the value of this work. Such an argument would challenge our sense of academic labor, however, in that it would acknowledge that the majority of academic workers, and of surplus labor, comes from students and not from faculty, returning us to the point that if academic labor is an activity and not a position, there is no reason to look for it only among academics. It also has implications for the politics of production, of course, transforming students from raw material worked upon by faculty to workers at the point of production. But in this argument, is the alleged circulation and realization of value during production any different from steelworkers talking to one another about making steel? It is. In academic labor there is often no product outside of the discourse about that product. This is so all the time in teaching, and often in research.

Where a distinct product is visible in a new chemical compound or piece of machinery or a new human relations model, once again it escapes a purely discursive life by its articulation with other sites of production where its value can be conventionally realized.

A Student and Worker Movement?

If students produce knowledge, if they are also so necessary to the making of the knowledge product, and they are essential to realizing its value, why do academic workers, or students for that matter, not see one another as coworkers? Perhaps the answer lies in the complexity of this very question. What could it mean to be involved in production, circulation, and realization as a student? Of course, nearly all of us in a society of producers are involved in all these operations. But the production of knowledge seems to both elide and disperse these operations. We know that selling airline tickets all day and then buying a car at the end of the day are different operations for us in time and space. We know that working as a travel agent has gained us a salary and moved our bosses' product and that buying a car with our wages has allowed another boss to realize the value of her or his product. But even this oversimplification would be very hard to map for an anthropology course. Who's working in this case? Who owns? Where does surplus go? And how is it realized? We can attempt some generalized answers about how a labor force is thus prepared to serve capital. But we cannot so easily individuate this production process. More important, those in the process have trouble keeping their individual roles straight and thus their liberal individualist identities. This trouble is where we can see the contingency of academic work and the ever possible agency contained in that worker. The insistence on the individuality of academic labor as a practice is always threatened by this trouble.

Students themselves are largely aware that at different moments they are interpellated as customers, products, workers, and owners in the university workplace. Like academic workers, they may not think of themselves as part of a process of production of knowledge within a wider system of profit. They do, however, know that market calculations are taking place around them and perhaps on them. They know that full-time and part-time academic workers are required to include more and more students in their classes, to speed up the line, allow credits to pile up faster and cheaper, with less attention to quality. But they also know that these market calculations risk constant disarticulation. They know they are produced as commodities, as quantifiable numbers of graduates who feed a labor market, and they work as producers of knowledge themselves on every term paper. Produced as workers, they act on their own subjectivity as workers but also have that subjectivity acted on. Working as producers, they assist professors, produce test results, and work on themselves. Yet they are also wooed not just as the customer as king but through a discourse of partnership, ownership, community, and domesticity. Like their parents, they are sold an education as a commodity where the tension of use value and exchange value cannot be resolved or hidden. Appeals to the value of an education are irreducibly contradictory in this way. This value must be realized in each student to support the university's sales pitch, but when students say, "What's the use of taking this course?" they may be saying a lot.

More and more students are also recognizably workers, outside and inside the university. They are employed in part-time and sometimes full-time work. More and more students are also entering into indenture. Through incurring debt, they have contracted to be workers and so are already thinking like people who must work. Graduates and dropouts who default on loans, on the other hand, are already regarded as lumpen, morally unfit for the rigors of wage labor. It is true, but not very helpful, to say that most academic workers do not view students primarily in this way, as part of the labor force. They do not regard them as coworkers. One can point to the documented unwillingness of professors to make common cause with, never mind join, graduate student labor-organizing efforts, despite some of the worthy exceptions noted in the recent collection *Will Teach for Food*.[10] And if academic workers do not regard graduate students as coworkers or even, in many cases, as workers at all, we can suggest that this has something to do with the way they view students in general.

Academic workers enter into relations with students at the same time as they enter into relations with universities, both state and privately held, as wage laborers hired to teach. These relations are contradictory.

They point both toward and away from the sociality of their labor and toward and away from its appropriation. The academic worker sees in the act of teaching the sociality of the knowledge commodity, but its attempted valuation and circulation by the student at the point of production, in production itself, leads the academic worker to believe he or she owns and controls that product. That is, teaching is not a product until the student also acts on it, and therefore the product is inherently social. It must be made in common, and its value must be realized in exchange. It becomes only through common labor, and it becomes a commodity only through the giving up of labor power. Yet the way it is presented to the student, as something only to be realized in them and taken away to use, also makes that product appear to be something that was created and possessed by the academic worker and then passed to the student. This latter appearance allows the academic worker to retain the imagined sense of individual artisanry and even ownership of the means of knowledge production. To maintain this imagined sense, it is important for the academic worker not to regard the student as coworker in any sense, because this view might lead to the necessity of the student's labor in the production of teaching.

This need to view the student as a passive individual who purchases and takes away the knowledge product helps us to understand why on the surface the relations of academic workers to students is so often described as disturbed or unhappy. Academic workers try to act toward students as if those students were only free-willed individuals entering into a contract to learn. They do not view this as purely or even chiefly as a market contract but rather one between liberal individuals. Many "progressive" universities actually use learning contracts to set up supposedly individual relations between students and teachers. Academic workers thereby take a moment of exchange and try to use it to establish stable identities and individuation. But this moment of exchange, as we have said, is highly problematic because its value is not so easily fixed. It hides the fact that students work on the product that is being exchanged. They create, with the professor, their knowledge of anthropology. Thus the student can sense at least two tensions. First, one often hears the exhortation to "get as much out of a class as possible." It would seem then that the value of a class as a commodity has to do not with how much you pay for it but with how much work you put into it. It would be a strange thing to say about a Saturn car or an airline ticket. At the same time, the value of a class or an education more generally does not seem to have to do with the individual or with individual effort. A student finds out how much a class or education is worth not in the exchange between her and the university or her and the professor. If she believes such worth can be calculated at all, she will likely determine it according to how much she later gets paid in a job. This is why education is often called an investment, an acknowledgment that its value cannot be known at the moment of exchange. Or she might say it cannot be measured at all and thus deny its status as a commodity. Either way something does not fit. How can an individual professor really know how much to "give" an individual student in either case? The learning contract invites the student to think of herself as an individual, and it helps the professor to believe she is passing a discrete product to the student. But, in reality, not only are the student and professor making the product together, not just exchanging it, but they are also both getting use value out of it and are unsure about its exchange value because its realization is deferred, perhaps indefinitely.

Students and professors are often aware of the problems created by trying to think of knowledge production as a series of singular enterprises relying on liberal individualism and market exchanges. We have all heard faculty complain of the "absurd" page counting in tenure committees or of the "meaningless" computer forms for student evaluations of classes. We have discussed the team concept in academia that makes this operative. Its basis is an evaluation of product that searches for equivalency and exchangeability of the academic worker or, more exact, his labor power. The irony is that academic workers encourage this valuation based on commodity exchange in precisely an attempt to individuate themselves. The price of individualism becomes the tyranny of the market, and many academic workers experience important self-referential moments when this circle closes.

Of course, not all academic workers regard their students through the contract of liberal individualism. Some show a kind of imagined attachment, a romantic link to the students as collective agents of human development or social change. They try to attach a putative worker status to the student that supposes they are not already in fact workers intrinsic to all the labor of academic workers. This putative notion of the student as worker or change agent takes the student to be someone other, outside the production process of knowledge, someone acted on and activated by that process. Although this position supposes a certain sociality and even a certain agency in learning, it is materially inconsistent and politically always flawed. The bafflement of the academic worker when she fails to mobilize the students as oppressed agents necessarily follows.

It is hard not to be sympathetic to this position, especially when the academic worker has a sense of the student as a class. Many of us know academic workers who are dedicated to helping students analyze and critique society where the object of that critique is actually existing capitalism. The academic workers are admirable for their faith in the human nature of these students and for their understanding of the subject of any such critique (what we would call socialism). Such workers are capable of viewing students as a social group, based on age, race, income, or their superficial place in the education system. They may attempt to teach antiracism, feminism, anti-imperialism, or pacifism. But it is necessary to be rigorous in critiquing the analysis that informs this position. The production of knowledge requires the student as producer. The student must manipulate the raw material of thought. She must expend labor time in this process. She must and she does add something to the product that the academic worker has not, no matter how insignificant, for the commodity to be formed. She is, therefore, a worker in the production of the teaching commodity. Now it is possible for an academic worker to hope for an agency from students not based on their position as workers, as one can hope for such agency among people in general. But it does not seem to us possible to devise a strategy for that agency which does not recognize, first, that the very act of strategizing implicates the students as workers and, second, that any strategy ignorant of these material conditions of production is at least incomplete.

Race and Academic Work

Thinking about your tools and your product as your own is both encouraged and undermined in the act of teaching students. But it can also be encouraged and undermined by teaching and working with colleagues.

The issue of race in the academic workplace, and especially the discourse on affirmative action, threatens to expose the sociality of the act of teaching and researching. Affirmative action threatens the ideology of individualism among academic workers precisely because it speaks about academic workers in social categories. It is regarded as an attack on the putative individual properties of the academic worker: his talents, choices, and motives. This underlying threat to individualism helps explain the widespread attack on affirmative action among liberal intellectuals and within an industry with an egregious record on racism (and sexism). The connections of the reserve labor pool to racism and sexism in the academic workplace are only one manifestation of racism and oppression in this venue. The academic workplace had to be integrated by federal and state law; legislated action against racism and sexism was augmented by recourse to court action. Together, these instruments forced some progress in the 1970s and 1980s on hiring practices in the university. But universities remained sites of entrenched racism, sexism, and oppression. Minorities, for instance, continued during this period to fare better in the automobile and steel industries, winning more concessions and enjoying more compensation relatively than has been available in the university workplace to the vast majority of minority professors. Schoolteachers unions during the same period developed female leaderships, bringing the conditions and concerns of the female elementary and high school teacher to a prominence they have never enjoyed in the university workplace. In a service sector increasingly occupied in its mass labor by minority women, the ease of recognizing solidarity stands in contrast to one part of that service sector where few minority women work and where little solidarity is in evidence, the colleges and universities (though the colleges stand closer to the rest of the service sector in both aspects). Although the argument that minorities cannot do certain kinds of work has long disappeared in the public discourse of other industries, it persists as a matter of course in academic labor. African Americans are hired to teach African American subjects, and East Asian scholars are asked to teach East Asian subjects. The minority candidate who is hired to teach Renaissance studies is rare, and the minority graduate student in the humanities who is not steered toward his "natural subject matter" is equally rare.

Such racial conditions would seem to be cause for outrage, not retreat.

But race is a social category, and affirmative action is a policy insistent of the sociality of race not just anywhere but in work. Consider the way race as a category within affirmative action has to be discussed. The fact of the social construction of racial communities always threatens to reveal the fact of the social construction of communities in general, including the community of academic workers. To discuss what the category Hispanic means, whether in California the category of Asian can contain meaning, or whether the City University of New York's affirmative action policy on hiring Italian Americans fits in the frame is to discuss potential workers as bearers of social relations that will operate in the act of work. The threat of the social category is that it will become a work category; that any minority academic worker can fill the category, can do the job (and by implications any academic worker in general can do any academic job); that the labor power of one equals the labor power of another; and that for such equivalencies to obtain commodity, production for profit must be in effect. Now the academic worker repels this threat by seizing on the moments of circulation and realization as he did with the student and trying to hold them steady as categories of individuality. In a sense they attempt to reracialize the minority worker as a way to fasten him to that idea of the academic worker as owner of his means of production and controller of his very singular product.

What we are calling "reracialization" is the contradictory act of individualizing the minority academic worker by assigning race to him anew. By individualizing him we mean trying to isolate his work and working conditions from the very sociality of affirmative action that brought him to the work site. Thus we hear the term "the black hire" or "the gay hire" in anthropology, English, or history.[11] This move simultaneously reinforces the very particularization of knowledge accompanying affirmative action that many on the left have turned against. And yet that particularization itself is not the same thing as this individualization through reracialization. The particularization of knowledge still affirms each area of knowledge, whether queer theory or critical race theory, as a social product and in fact by its very manufacture reconfirms the sociality of all knowledge products. Reracialization attempts to create distance and difference in the minority worker to avoid possible comparisons with other academic workers. Such comparisons risk the recognition that both minority and nonminority workers possess the same tools, only usable in common. This distance and difference is accomplished by the invidious opinion that minority workers have been hired to do only certain kinds of work, that they are special cases, highly isolated cases, and that they do a kind of work unlike other workers. They have been hired by this argument for political reasons. That is, they have been hired to enforce a sociality that is not actually inherent, in this view, in academic work.

This reracialization is a trap for both the minority worker and other workers. It seizes on that disarticulation in knowledge production that reflects what Manthia Diawara calls in relation to the African diaspora "the circulation of black things" and attempts to fasten a worker to these "black" commodities of knowledge.[12] But every commodity leads to the next and to fetishization of these relationships. The minority worker experiences the alienation of comparison to things and not other workers, and the other workers experience the alienation of invoking the fetish to dehumanize and reracialize the minority worker. For instance, the Latina who will be considered only for positions in Latina studies is asked if she is willing to be responsible for Latina content in the curriculum and for teaching a course on the Latina experience. If she accepts this reracialization, she accepts not the obvious, a division of labor by race, but the opposite, the fiction that there is no division of labor that in turn can be harnessed to race. That is, if she accepts that it is possible for her to be responsible for these things, to associate with these things, to be compared to these things, she accepts a moment of disarticulation in her conditions of work and her relations to other workers. When she fails, she will say she was not given the backing to succeed as an individual, completing the confused picture of her position in production. That the production of Latina knowledge fails in this workplace to be liberatory has to do neither with deficiencies in a worker nor with a worker's ability to make this product. She is not the author of the Latina knowledge produced in the university workplace and never was. She is a worker in a system of knowledge production whose constraints easily absorb individual or small collective efforts by those workers. The reracialization encountered by these workers reinforces and is reinforced by its inevitable failure to hold in its valuation against minority things. The social reemerges at the moment of failure only to be accused of a politics incompatible with the kind of labor in which academic workers claim to be involved. Thus we have the return of the invidious moment of reracialization, when other workers insist on the individual failure of the minority worker and reject the discourse of affirmative action that would lay a social claim on their work.

But the attack on affirmative action or affirmative action workers is not always successful, of course. Moreover, when such workers succeed in producing with a sense of the sociality of their task, they not only subvert the presumed individual nature of academic work but also build the solidarity of such work beyond the academic work site. Solidarities have been built around multicultural curriculums, for instance, that acknowledge the common process of production among professors, students, and communities beyond the walls of the university. The possibility of such solidarity reminds us that despite our focus on the act of producing academic knowledge, the social place of the academic in society does indeed play a role in her subjectivity. The Latina academic worker can use her social place in her community as an academic worker, and that place can militate against a false individualism in the act of work. We are reminded that our focus on that act of work cannot presume that we can always identify where that work takes place or how, anymore than it can presume who is capable of such work.

Community Struggle

In the fall of 1996, a group of academic workers arranged a conference at Columbia University in cooperation with the new leadership of the AFL-CIO. Over eight hundred people, mostly academic workers and students, attended the conference, which was consequently divined as a sign of labor's resurgence and the start of a new labor-intellectual alliance.[13] Academic workers asked how they could contribute to the labor movement, what role they could play in its rebirth. The announced rebirth of the labor movement occurs at the same time that workers in the academy are beginning to discuss again the relationship between their work and what they perceive to be the world outside of their work. Discussions of becoming more relevant, of writing so that nonspecialists can understand, and of creating links with business outside the site of the university fill the hours of university administrators and departmental chairs. In his introduction to *After Political Correctness: The Humanities and Society in the 1990s*, coeditor Christopher Newfield suggests that the university should call out to its many publics and ask how it can be helpful.[14] But if the nascent labor-intellectual alliance at Columbia is any example of this interpellation, we must raise several questions about the ability of academic workers to call out.

First, if the social relations of labor for academic workers are approximately as we have described them, we are left with real questions about whether the most urgent point of action for such workers is to build solidarity with others or to build it with one another. At the very least, it would seem that two projects should and must run apace. Second, although Newfield and Strickland do not single out the labor movement, the question of calling out to that movement given the conditions of work for academic laborers begs the question of whether it is a call to help or a call for help. Moreover, to borrow from the language of therapy, such books as Cary Nelson's recent *Manifesto of a Tenured Radical* (1994) suggest that, as academic workers, we do not know how to ask for help.[15] Nelson's attitude toward the labor movement seems to be that it is all right for some (graduate students and perhaps part-time workers) but that he can handle his addiction to liberal individualism and craft unionism.

Second, the discourse on affirmative action on campus can be read in two ways. Either we can be hopeful that such a discourse even exists, in which case we may have something to say to communities. Or this may be another area where we should receive expertise from community organizations working on social justice issues, not dispense it. Calls to "popularize" academic research and "put to use" this knowledge for social movements resonate differently in light of this discussion. At the very least, rethinking the conditions and practice of academic labor would have to be a part of any such strategy. The popularizing of academic work, without rethinking it, risks spreading ways of thinking about it that could increase invidious social differentiations, not attack them.

Such a rethinking of academic labor in relation to community might start by questioning the distinction itself. Again we are speaking not just of social positioning, of the problem of stable borders and identities of academia and community, but also of the fragile distinctions in the act of knowledge production itself. We can see academic research as the social act that brings the world outside the academic worker into the center of her labor process and brings her labor process out into the center of that world. If one undertakes to write and teach about Work-to-Employment Program (WEP) workers, for instance, one immediately enters into certain relations with those workers at the moment any recognizable knowledge commodity is produced. The observations of the labor of those WEP workers, interviews with workers, city documents, and social theories in circulation are valued by the academic worker in a process of production. Of itself, this would not necessarily prove the relations we are positing, unless we simply wish to say that all thinking, talking, and writing is inherently social. But this thinking, talking, and writing is work for the academic laborer, and it forms a commodity containing sometimes nothing but this discursive activity. (Of course, contained in books, journals, and conference programs it has a physicality sometimes as well.) In this sense, such work is impossible without the communities that simultaneously make up this work activity in the solitude of the university office and disperse it in the public space of the city park. In some moments, the academic worker may see this relationship as only his ability to represent the world of the WEP worker. But at other moments, moments of conjuncture brought on by the play of articulation and disarticulation, it is clear that the WEP workers are present at the point of production in what is essentially the social act of making the knowledge commodity. At this moment the oral testimony of a worker and the past work of a colleague are necessary contributions of labor at the point of production, and necessary points in the circulation and realization of that product thereafter, asserting the sociality of the enactment and reenactment of academic labor. We can see, then, that to approach communities as an academic laborer, just as to approach students or other academic workers, it necessary to acknowledge certain interdependencies that make work possible. We think seeing that there is no steady distinction between our work and our relations with others is always possible for academic workers because of the nature of our work. The production of knowledge as a commodity affords us an extraordinary encounter with the sociality of production under capitalism. But it simultaneously assaults us with the most idealized images of the self in the moments of disarticulation inherent in this kind of production. Whether academic workers seize the conjunctures of this labor process remains to be seen. Such conjunctures will not offer a purity of social vision, but they may offer us images of an expanding solidarity.

Notes

1 The literature on the social position of intellectuals, producers of knowledge, is large-ranging, from Karl Mannheim, *Essays in a Sociology of Knowledge* (New York: Oxford University Press, 1952), to Andrew Ross, *No Respect: Intellectuals and Popular Culture* (New York: Routledge, 1989).

2 Michael Burawoy, *The Politics of Production* (London: Verso, 1985, 1990). Burawoy is correcting for what he regards as Harry Braverman's overly dichotomized scheme of deskilled worker facing taylorizing manager (*Labor and Monopoly Capital: The Degradation of Work in the Twentieth Century* [New York: Monthly Review Press, 1974], 90–109). But neither Braverman nor Burawoy is focused on the point of knowledge production, rather than knowledge produced for production. We find it necessary to implicate moments of circulation and realization in this kind of productive process, moments that break us away from the dichotomy of worker and manager and into a managed self that is made in the act of work but not composed of it alone.

3 The implication of looking at academic labor primarily as activity and not position is that academic labor does not have to be performed by traditional academics. But for the purposes of this paper we will confine ourselves to academic labor in the academic workplace.

4 Stephen Watt, *On Apprentices and Company Towns*, in *Will Teach for Food*, ed. Cary Nelson (Minneapolis: University of Minnesota, 1997), 229–63. Watt does not remark much on the unusual length and insecurity of these apprenticeships, though he does draw the comparison with trades.

5 Alexander Cockburn, *Wall Street Journal*, Thursday, August 14, 1997, Op-Ed.

6 See, for instance, the *Labor Notes* newsletter and publications for a trade union critique of new managerialist models such as "teams," especially Kim Moody, *Workers in a Lean World: Unions in the International Economy* (London: Verso, 1997).

7 Karl Marx, "Results of the Immediate Process of Production" in *Karl Marx: Selected Writings*, ed. David McClellan (London: Oxford University Press, 1990), 509.

8 Cary Nelson, *Manifesto of a Tenured Radical* (New York: New York University Press, 1997), 185–86.

9 Michael Brown, *The Production of Society* (Totowa, N.J.: Rowman and Littlefield, 1986), 127.

10 Nelson, *Will Teach for Food*.

11 Although the natural sciences escape some of this race-ing of academic posts for minorities, they are often complicit in race-ing posts for non-minorities and indeed race-ing undergraduate and graduate majors.

12 Diawara in Mathia Diawara, Arjun Appadurai, Lauren Berlant, and Carol A. Breckenridge, "Editorial Comment on Thinking the Black Public Sphere," *Public Culture* 7, no. 1 (fall 1994): 11–14.

13 In an editorial in the *Union Democracy Review* (New York: Association for Union Democracy [AUD], January 1997), Herman Benson, founder of the AUD points out the need for academics not to accept the new labor movement uncritically but to analyze the real conditions of work in labor unions and the necessity of democratizing those unions.

14 Christopher Newfield, introduction to in *After Political Correctness: The Humanities and Society in the 1990s*, ed. Newfield and Ronald Strickland (Boulder, Colo.: Westview, 1995), 16–19.

15 Nelson, *Manifesto*.

Adjuncts and More Adjuncts

Labor Segmentation and

the Transformation of Higher Education

Vincent Tirelli

The nation's higher education faculty have not been immune to the trend toward low-paying, part-time, and temporary work. Colleges across the country, especially community colleges and municipal colleges attempting to balance their budgets, have made use of a buyer's market for teachers during the last two decades. The conflicts and issues surrounding the use of part-time and temporary faculty are complex and have become increasingly volatile, exposing discord and fueling schisms that have lain dormant beneath the surface of academe. Recent activity indicates that a more organized response to these exploitative conditions is now emerging. This is an interesting development from many perspectives, but especially from the perspective of labor organizing. After all, the likelihood of success in organizing a fragmented labor force in a post-Fordist society is, on the face of it, not very good. The fragmentation of work roles in the post-Fordist era places obstacles in the path of successful mobilization of workers and raises the question of what, if any, strategies and tactics might help to alleviate exploitative conditions. New categories of contingent workers are difficult to organize, frequently ignored, and left unprotected by most mainstream labor unions, and they are a growing population. This essay is an attempt to define the political and social context of the segmentation of higher education faculty, provide a description of the part-timer experience, and explore the problems that hinder collective action as well as the activities or dynamics that enhance it.

Teachers and Unions: A Marriage Made in Limbo

The situation for college teachers has never been very good in terms of remuneration—the rewards have always been heavy on the personal satisfaction side of the scale. The formation of teachers unions in the 1960s following the unprecedented postwar expansion of higher education can now be viewed as the golden age of the university from the perspective of the career seeker. Teaching conditions today, especially for those trying to eke out an existence combining part-time jobs in the hope of finding a niche in which to survive, bear more of a resemblance to the impecunious academic life described by Thorstein Veblen in The Higher Learning in America[1] than to the "multiversity" described by Clark Kerr at the height of the 1960s.[2] Still, teachers have a difficult time thinking of themselves as typical employees.

The collective sense among faculty as being part of an organized labor force is often undeveloped and weak. Teachers do not usually come to mind when most people think of organized labor. We tend to have images of hard hats and sledgehammers, coal miners and coal miners' daughters, not academics and intellectuals. Within the more traditional sectors of organized labor, unionized manual workers have usually not considered educators as fully a part of the labor movement because they do not "dirty their hands." Likewise, many teachers in the United States historically have shunned organized labor unions because they were not considered to be for professionals. As Veblen points out, teachers tend to "balk at rating this work as a frankly materialistic and pecuniary occupation," thus their aversion to organized labor unions and the piece-wage demands for which they bargain.[3]

Though there is resistence in academic circles to the characterization of higher education faculty as *employees*, the expansion and bureaucratization of the university system makes this a logical term to describe faculty's relationship with administration, especially as it pertains to those on the lower rungs of the academic ladder. Teachers have come to wear the union label long after the major labor upheavals of the 1930s. Their relationship to organized labor may be unique in some ways, but it may well be that this uniqueness is what will serve to reinvigorate the labor movement. The part-time faculty can play a critical role in this process. Barring a dramatic shift in the global economy that would favor a seller's market for teachers, success in organizing teachers will likely depend on their ability to develop activist, democratic unions that will help them to deepen the collective sense of purpose and identity between themselves and their constituents. The history of teacher unionization in the university suggests that part-timers' involvement is necessary for this possibility to occur.

The earliest teachers' organizations served as guilds or professional associations rather than as collective-bargaining units. It was not until 1962 that the United Federation of Teachers won its first contract in New York City, making it "the first metropolitan school district in the country to engage in formal collective bargaining."[4] In 1968, the City University of New York (CUNY) held the first election "in an integrated, heterogenous, multicampus system."[5] Interestingly, the results showed that "the lower the tier of academe"—that is, those with less security, prestige, income, and involvement in graduate research—the greater the likelihood of a vote for strong union representation (that is, of a vote for the United Federation of College Teachers, the AFT affiliate); conversely, the majority of upper-tier faculty voted for either the Legislative Conference, which had not previously operated as a union, or for "no representation."[6]

Taken together, the formation of faculty unions in higher education, the increase in the size of these institutions, the ensuing bureaucratization, and the results of the CUNY election of 1968 suggest that the relationship of the faculty to the administration has become less collegial and more like traditional employer-employee relationships, especially for the expanding lower tier.[7] This shift suggests a "sharp reversal of the historic position of academics" regarding their attitudes about trade unions.[8] The past generation, however, has witnessed an overall weakening of organized labor unions, and many higher education teachers still carry with them an ambivalence toward collective bargaining.

A common explanation for the success or failure of unionization has been that the fate of workers and their organizations is strictly tied to the business cycle.[9] This argument asserts that workers' organizations do well in an expanding market in which demand for labor is great and, conversely, that they do poorly in times of slump when there is high unemployment. The struggles of the 1930s, however, have shown that even when economic conditions are unfavorable to labor, political mobilization of workers can serve as a barrier against the worst effects of rapid economic transformation.[10]

The emergence of the labor movement in the 1930s fueled the success of labor unions for years to come. This success was at least partially due to the development of shared attitudes among the working class that facilitated their collective political mobilization.[11] These labor victories resulted in increased labor union membership, a trend which peaked in the mid-1950s and which has since been in decline (although the growth of public sector unions in the 1960s and early 1970s offset the intensity of the decline).[12]

The success that teachers had with unionization came at a time of unprecedented support for the expansion of higher education. The favorable market for teachers, resulting from the demand caused by this expansion, facilitated their unionization. From 1960 to 1976 public employment grew at an average rate of 5 percent per year.[13] In 1962 President Kennedy issued an executive order encouraging organization and collective bargaining by federal employees.[14] Many states passed similar measures. By 1976 public sector unions claimed over 40 percent of government employees.[15] The expansion of the scope of government took place in the context of the post–World War II development of urban areas, fueled by urban growth coalitions.[16] This expansion, along with the social upheavals of the 1960s that led to the open admissions policies (at CUNY and elsewhere), contributed to the expansion of the market for higher education teachers. It was in conjunction with this growth and the rise of the big public university systems that college teachers—mostly public university teachers—successfully organized into recognized collective-bargaining units.

Public sector unions bear some similarity to their counterparts in the private sector, but there is a fundamental difference: rather than negotiating the terms for the sale of labor power, "demands in the public sector are framed as public policy." [17] After the 1960s the public policy winds had shifted. By the mid-1970s the economic crises faced by states and municipalities led to budget cuts that have challenged public employees and their unions. In the university, especially in the lower tiers (that is, municipal colleges and community colleges), these budget cuts have led to the creation of an academic underclass, that is, the part-time faculty.

Higher Education in the Post-Fordist Era

Desiring to maintain flexibility in hiring during uncertain and unstable periods of funding, public and private higher education institutions began in the 1970s to adopt the post-Fordist mechanisms that private industry had implemented: increased flexibility in the management of work roles, a two-tiered workforce, and a deskilling or degradation of labor. This system leaves the workers on the bottom with low status, no benefits, and little job security. It also has a negative effect on those students who are most disadvantaged.

The percentage of part-time faculty among the nation's higher education faculty overall is, by conservative estimates, slightly over 40 percent.[18] This figure does not include graduate teaching assistants. In this two-tiered workforce the flexible workers occupy the lower-tier colleges, that is, the urban four-year colleges and the community colleges where the most socially disadvantaged students are found. Between 1972–73 and 1976–77 the ranks of part-timers at community colleges in the nation rose from 40 percent to approximately 50 percent of the total number of faculty.[19] More recent figures indicate that the average number of part-timers used at community colleges has risen to 64 percent.[20] Vermont has the distinction of using 100 percent part-time faculty in their community colleges. Nevada and Colorado are close behind with 80.5 percent and 74.1 percent, respectively. New York State falls in with the next ten states that use over 60 percent part-time faculty in their community colleges.[21]

Jagna Wojcicka Sharff and Johanna Lessinger suggest that the "reorientation of U.S. corporations toward global, rather than domestic, economic interests is a major factor" in the construction of an academic underclass. They build on the concept of the "casualization" of work that Saskia Sassen put forward in The Global City, and they extend her thesis to include academic work.[22] They argue that the removal of the corporate tax base and the shifting trends in corporate funding of university research have contributed to conditions that favor research over teaching. The result of these trends is that "teaching . . . is increasingly transferred to an underpaid academic underclass."[23]

June Nash compares these changing patterns of the academic workforce to the "Babbage principle," originally introduced by nineteenth-century capitalists:

The principle is simple: segment the workforce in jobs where subordinated workers undertake the denigrated, low-paid portions of the task structure, thereby preserving the privileges of a core group who monopolize the prestigious, more highly compensated sector. But in the case of academia, a method that has proven counterproductive in the U.S. industrial scene, with the debasement in the organization of work and the alienation of the workforce, is now being tried with faculties charged with instilling the highest levels of aspiration in training future generations who will undertake the most responsible roles in the society.[24]

This segmentation presents problems not only for part-time faculty but also for full-time faculty prerogatives, for women and members of racial and ethnic minorities in the teaching workforce, and for the ability of the general public to gain a quality higher education. At the same time, this convergence of interest between the faculty, those seeking affirmative action, and the interests of the public holds out the possibility of alliances on behalf of higher education.

First, in terms of faculty prerogative, the extensive use of part-time faculty changes the environment of higher education. The flip side of the part-timer coin is the expansion of the administrative apparatus. In the process, faculty prerogative is slowly eroded as full-timers are increasingly marginalized from university policy-making. In part, this is due to the fact that part-timers do not go as far as full-timers in maintaining program continuity and integrity.[25] They are often unavailable to students outside the classroom, and they usually avoid the "onerous duties of running the institution by committee."[26] Thus a significant proportion of part-timers in any program *increases* the workload for full-timers.[27] According to Judith M. Gappa and David W. Leslie, this bifurcation of the faculty is damaging to the "general ethic of community" and to the quality of education.[28]

It should be pointed out that this does not mean that part-time teachers are incompetent or even less competent than their full-time colleagues. In fact, Gappa and Leslie have found that part-time faculty are "superbly qualified."[29] Though they are "often unavailable for advising, committee work, or other noninstructional duties, this is also not part of their assignment."[30] There is a significant amount of evidence to indicate that part-timers are often outstanding teachers and at least as effective in classroom performance as full-timers.[31]

Second, higher education suffers from gender bias in ways similar to the rest of the lower tier of the post-Fordist workforce. The rights and privileges of faculty are being eroded just as women join their ranks in large numbers. The increase of women in the lower tier has been accompanied by a stasis in their ranks at the top.[32] Mary Edwards writes, "The feminization of academe may coincide with the larger impoverishment of the profession."[33] According to Gappa and Leslie's analysis of the National Center for Education Statistics' 1988 National Survey of Postsecondary Faculty (NSOPF 1988), women are disproportionately represented in the part-timer ranks, although they are not a majority in either the part-time or the full-time categories (that is, among the full-time faculty women constitute 27 percent, whereas among the part-time faculty they constitute 42 percent).[34]

In terms of racial and ethnic minorities, the faculty composition, according to NSOPF 1988, shows a lack of diversity among full-timers that is matched by a lack of diversity among part-timers.[35] According to the data, racial and ethnic minorities constitute 9.2 percent of part-time faculty and 10.7 percent of full-time faculty.[36] Gappa and Leslie express some perplexity with this outcome, because they believe that hiring part-timers who are members of racial and ethnic minorities would be a good opportunity for higher education institutions to diversify their faculty. This needs further study and more specific data.

Finally, some would argue that there are broader implications to segmentation as well. The growing use of part-time faculty has important consequences for the overall quality of higher education. Nash explains that "the degradation of professional roles is linked to global processes promoting research over teaching, physical sciences over social sciences and the humanities, and profitable ventures that promise high returns over education."[37] These distinctions are reflected in the breakdown of categories by academic department. Whereas in community colleges part-timers are used extensively in *all* programs, in four-year colleges part-timers are most commonly found in the fine arts, education, the humanities, and the "basic, lower-division core courses of the under-graduate curriculum."[38] Although to some degree the use of part-timers may be budget driven and chaotic, discernible patterns can be uncovered. Gappa and Leslie help us to understand these patterns better when they say, "The more an institution 'looked like' a community college, the more likely it was to make extensive use of part-timers. For example, part-timers were commonly used to staff evening division and extended education programs."[39] This use of part-time teachers suggests hidden disparities in higher education.

On the one hand, it may seem, on the face of it, unduly pessimistic to say that using part-time teachers to staff the postwar expansion of higher education (that is, community colleges, extended education, and so on) constitutes a "disparity" in higher education. It is clear that the American system of higher education since the nineteenth century has had a reputation for its egalitarian character and openness, especially when compared with its European counterparts.[40] From the Morrill Acts of 1862 and 1890 to the G.I. Bill of 1944 to the open admissions policies that emerged from the 1960s, American higher education has continued to expand and to become increasingly inclusive. In the 1970s, universities across the country responded to the fiscal crisis that followed open admissions by relying more heavily on part-time teachers. This use of part-timers has helped to make continued expansion possible by holding down costs and allowing greater access to higher education than would be otherwise possible under the existing conditions.

On the other hand, some scholars argue that the American system of higher education perpetuates or reproduces social inequality.[41] In *Education under Siege*, Stanley Aronowitz and Henry A. Giroux point out the following about open admissions: "[It] did not signify full democratization of higher education because reformers did not demand integration at all levels of the academic system. It did signify, though, a sharp rise in college enrollments in vocational programs, particularly in community colleges. Open admissions meant a new era for those historically left out of college, but [it] also reinforced the hierarchical character of higher education."[42]

At the lower end of the hierarchy are the community colleges, which act as a buffer between the four-year colleges and the demands of open enrollment. In the middle of this hierarchy are some private colleges and the state universities, and at the top are the elite colleges. This perspective views the role of the community college as being one of deflection, that is, it serves to dampen the academic aspirations of underprivileged students by directing them toward more vocational pursuits. Thus, whereas the educational system has been expanded, this expansion can be seen as "not reducing but actually reinforcing and extending the inequality of opportunities between students from different social backgrounds."[43]

To add to this argument, evidence shows that there is a significantly enhanced impact on student advancement when there is greater interaction between faculty and students.[44] Outside of paid classroom hours, part-timers have a limited amount of time for their students, and as indicated above, in those colleges that rely on them to do a high percentage of their teaching, it is left to the full-timers and a growing administrative staff to shoulder the committee work and other departmental responsibilities, thus leaving them, too, with less time to meet with students.[45]

The high concentration of part-time faculty at community colleges and at urban public four-year colleges with large populations of disadvantaged students and the distribution of part-time faculty within these colleges by type of program reinforces the argument that the higher education system systematizes and legitimates inequality. Thus, the cutbacks to education, which have resulted in the development of the part-timer system, are nothing short of an institutional undercutting of the democratic demands for education that were won in the 1960s. At the same time, however, we are not totally bound by the structural parameters of the institutions in which we live and work. We can shape them as well. Countermovements inevitably will emerge and create new parameters. We can look for these countermovements to emerge from the contradictions of the existing system and from those who are affected by it.

Flexible Labor and the Reserve Army of the Underemployed

Those who make up the contingent faculty workforce are a diverse group, but they share the lower-tier status and all the indignities that accompany it. Some are adjuncts who have terminal degrees. Some have full-time jobs elsewhere. Many are piecing together part-time jobs and trying to remain optimistic. Some are graduate students working as teaching assistants. Among the latter group, some have complete responsibility for their classes, whereas others are being mentored. Then there are graduate students who double as adjunct instructors independent of their student status. There are probably other configurations that are being overlooked, but the point is that from whatever place they enter this system, they all share the experience of second-class citizenship in the university. Full-time faculty also feel the effects of this system, although they are relatively privileged and are not always aware of the part-timer standpoint.

Adjuncts surveyed at CUNY have commonly complained about the working conditions: many do not have office space, or they share it with many other adjuncts; they often do not have a desk or even a locked drawer. These are conditions shared by adjuncts all over the country. On their own they may not seem like such hardships, but they speak to the issue of status, and they make it more difficult to serve one's students. They are also a constant reminder that adjuncts are not fully a part of university life and may lose their job without any recourse at a moment's notice. Thus, the most common demand put forward by adjuncts is job security. Next comes increased pay and some type of benefits, most notably health insurance.

The low pay, the lack of benefits, and the low status indicate the university's unwillingness or inability to make a commitment to those who teach its bread-and-butter courses. Adjuncts, however, are usually too atomized to be able to recognize their own worth collectively. Thus, they usually have little or no role in the decision making that affects them and the classes that they teach; they are sometimes handed a syllabus at the last minute and expected to step in and teach the huge introductory classes that serve as a feeder to the upper-level courses. In the most extreme cases, they do not have the time or opportunity to choose their own texts or, even worse, are expected to use a book written by a member of the full-time faculty from the department. This is not done coercively, usually, or even consciously, for that matter, but it is difficult for a pieceworker to say no when a job is at stake.

Given the instability of the employment and the weakness of the adjunct bargaining position, the voice of the labor representative, when one exists, is important. The development of this fundamental component often presents the greatest challenge for part-time faculty organizers. For example, the faculty union at C U N Y, the Professional Staff Congress (P S C), which represents full-time faculty, part-time faculty, and staff, has been openly criticized by adjuncts and their supporters for its lack of outreach to the part-time faculty who often do not even know that they have a collective-bargaining agent. Several adjuncts have indicated privately that they were unwilling to even talk to the union about a grievance issue because they did not trust the representative process and they feared that they would be fired if they tried anything. They also did not have much hope of winning, even though they felt that they were in the right. When one has zero job protection and the other has both tenure and decision-making power over whom to hire and over classroom evaluations that determine one's future, then the space for the adjunct to speak his or her mind candidly does not exist.

Research and education about the workforce would help adjuncts overcome the segmentation that restricts their ability to mobilize. The segmented nature of the labor force in the part-timer system hinders communication and dialogue, perpetuating myths and attitudes about part-time faculty that destroy their organizing efforts. The isolation of the part-time faculty and the full-time faculty's relation to this condition are key obstacles to the development of strong collective action by university faculty. The problems inherent in this relationship need to be examined.

Anecdotally, the attitudes of department heads toward their part-time faculty range from "I love my adjuncts and don't want to lose them" to a suggestion that adjuncts should not have seniority or job security rights because they eventually get "burned out" and need to be replaced. Findings from initial stages of research (for example, a pilot survey, a dozen interviews, and my observations from a decade of participation in adjunct organizing) suggest that most adjuncts have good relations with their full-time faculty colleagues and with the departmental chair (to the extent that they have any relations with them at all!). However, as one adjunct instructor has said, "it's the system" rather than conflicts with particular full-time faculty that creates problems for the part-time workforce.

One of the common claims about adjuncts is that they are "apprentices." This claim undercuts the momentum of adjuncts in their organizing efforts. It implies a kind of guild system, whereas the adjunct system bears more of a resemblance to the industrial model. It justifies the adjunct's low wages and shabby treatment as part of a rite of passage into the upper ranks. Most part-time faculty, however, have many years of experience, are not in any kind of mentoring relationship, and do not have a career path, per se. Calling them "apprentices" is a means of ignoring and denying their real relationship to the university.

Another common explanation used to describe the part-timer system is to say that adjuncts are used to provide "flexibility" in times of shifting enrollment. Alberta Grossman, an adjunct professor of English as a second language (ESL) at CUNY and a union activist, responded to this point when she said at a 1997 public forum, "It is said that the university uses adjuncts because they need 'flexibility.' There are 800 adjuncts at BMCC [Borough of Manhattan Community College] and 275 full-timers. I ask you, how much flexibility is needed?" Obviously most of these teachers are needed on a permanent basis. The argument that the university needs flexibility is not about shifting enrollments, but it is a means of cutting labor costs.

Another notion commonly propounded is that most adjuncts have full-time jobs elsewhere. Analysis by Gappa and Leslie of the NSOPF 1988 data shows that this is true, as of 1988, but that it must be understood in the proper context: "According to NSOPF '88, over half of the part-time faculty in all institutions (52.5 percent) have other full-time employment. This ranges from a low of 37 percent at liberal arts colleges and public doctorate-granting institutions, to a high of 67 percent at private doctorate-granting universities. There is also variation among disciplines. Only 19 percent of those in the humanities have full-time positions elsewhere, while 59 percent of those in education, 67 percent in business, and 73 percent in engineering work full-time at other jobs." [46] These data do not include graduate teaching assistants, and since 1988 there has been an overall growth in the proportion of part-time faculty.

The assumption is that if an adjunct has full-time employment elsewhere, then it is not so awful that he or she is providing a service to the university for token wages and, usually, no benefits. This assumption makes it difficult to gain full-time support for organizing part-time faculty, especially if tight budgets pit the short-term interest of full-timers against the interests of their part-time colleagues. Experience with organizing adjuncts leads me to believe that in urban institutions with a large pool of underemployed academics to choose from, such as C U N Y, the proportion of adjuncts who are otherwise employed full time is much less than 50 percent. More specific and more current data are needed to clarify this point.

Susan DiRaimo, an adjunct instructor of E S L at C U N Y and a longtime adjunct activist, spoke with me about some of these issues. She reported on two personal incidents that provide some insight into the conflicts that exist between the two tiers of faculty. The first incident occurred when a full-timer in the department sent around a memo asking everyone to contribute money for a fund for gifts (for example, if someone gets sick). Full-timers were asked to contribute twenty-five dollars, and part-timers were asked to contribute ten dollars. She said that many of the part-timers were very resentful of this. One part-timer wrote "a long and nasty letter, which is not like her, but she was so upset." The attitude among the part-timers toward the request was generally along the lines of "you have some nerve asking for that kind of money." The memo, innocent though it was in its intention, had touched a nerve.

The second incident occurred one day when Susan was on the payroll line with a friend who is a full-time faculty member. The full-time friend complained to her about not making the big bucks (about seventy-eight thousand dollars per year) that another colleague was getting. Instead, she was making only forty-five thousand per year. Susan was taken aback by this, so she reminded her friend that as an adjunct she teaches nearly a full-time load and gets only one-third of the forty-five thousand dollars her friend makes. She thought that her friend, who acknowledged that this was unfair, was being oblivious to her working conditions and to the great disparity that exists. Again, the lack of awareness was fairly benign in intent, but it provoked Susan to the point where she had to provide a firm reminder.

These casual observations may seem inconsequential, but adjuncts' interests are too often dismissed based on erroneous assumptions about who they are and what their lives are like. Thus, even a seemingly innocuous memo or a casual comment about pay can generate intense anger in part-timers, who are often reluctant to express this to those who might have decision-making power over their employment. The obliviousness to adjunct conditions and the characterizations that downgrade their working identity (for example, "apprentices") are means of avoiding the changing conditions of academic labor that confront adjuncts directly. More detailed information regarding the composition of the part-time faculty can help to dispel the myths, change the attitudes, and overcome the obstacles to faculty mobilization.

Information alone, however, is not enough. The suspicion, resentment, and distrust generated bidirectionally in the two-tiered system is probably its most destructive aspect. It complicates the possibility of forging a collective identity among faculty. A full-timer could be perfectly fair-minded, but if he or she does not make this absolutely clear, then a part-timer who is subject to his or her good graces is likely to be somewhat cautious. Unequal relations of power can be a breeding ground for the kinds of projections and psychological transference that make dialogue difficult. To get past this, one would need to be secure and confident and to have strong self-esteem—not an easy task when one is broke, in debt, facing a bleak employment future, and locked into a system that is demoralizing and does not provide any job security. However, given that a large number of adjuncts in any department increases the administrative workload of the full-timers and that the growing lower tier will, over time, diminish the collective-bargaining power of all faculty, then it stands to reason that there is an increasing convergence of interest between the upper and the lower tiers, and it is that convergence, if properly understood, that will provide a basis for dialogue and for mobilization.

In view of the shape of contemporary politics and the direction of the economy, it would seem nearly impossible to organize a workforce that is fragmented and isolated, but there has been some movement that is encouraging. The more recent victories by graduate student employees and the spate of conferences on the topic of academic labor may prove to be the spark that is needed.

In November 1996 the General Counsel of the National Labor Relations Board determined that Yale teaching assistants are employees under federal law and therefore have rights to collective bargaining. They also indicated that a complaint would be issued against Yale for violating federal labor law in its threats against strike participants the previous winter. In a November 19, 1996, press release issued by the Federation of University Employees at Yale, David Montgomery, the noted professor of labor history at Yale, was quoted as saying, "We are witnessing labor history in the making. . . . Universities across the country have come to rely more and more on both teaching assistants and adjunct professors as part-time workers carrying out more and more of the teaching responsibilities. This decision puts the protection of the law securely behind their efforts to improve their conditions and that should improve the security of everyone in the academy." [47]

In April 1996 graduate student employees at the University of Iowa voted to unionize and have since been successful in negotiating for improved pay and working conditions. In late November 1996, teaching assistants at the University of California at Los Angeles, San Diego, and Berkeley were joined by readers and tutors for a week of protest owing to the university's unwillingness to acknowledge their collective-bargaining rights. The Yale decision and the activities at the University of Iowa and at the University of California have been highly publicized and have encouraged other graduate student employees to organize.

Graduate students and part-time faculty may be a diverse group, but they share the contingent status on the lower tier of the contemporary university. Part-time faculty have not been as publicly visible as the graduate employees in the past year, but they have been involved in a long and continuing struggle for fair representation and improved working conditions. Some examples follow that represent the different bargaining unit configurations in which part-time faculty can be found.

At Rutgers University they have a separate chapter that is a local of the American Association of University Professors (AAUP). They have a good relationship with the full-timers union at Rutgers, which is also an AAUP chapter. The graduate teaching assistants there are part of the full-timer chapter. Another example is Long Island University (LIU), where the adjuncts are part of the same union as the full-timers. They even outnumber full-timers as union members by over two to one, thus giving them some electoral clout in the union. In the fall of 1994 at LIU, both full-timers and part-timers together waged a partially successful strike. Finally, at CUNY the part-timers are part of the same collective-bargaining unit as the full-timers and the graduate teaching assistants, but only a fraction of the part-timers are dues-paying, voting members of the union. If they joined the union proportionate to their numbers, they would be the largest group in the union. The union leadership has refused to collect the agency shop fee from the part-timers and has only halfheartedly encouraged them to join. A recent campaign by an insurgency group, the New Caucus, has put the issue of adjunct representation and the transformation of the professoriat on the front burner.

If communication and organization are, indeed, a means to desegment the workforce, then recent activities give reason for hope. In addition to the graduate student activities noted above, there has been a flurry of conferences and forums on issues related to adjuncts, teaching assistants, and academic labor in the past year. The frequency of these events has been encouraging.

In October 1996 Columbia University hosted a massive conference titled "The Fight for America's Future: Teach-In with the Labor Movement." It brought academia together with the labor movement to discuss the problems faced by workers both in and out of the university. The next month it was New York University's turn to host a big conference on labor. "Between Classes: A Conference on Academic Labor" focused specifically on the university. The discussions explored strategies for organizing part-time faculty, including a discussion of the formation of a regional labor organization to advocate for adjuncts and to coordinate adjunct unionization, similar to the industrial union hall model.

In late December 1996 in Washington, D.C., the National Congress of Part-Time, Non-Tenure-Track, Adjunct, and Graduate Student Faculty held its first national meeting. On the agenda were issues such as adjunct and graduate teaching assistant unity, unionization, and building a national teach-in. Across town, at the same time, the Modern Language Association held its annual conference, which included panels on adjunct and graduate student organizing. The following week brought the National Adjunct Faculty Guild to Washington, D.C., for its "Second Annual Conference on Adjunct Faculty: Adjuncts and Empowerment." This group was formed in 1993 and is based in Ann Arbor, Michigan. Whereas the national congress is focusing on political issues and unionization, the guild is also interested in promoting means of professional development for adjuncts.

There is no end in sight to the conferences and colloquia on this topic. In early spring 1997 there was a conference on higher education politics sponsored by the Brecht Forum in New York City, and the New Caucus of the PSC also held a conference on academic labor in February 1997.[48] All who are concerned about the future of higher education have been keeping a close eye on these events.

Conclusion: Whither the Lonely Adjunct?

Emily Abel has done extensive interviews with part-time, temporary, and untenured faculty. In her pioneering work she provides some glimpses of both despair and hope. Interestingly, when she compares the relationship between those who occupy the different levels of the contemporary two-tier system with the relationship that existed between the early craft-workers and the unskilled workers who were entering the workforce in the early part of this century, she implicitly recalls that these masses, too, were fragmented, exploited, and isolated.[49] Most had few skills and little education, and sometimes they could not even speak the same language as that spoken by their labor movement allies. They overcame these obstacles and developed a group identity. They were thus able to act collectively and to secure a beachhead against the worst aspects of industrialization.

Given the effects of division and fragmentation on the workforce in general, it would seem logical that demands for much-needed improvements in terms such as pay, job security, and so on will have only limited success if they are not part of a broader movement on behalf of higher education. To this end there needs to be developed a collective sense of purpose among the faculty, staff, and the community that the university serves.

Perhaps the beginning of an answer to this problem can be found in the idea of a regional hiring hall, discussed at the NYU conference, a national adjunct union, or some hybrid form of these older models that brings together local concerns with the need to organize broadly. Whatever the mechanism, it will need to overcome the division and fragmentation of the workforce that is engendered by post-Fordism. My experiences with adjunct organizing leave me hopeful. College faculty—whether graduate student, part-time, or full-time—are skilled, resourceful, and talented. Even the most apolitical and conservative among them have been known to transform into savvy political activists after a couple of seasons in the fray. They may yet prove to be the unique element needed to reinvigorate the labor movement.

Notes

1 Thorstein Veblen, *The Higher Learning in America* (1918; reprint, New York: Augustus M. Kelley, Bookseller 1965).
2 Clark Kerr, *The Uses of the University* (Cambridge: Harvard University Press, 1963).
3 Veblen, *Higher Learning*, 117.
4 Thomas R. Brooks, *Towards Dignity: A Brief History of the United Federation of Teachers* (United Federation of Teachers, Local 2, American Federation of Teachers, AFL-CIO, 1967), 81.
5 Everett C. Ladd Jr. and Seymour Martin Lipset, *Professors, Unions, and American Higher Education* (Carnegie Commission on Higher Education, 1973), 48.
6 Ibid., 48–49.
7 Ibid., 4.
8 Ibid., 2.
9 John R. Commons, *History of Labour in the United States* (New York: Macmillan, 1918).

10 Irving Bernstein, *The Turbulent Years: A History of the American Worker, 1920–1933* (Boston: Houghton Mifflin, 1971); Frances Fox Piven and Richard A. Cloward, *Poor People's Movements: Why They Succeed, How They Fail* (New York: Vintage Books, 1979); James R. Green, *The World of the Worker* (New York: Hill and Wang, 1980).

11 Jeremy Brecher, *Strike!* (Boston: South End Press, 1972), xi–xii; Piven and Cloward, *Poor People's Movements*, 3–5; Green, *World of the Worker*, 139–40.

12 Green, *World of the Worker*, 210–48; David Lewin, "Public Employee Unionism and Labor Relations in the 1980s: An Analysis of Transformation," in *Unions in Transition*, ed. Seymour M. Lipset (San Francisco: Institute for Contemporary Studies, 1986); Michael Goldfield, *The Decline of Organized Labor in the United States* (Chicago: University of Chicago Press, 1987).

13 Lewin, "Public Employee Unionism," 243.

14 Green, *World of the Worker*, 234.

15 Leo Troy, "The Rise and Fall of American Trade Unions: The Labor Movement from FDR to RR," in *Unions in Transition*, ed. Lipset, 80–81.

16 John Mollenkopf, "The Crisis of the Public Sector in Americas Cities," in *The Fiscal Crisis of American Cities*, ed. Roger E. Alcaly and David Mermelstein (New York: Vintage Books, 1977).

17 Paul Johnston, *Success while Others Fail: Social Movement Unionism and the Public Workplace* (Ithaca, N.Y.: ILR Press, 1994), 209.

18 The latest data were supplied to me via electronic mail from Ernest Benjamin of the AAUP, Washington, D.C. He relies on the National Center for Education Statistics 1992–93 survey recently published as "Institutional Policies and Practices regarding Faculty in Higher Education" (Washington, D.C.: Department of Higher Education, 1996).

19 Howard P. Tuckman, Jaime Caldwell, and William Vogler, "Part-Timers and the Academic Labor Market of the Eighties," *American Sociologist* 13 (November 1978): 184–95; David W. Leslie and Ronald B. Head, "Part-Time Faculty Rights," *Educational Record* (winter 1979): 46–67.

20 U.S. Department of Education (USDE)/National Center for Education Statistics (NCES), *Fall Staff in Postsecondary Institutions, 1993* (NCES: Washington, D.C., 1996), 24–25.

21 Perry Robinson, deputy director, Higher Education Department, American Federation of Teachers, "Part-Time Faculty Issues, Item no. 607," 1994, 9.

22 Jagna Wojcicka Sharff and Johanna Lessinger, "The Academic Sweatshop: Changes in the Capitalist Infrastructure and the Part-Time Academic," An-

thropology of Work Review 15, no. 1 (spring 1994): 2; Saskia Sassen, *The Global City* (Princeton, N.J.: Princeton University Press, 1991).

23 Sharff and Lessinger, "Academic Sweatshop," 4.

24 June Nash, preface to *Anthropology of Work Review* 15, no. 1 (spring 1994): 1.

25 Leslie and Head, "Part-Time Faculty Rights," 64.

26 Ibid., 50.

27 Ibid.

28 Judith M. Gappa and David W. Leslie, *The Invisible Faculty: Improving the Status of Part-Timers in Higher Education* (San Francisco: Jossey-Bass Publishing, 1993).

29 Ibid., 6.

30 Ibid.

31 Ibid., 126–28.

32 Nancy Cadet, "Marginalia: Women in the Academic Workforce," *Feminist Teacher* 4, no. 1 (spring 1989): 16–17; Ana Maria Turner Lomparis, "Are Women Changing the Nature of the Academic Profession?" *Journal of Higher Education* 61, no. 6 (November–December 1990): 643–77.

33 Mary Edwards, "The Decline of the American Professoriate, 1970–1990," *Anthropology of Work Review* 15, no. 1 (spring 1994): 26.

34 Gappa and Leslie, *Invisible Faculty*, 24.

35 Ibid., 22.

36 Ibid.

37 Nash, preface, 1.

38 Gappa and Leslie, *Invisible Faculty*, 118.

39 Ibid., 113.

40 Frederick Rudolph, *The American College and University* (New York: Alfred A. Knopf, 1962); John S. Brubacher and Willis Rudy, *Higher Education in Transition—a History of American Colleges and Universities, 1636–1968* (New York: Harper and Row, 1968). This position is also discussed, with some important qualifications, by Alain Touraine in *The Academic System in American Society* (New York: McGraw-Hill, 1974).

41 Touraine argues that despite relative openness in the American system, as compared with European models, it still reproduces inequality. See also Stanley Aronowitz and Henry A. Giroux, *Education under Siege* (South Hadley, MA: Bergin and Garvey Publishers, 1985), and Steven Brint and Jerome Karabel, *The Diverted Dream: Community Colleges and the Promise of Educational Opportunity in America, 1900–1985* (New York: Oxford University Press, 1989).

42 Aronowitz and Giroux, *Education under Siege*, 3.

43 Touraine, *Academic System in American Society*, 59.

44 Ernest T. Pascarella, "Student-Faculty Informal Contact and College Out-comes," *Review of Educational Research* 50 (winter 1980): 545–95; Vincent Tinto, "Stages of Student Departure: Reflections on the Longitudinal Character of Student Leaving," *Journal of Higher Education* 59, no. 4 (July/August 1988): 438–55. For a comprehensive and useful source, see Ernest T. Pascarella and Patrick T. Terenzini, "How College Affects Students: Findings and Insights from Twenty Years of Research" (San Francisco: Jossey-Bass Publishing, 1991).

45 Leslie and Head, "Part-Time Faculty Rights"; Gappa and Leslie, *Invisible Faculty.*

46 Gappa and Leslie, *Invisible Faculty,* 50–51.

47 David Montgomery, press release, Federation of University Employees at Yale, November 19, 1996.

48 On April 3–5, 1998, the second National Congress of Adjunct Nontenure Track and Graduate Teaching Assistant Faculty was held in New York City. Workshops and meetings were directed at elaborating a national organizing network. At this congress, the electronic journal *Workplace* was officially launched. It was started by graduate student activists and can be found at http://www.workplace-gsc.com.

49 Emily K. Abel, *Terminal Degrees: The Job Crisis in Higher Education* (New York: Praeger, 1984), 211.

The Last Good Job in America

Stanley Aronowitz

Prologue

There is a wonderful museum of eighteenth- and nineteenth-century material culture in Shelburne, Vermont. Last summer our family joined thousands who marveled at exhibits of toys, miniature soldiers and battle scenes, and the many transported authentic artifacts or replicas of living rooms, kitchens, pantries, and other objects of everyday life. My favorites were the working blacksmith's and print shops. The print shop reminded me of old movies about courageous small-town editors crowded into a single room with their presses. The Shelburne presses were more industrial, but the technology was the same. Amid the fire and the heat and the clanging hammers hitting the forge, one had a vivid picture of what skilled manual work might have been like before the automobile displaced the horse and buggy and cold type all but destroyed the old printer's craft.

These were good jobs. They paid well and, perhaps equally important, engaged the worker's mind and body. Apart from the laborious task of typesetting, which was done by hand, the printer had to carefully set the controls on the machine just right. It was a time-consuming but supremely intellectual activity. Through reenactments of popular material culture—for example, the blacksmith let our daughter participate by forging a metal hook—as well as through artistic representations, the Shelburne museum reminds us how rural and small-town people once lived and worked.

Walking through the museum's sprawling acres, I could not help drawing an analogy with the disappearing professoriat. One day some academic entrepreneur—a *Lingua Franca* publisher Jeffrey Kittay of the future —will hit on the idea of exhibiting mid-twentieth-century academic material culture. There will be a replica of a professor's study: On her desk sits the old Olympia typewriter, an ashtray, and some yellow pads filled with notes for an article or book or the next day's lecture. The study is book-lined, many volumes surfeited with dust. A leather jacket and denim work shirt hang on the door's hook.

The magazine rack is filled to the brim with scholarly journals, along with the *New York Review of Books* and *Lingua Franca*, those quintessentially academic feuilletons which went out of business about 2010 because there were too few professors around to read them. By then most of us had been retread as part-time discussion leaders—freeway or turnpike flyers—and could manage only to scan the day's video of the famous scholar's lecture on whatever before meeting the fifty students at the local American Legion hall where the group meets. The actual postsecondary faculty member of the future may still own a desk, but the shelves may contain as many video cassettes as books and there might or might not be a magazine rack.

Diary

It's Wednesday, one of my writing days. Today I'm writing this piece, for which George Yúdice and Andrew Ross have been nudging me for a couple of days. Nona will return home about three o'clock, and it's my turn to get her to her after-school music class and prepare dinner. As it turns out she brings a friend home so I have a little extension on my writing time. I couldn't begin working on the piece yesterday because on Tuesdays I go to the City University of New York (CUNY) Graduate Center. Even so, after making Nona's breakfast and sending her off to school (as I do every other day), reading the *Times* and selected articles from the *Wall Street Journal* and the *Financial Times,* and checking my e-mail, I usually spend the morning editing my Monday writing. But yesterday Nona was home with a stomach bug, and because Ellen, her mother, had umpteen student advisements at New York University (NYU), it fell to me to make her tea, minister to the puking, get some videotapes, and commiserate. Anyway, Monday morning after my usual reading routine I had finished an op-ed for the *Nation* on the future of the Left. Otherwise I would have started this article a day earlier.

I was somewhat out of the writing mode on Monday because I had a second (oral) exam to attend. I'm chair for a candidate who was examined in cultural studies, psychoanalysis, and feminist theory. She knew her stuff but took some time to get rolling, after which the exam was quite good. After the exam I answered my calls, wrote two recommendations for job applicants, attended a colloquium in the early evening given by Elizabeth Grosz and Manuel De Landa, and arrived home about nine o'clock, after which Ellen and I prepared our dinner (Nona eats earlier).

On Tuesday afternoons I meet with students. At this time of year (mid-December) many sessions are devoted to discussing their papers, which are due at the end of January. This semester I preside at a seminar on Marx. We are reading only four texts but a lot of pages: the early manuscripts, *Critique of Hegel's Philosophy of the State, Capital,* and the *Grundrisse.* There are about twenty-five students in the group, who form three study groups that meet weekly to address the critiques and commentaries as well as to study the texts more extensively than the two-hour session with me could possibly accomplish. Sometimes after class I meet with one of the study groups to help with the reading. Yesterday I did some career counseling in the early evening for a friend who is thinking about quitting his job and trying to work for the labor movement.

Tonight I'll read in the *Economic and Philosophical Manuscripts* because tomorrow one of the groups is making a presentation. Yesterday, a few of my students met with me individually to discuss, among other things, the merits of Althusser's argument for an epistemological break between the early and late Marx, the state/civil society distinction, and whether Marx's *Capital* retains the category of alienation in the fetishism section of volume one. Tomorrow after checking my e-mail I will edit some of this stuff I am writing and arrive at school around noon to meet with a student about last semester's paper for a course called "Literature as Social Knowledge." Then I'll try to work on this piece until my office hour, which is simply a continuation of what I do on Tuesday, except some of my dissertation students may drop in to give me chapters or to talk. At 4:15 I'll meet my seminar, after which a small group of students has asked to meet about publication chances for a collective paper they wrote on what the novels of Woolf, Lessing, and Winterson tell us about the gendering of social life. I'll probably get home by nine o'clock.

Friday is committee and colloquium day in the sociology Ph.D. program in which I work. While I serve on no departmental committees, I am involved in seventeen other committees this year, either as dissertation adviser or as chair of a CUNY-wide committee that raised some money to help faculty do interdisciplinary curriculum planning. But I will try to attend the colloquium. I often invite my advisees to meet me at home because life is too hectic in my office. My office is a place where students hang out, where there are myriad telephone interruptions, and where I am called on to handle a lot of administrative business, such as change-of-grade forms, recommendation letters, and so on.

Over the weekend I'll have time for my family, having hopefully finished a draft of this piece. I also have to finish a longer, collectively written article for a book called *Postwork*, which came out of a conference sponsored by the Center for Cultural Studies, of which I am director. The group will meet on Monday evening to go over my collation. I may get it done on Sunday or Monday. And next week Jonathan Cutler, the coeditor of the volume, will work with me on writing an introduction.

I am one of a shrinking minority of the professoriat who have what may be the last good job in America. Except for the requirement that I teach or preside at one or two classes and seminars a week and direct at least five dissertations at a time, I pretty much control my paid work time. I work hard, but it's mostly self-directed. I don't experience "leisure" as time out of work because the lines are blurred. What is included in this form of academic labor anyway? For example, I read a fair amount of detective and science fiction, but sometimes I write and teach what begins as entertainment. The same goes for reading philosophy and social and cultural theory. I really enjoy a lot of it and experience it as *recreation* but often integrate what I have learned into my teaching and writing repertoire. In any case, much reading is intellectual refreshment. And even though I *must* appear for some four hours a week at a seminar or two, I don't experience this as institutional robbery of my own time. It's not only that I like to "teach" or whatever you call my appearance in the classroom. I'm not convinced that even the best of my lectures "teaches" anybody more than providing some background on the topic. (I hardly ever give a "talk" in class that lasts more than ten minutes without student interruptions, either questions or interventions.) Most of the time I work from texts; I do close readings of particular passages, inviting critique and commentary and offering some of my own.

When I meet with study groups I do so voluntarily. Needless to say, the job description really doesn't require it, since few of my colleagues encourage such groups to form. And my assent to serve on more than twenty dissertation committees, about a quarter of those outside the sociology program, and to direct a number of tutorials and independent studies is by no means "required" by some mandated workload. Whatever I take on is for the personal and intellectual gratification or obligation which I have adopted.

As a professor in a research school and a teacher of Ph.D. students, I feel I should also raise money to help support students in addition to doing whatever I can to help them find jobs and get their dissertations published. And as director of a center, I need to find money for its public life: talks, conferences, and postdoctoral fellowships. Now, in my situation I don't have to do any of this work, but I feel that I should go back to undergraduate teaching if I won't or can't contribute to meeting these urgent student needs. So I raise between fifteen and fifty thousand dollars a year for student support and for conferences and research projects.

Finally, for all practical purposes my career is over, so none of this work is motivated by the ambition or necessity of academic advancement. I am a full professor with tenure and have reached the top of a very modest salary scale, at least for New York. I earn more by some five thousand dollars a year than an auto worker who puts in a sixty-hour week but less than a beginning associate in a large New York corporate law firm or a physician/specialist in a New York health maintenance organization (HMO). But most of them work under the gun of a manager, and in the case of the law firm, only five of every hundred attorneys will ever make partner. With a two-paycheck household we can afford to eat dinner out regularly, send Nona to camp, give her the benefit of piano lessons, fix the car, and own and maintain a couple of early and late-model computers and a decent audio system. And we pay a mortgage on an old, ill-heated farmhouse in upstate New York, where we spend summers and some autumn and spring weekends. But because in my academic situation I have nothing careerwise to strive for, I'm reasonably free of most external impositions. Before every semester my chair asks me what I want to teach. What's left is the work, and with the warts—administrative garbage, too many students (a result of my own hubris), and taking on too many assignments, writing and otherwise—I enjoy it.

What I enjoy most is the ability to procrastinate and control my own work time, especially its pace: taking a walk in the middle of the day, reading between the writing, listening to a CD or tape anytime I want, calling up a friend for a chat. And I like the intellectual and political independence the job affords. I can speak out on any public issue without risk of reprisal from the administration or from my program. Organizations such as the American Association of University Professors (AAUP) originally fought for tenure because, contrary to popular, even academic, belief, there was no tradition of academic freedom in the American university until the twentieth century, and then only for the most conventional and apolitical scholars. On the whole, postsecondary administrations were not sympathetic to intellectual, let alone political, dissenters, the Scopeses of the day. Through the 1950s most faculty were hired on year-to-year contracts by presidents and other institutional officers who simply failed to renew the contracts of teachers they found politically, intellectually, or personally objectionable.

For example, until well into the 1960s the number of public Marxists, open gays, blacks, and women with secure mainstream academic jobs could be counted on ten fingers. And contrary to myth it wasn't all due to McCarthyism, although the handful of Marxists in American academia were drummed out of academia by congressional investigations and administrative inquisitions. The liberal Lionel Trilling was a year-to-year lecturer at Columbia for a decade not only because he had been a radical but because he was a Jew. The not-so-hidden secret of English departments in the first half of the twentieth century was their genteel anti-Semitism. For example, Irving Howe didn't land a college teaching job until the early 1950s, and then it was at Brandeis. Women fared even worse. There's the notorious case of Margaret Mead, one of America's outstanding anthropologists and its most distinguished permanent adjunct at Columbia University. Her regular job was at the Museum of Natural History. She was a best-selling author, celebrated in some intellectual circles, but there was no question of a permanent academic appointment. Her colleagues Gene Weltfish and Ruth Benedict, no small figures in anthropology, were accorded similar treatment.

It is not surprising that the University of Minnesota administration recently decided to try to turn back the clock forty years and rescind tenure. Only the threat of an AAUP-conducted union representation election caused the board of trustees and the president to withdraw (temporarily) the proposal. In the absence of a powerful-enough Left there is little, other than market considerations, to prevent university administrations from abrogating the cardinal feature of academic work: the promise that, after five or six years of servitude, mainly to the discipline and to the profession, a teacher may be relatively free of fear that fashion will render his or her work obsolete and, for this reason, not worthy of continued employment. The irony of the current situation is that many who win tenure nonetheless risk not being promoted, harassment, and, probably most painful of all, utter marginalization for dissenting intellectual work. For those who have been incompletely socialized into their professions, tenure turns out to be a chimerical reward. With some notable exceptions, by the time the teacher has achieved tenure, at least in the major schools, internalized conformity is often the condition of long-term survival.

In this respect, in addition to protecting genuine political dissent in conventionally political terms, tenure can protect academic dissidents — scholars and intellectuals who depart, sometimes critically, from the presuppositions of conventional science, literature, or philosophy. But tenure is job security only in the last instance. Typically the successful candidate must demonstrate her or his lack of independence, originality, and hubris. Peer review is often used as a way to weed out nonconformity. It works at all levels: getting tenure and, in many systems for which pay raises depend almost entirely on "merit," climbing the pay scale often entail publishing in the "right" journals (in the double-entendre sense) and prestigious academic presses. For example, I know a wonderful younger scholar coming up for tenure in a quasi–Ivy League college who decided to accept an offer from Stuffy University Press rather than one from an aggressive, hotter house. He admitted his book might end up in annual sales, but it would do the tenure trick. It's hard to say whether the other choice would have been as efficacious. But he felt in no position to take a chance. The second question is, How much did this decision take out of his chance to become an intellectual rather than a professional clerk of the institution?

Now, it must be admitted that most faculty have long since capitulated to the strictures of the conservative disciplines and to the civility and professionalization demanded by academic culture. Many define their intellectual work in terms of these strictures and, in the bargain, measure their contribution not by the degree to which they might be organic intellectuals of a social movement but, at best, how they might make piecemeal, incremental changes in the subfield to which they are affiliated. The overwhelming majority do not aspire to genuine influence. Moreover, they disdain any discourse or activity that cannot be coded as civil: the idea of confrontation as a means of clarification is beyond the bounds of acceptability. Insofar as institutional power continues to reward conformity, tenure is quite beside the point for the overwhelming majority of the professoriat.

I have a "central line" appointment, which means that I teach exclusively in the graduate school and nearly all of my students are working toward the Ph.D. With the exception of approximately one hundred others, most of the teaching and advising at the school is performed by college-based faculty who rarely teach more than one graduate course a year. My situation is enviable by CUNY and most other colleges' standards.

For the time being I write what I please without the sword of unemployment or ostracism hanging over my head. If I were on the job market today, most sociology departments would not hire me because I don't follow either the discursive or the methodological rules of the discipline and first and foremost I'm a *political* intellectual whose views occasionally are in public view. I doubt I would have gotten a tenured professorship at the University of California at Irvine in 1977 if the program into which I was hired, although sympathetic with my political views, grasped that my work on labor was informed by cultural studies and what it has come to mean. But I did, and they were stuck with me until I left in 1982 to teach at CUNY. CUNY Graduate School hired me because they believed I was a labor sociologist, even though I had published several articles in social and cultural theory during the late 1970s. They had good reason to focus on my work on labor. I had helped organize the Center for Worker Education at City College while teaching at Columbia during 1980–81. It is a thriving B.A. program for working adults, many of whom are union members or their family members. Then I became a visiting professor in the Center. Shortly after I was hired in the sociology program at CUNY, I organized a cultural studies center, and in addition to what I had been hired to teach—political economy and labor—I began teaching courses in cultural studies, social studies of science and technology, and social theory. Some of my colleagues were astonished and some were chagrined. I am glad to report most got used to my eclecticism, but not immediately or easily.

Now there are some who view my teaching and writing as a luxury that should be ended at the earliest possible convenience and, indeed, are waiting for me to retire or leave by any other possible circumstance. Sometimes it's about me, but mostly it's about the structural position of the full professor in research institutions. According to some, they/I have too many privileges. I offer another perspective on this position. I am a radical because I believe that people work too hard for too little and that their work is more like labor, not under their control. The situation of the few holding the last good job should be universalized, not suppressed. I do not hold to the view that there should be an equality of misery; on the contrary, we need a movement for less externally imposed labor and more self-directed activity. People should be able to write their stuff independent of whether it is necessary for promotion, tenure, or anything except to share their knowledge or their art. People would be better served by cutting working hours for more pay rather than by working without end. I believe that the work ethic is, literally, a cornerstone of the prevailing ideology of capital. That some are swimming against the stream should be defended, not attacked on phony populist grounds.

In fact, the salaries and working conditions that some enjoy in universities should be held up as a standard for everybody. Work without end is the scourge of every radical idea because it colonizes our most precious possession: time. Participatory governance at the workplace, in the community, and in the home; free time for personal development and pleasure; and social and cultural equality are next to impossible when work time is so long that the worker (intellectual as well as manual) can barely keep her or his eyes open at the end of the day. Backbreaking manual labor and work that separates body and mind should be eliminated by technology and democratic work organization. And rather than excoriate those who are able to avoid the most degrading jobs, the Left should excoriate those jobs and not romanticize them. In a word, most paid labor is shit, and those who are lucky enough to avoid it, make it more pleasant and self-managed, or reduce it to the barest minimum should be emulated.

A Little Political Economy of Teacher Work

Most of us who work for wages and salaries are subject to external compulsion throughout the workday. Signifying one of the most dramatic shifts in work culture, the ten- and twelve-hour workday has become almost mandatory for many factory, clerical, and professional employees. Forty years ago looming automation was accompanied by the threat of unemployment and the promise of shorter hours. It was also a time when the so-called mass culture debate exploded in universities and in the media: Would the increased leisure made possible by technological change be subordinated to the same compulsions as paid labor? Would television, for example, crowd free time? Or would the late twentieth century become an epoch of such innovations as lifelong education, the recreation of civil society (imagine all the cafés filled with people who have the working lives of full professors), a flowering of the participatory arts, a golden age of amateur sports?

One of the predictions of that period has been richly fulfilled. World unemployment and underemployment reached a billion in 1996, 30 percent of the working population. And this is the moment when part-time, temporary, and contingent work is threatening to displace the full-time job as the characteristic mode of employment in the new millennium. But the part-timers have little space for individual development or community participation. You may have heard the joke: the politician announces that the Clinton administration has created ten million jobs in its first four-year term. "Yeah," says the voter, "and I have three of them."

This is a time of work without end for many Americans and a work shortage for many others: youths, blacks, other "minorities," and women (whose jobless rate is higher by a third than men's). Behind the statistics lies a political and cultural transformation that has already wiped out the gains of three generations. A hundred years ago the dream of the eight-hour day animated the labor movement to a new level of organization and militancy.

In the main, unions embraced technology because, if its benefits were distributed to producers, it could provide the material condition for freedom from the scourge of compulsory labor and the basis for a new culture where, for the first time in history, people could enter into free associations dedicated to the full development of individuality. In the aftermath of the defeat of the Paris Commune, where for a brief moment workers ran the city, Marx's son-in-law railed against the dogma of work and insisted on the right to be lazy. Some workers, imbued with the Protestant ethic, vehemently disagreed with this utopic vision—many of the best labor activists were temperance advocates—but did not dispute the goal of shortening the workday so they could fix the roof or repair the car. Whether your goal was to spend more time fishing or drinking or at "productive" but self-generated pursuits, nearly everyone in the labor movement agreed, mediated for some by the scurrilous doctrine of a "fair day's pay for a fair day's work," to do as little as possible to line the bosses' pockets.

As everyone knows, we are having our technological revolution, and the cornucopia of plenty is no longer grist for the social imagination; it is a material possibility. As, among others, Robert Spiegelman, Herbert Marcuse, and Murray Bookchin have argued, scarcity is the scourge of freedom and, from the perspective of the rulers, must be artificially reproduced to maintain the system of domination. Hence, working hours are longer, supervision—call it surveillance—more intense, accidents and injuries more frequent, and wages and salaries lower. Marx's belief that the more the worker produces the more he or she is diminished, enriching only the owners, seems more relevant today than it did in 1844 when he first wrote this idea.

Technology is deployed as management's weapon against its historic implication of freedom. It permits radically shorter working hours but, instead, has been organized to produce a three- or four-tier social system. At the bottom, millions are bereft of the good life because computer-mediated work destroys jobs faster than the economy creates them. Many are fully unemployed, some still receive government support. Others are casual laborers who "shape up" everyday at the docks of companies such as United Parcel Service and FedEx for a day's work or are migrant farm-workers. You can see the shape-up any morning in the South Bronx or on Chicago's West Side where mostly Latino workers await a furniture or vegetable truck for a day's hard labor.

At the pinnacle of the working class a shrinking elite—industrial workers in the large enterprises, craftspersons, and technical employees—still have relatively well-paid, full-time jobs and enjoy a battery of eroding benefits: paid vacations, health care (with the appropriate deductibles), and pensions. In between are the at-risk categories of labor: laid-off workers rehired as "contractors" or "consultants," both euphemisms for contingent workers; workers in smaller enterprises with lower-paying, full-time jobs and fewer benefits; and, of course, the bulk of college teaching adjuncts.

As capital reorganizes and recomposes labor, the idea of a job in contrast to paid labor is increasingly called into question. Here I will not dwell on the political economy of capital's offensive. Many of its salient features are well known: sharpened international competition, declining profit rates, global mergers and acquisitions. But it is important to underline the crucial fact of the decline, even disappearance, of the opposition and alternative to capital. It is not only the disarray into which the socialist project has fallen but also the inability of powerful national labor movements to confront global capital with more than sporadic resistance.

Corporate capitalism and its fictions, especially the "free market," have become the new ideological buzzwords of world politics and culture. They penetrate every itch and scratch of everyday life. Under the sign of privatization public goods are being disassembled: health care, environmental protection, and, of course, state-sponsored culture, signified by, among other things, the legislative evisceration of the National and State Endowments and Councils on the Arts and Humanities and their replacement by corporate-sponsored arts programs, notably those aired by PBS (the Petroleum Broadcasting System), countless corporate-funded museum exhibits, and the reemergence of corporate sponsorship of all kinds of music, especially middlebrow classical music. Sixty million Americans obtain their health care from HMOs, private consortia of hospitals, managers, and owners. The mission of these groups is to get rid of patients, not disease. And they operate under the sign of cost containment, with ultimate success measured by the number of subscribers turned away from service.

No more startling change has occurred than the growing tendency by local school boards to use their funds to outsource instruction, curricula, and other educational services to private contractors. Meanwhile, the drumbeat of vouchers gets louder as public perception that elementary and secondary schools are "failing" prompts an orgy of straw grasping. As a recent report using standard measures indicated, these arrangements do not seem to have a noticeable effect on improving school performance, but it is not clear that panic will not overcome reason. Teachers unions have resisted privatization, but the propaganda campaign on behalf of "free choice," the euphemism for privatization, appears, at times, overwhelming.

It was perhaps inevitable that the steamroller should have arrived at the doorstep of America's universities and colleges. By 1990, in contrast to the general decline of the labor movement's density in the workforce, faculty and staff were joining unions in record numbers. By the 1990s some 130,000 faculty and staff (exclusive of clerical workers) were represented by the three major unions in higher education, the American Federation of Teachers (AFT), the AAUP, and the National Education Association (NEA). Thousands of college and university clerical workers organized into a wide diversity of organizations, including AFT, but mostly others such as the United Auto Workers (UAW) and, in public universities, the American Federation of State, County, and Municipal Employees (AFSCME). To pay for rising salaries for clerical workers and faculty and to compensate for falling revenues for research, many administrations imposed tuition increases that exceeded the inflation rate and beefed up their endowments from—you guessed it—large donations from corporations and the individuals who headed them.

The growing influence of corporate giving on private and public research universities has been supplemented by a cultural corporatization of higher education. Once limited to community and technical colleges, vocationalization has become a virus infecting the liberal arts undergraduate curriculum. In many institutions social science and humanities departments have been reduced to service departments for business and technical programs. Many colleges have agreed to offer degrees, majors, and specially tailored courses to corporate employees in return for company reimbursements of tuition and other revenues and have accepted money from corporations to endow chairs in vocationally oriented fields. In some cases, notably the Olin Foundation, not only chairs are offered to universities but also the right-wing professors to sit on them.

This configuration is not confined to technical and managerial areas: it has become one of the solutions for the sciences, which have progressively lost public funding for research in fundamental areas. Now, many scientific departments must justify their faculty lines by raising outside money to perform (mostly) product-oriented research. Most famous, Massachusetts Institute of Technology molecular biologists entered a hotly contested Faustian bargain with drug companies, which have subsidized research in return for patent ownership. This model has been reproduced in many other institutions and has, to some extent, become the norm. Of course, American scientists are accustomed to subordination to higher authorities; their involvement with the defense establishment is a sixty-year marriage.

Faculty unions are not entirely a solution to the conditions that generate them: an acute power switch from the faculty to administration and to government and corporations over some hiring, curricular, and academic priorities; sagging salaries except for the high-profile stars and top administrators; and, at least in the public universities, legislatively mandated budget cuts that, in most instances, buttressed the power switch and resulted in some layoffs, a much tighter market for real jobs, increased workloads for those who have them, restrictions on promotions, and pay raises calibrated to the inflation rate. In sum, faculty members see their unions as a means to restore their lost autonomy and shrinking power as well as to redress salary and benefits inequities.

Academic labor, like most labor, is rapidly being decomposed and recomposed. The full professor, like the spotted owl, is becoming an endangered species in private as well as public universities. When professors retire or die, their lines frequently follow them. Instead, many universities, even in the Ivy League, convert a portion of the full line to adjunct-driven teaching, whether occupied by part-timers or by graduate teaching assistants. At the top, the last good job in America is reserved for a relatively small elite. Fewer assistant and associate lines are being made available for newly minted Ph.D.'s. As the recently organized Yale University graduate teaching assistants discovered, they are no longer, if they ever were, teachers-in-training. Much of the undergraduate curriculum in public and private research universities is taught by graduate students who, in effect, have joined the swelling ranks of part-timers, most of whom are Ph.D.'s. Together they form an emerging academic proletariat. They make from twelve to twenty thousand dollars a year, depending on how many courses they teach and where, whether they teach summers, and whether they are hired as adjunct instructors or assistant professors. Except for those termed *graduate teaching assistants*, most do not get benefits or have offices or, indeed, any of the amenities enjoyed by full-time faculty.

It reminds me of my semester teaching at the University of Paris at Saint Denis. Only the chair of the department had an office. Faculty from part-timers to full professors crowded into a single large room where they deposited their outer clothing and some papers while they taught. After class, they picked up their belongings and headed home. In most French universities the university as a public sphere is simply unthinkable, a situation that once described the American community or technical colleges. The postsecondary scene of the future may, unless reversed by indignant and well-organized students and faculty, resemble more the second-tier European and third world universities than the "groves" celebrated in the popular press.

Administrators offer contradictory accounts of this emerging configuration of academic teacher work. They claim teaching is merely part of the academic apprenticeship of graduate students and a means to support them through school. On the other hand they are wont to claim that the proliferation of adjuncts is a sad but necessary aspect of the imperative of cost cutting. According to this line, if they could they would create many new full-time lines. But they can't. At CUNY, where the number of new full-time lines has slowed to a slow faucet leak, approximately half of all courses in the undergraduate curricula are taught by adjuncts; in community colleges the figure is 60 percent. Even in schools such as New York University, which has made substantial efforts to rebuild its full-time faculty, some key programs such as the School of Continuing Education and many traditional departments' undergraduate lower-division offerings are largely taught by adjuncts.

In the largest middle-level state systems such as California State University and CUNY, research is not genuinely encouraged except in the natural sciences. Nonetheless, it remains a sorting device to get rid of faculty by denying tenure to those who fail to meet the criterion of producing the requisite quantity of publications. In these schools, many full-timers teach four and five courses a semester and have dozens of student advisees. In some instances, the professor who defies gravity's law by remaining intellectually active is labeled a rate-buster by the exhausted or burned out majority of her or his colleagues. When combined with committee work, many faculty are transformed into human teaching machines, whereas others, in despair, desperately seek alternatives to classroom teaching, even stooping to accept administrative positions, and not just for the money or power. The old joke that the relationship between a tenured professor and a dean is the same as that between a dog and a fire hydrant has become one of the anomalies of the waning century. Now the administrators are the cat, and the faculty, the catbox.

A Margin of Hope?

In The Jobless Future William DiFazio and I have argued that academic teacher work is heteronomous. Salaries, working conditions, and expectations are crucially shaped by where the teacher is employed and in what capacity. I have already alluded to the heavier teaching loads in middle- and lower-tier colleges. In community colleges and state nonresearch four-year institutions, teaching loads and student advisement have been rising in the 1990s. And many more professors are teaching introductory courses where texts are prescribed by the department, especially but not exclusively in community colleges, which enroll half of the fifteen million students in postsecondary education. As teacher/student ratios skyrocket, class size increases; at one CUNY campus an introductory course enrolled eighty students. The graduate assistant told me that she had no teaching assistant or grader. And this narrative is fairly typical of many public four-year colleges. When the course load was three for full-time faculty and classes enrolled no more than thirty students, the professor had time to read and write and pay close attention to students' work. It was at least one of the better jobs. Now many institutions of post-secondary education have an industrial atmosphere, especially with the increasingly vocational curricula in the liberal arts.

Research universities have smaller classroom teaching loads in order to facilitate faculty research, at least in the social and natural sciences. Apart from composition and other required introductory courses that have increasingly become the meat and potatoes of English departments in community colleges and middle-level universities, philosophy, criticism, and history are activities treated as ornaments. The leading figures in these disciplines enhance the institution's prestige, which has implications for fund-raising and, in some instances, provides administrative leaders for elite schools. Deans, provosts, and presidents are frequently recruited from the humanities in high-prestige liberal arts colleges and private research universities, although the public universities lean toward natural scientists.

Many faculty maintain their intellectual and social distance from students, even graduate students. It is not only that they are busy with their grant-funded research, their writing, and their narrowly circumscribed celebrity. The distance is produced by the growing gap between the professoriat, who in the elite universities almost completely identify with the institution, and graduate students' growing recognition that collective action rather than individual merit holds the key to their futures. For example, when I was invited to address a meeting of hundreds of members of the recently organized Yale graduate assistants union in spring 1995, I was dismayed but not surprised to find only three senior faculty in attendance, one of whom promptly resigned his job in the sociology department to return to the labor movement. The other two, David Montgomery and Michael Denning, and a few others who could not make this particular event, are union stalwarts in this otherwise snow-blinded community of scholar-managers. "Left" critics and scholars, along with more conservative faculty, were prominent by their absence. A year later I was informed that a distinguished historian turned in a graduate assistant who had participated in an action to withhold grades as a protest against the administration's refusal to recognize the union.

The formation of an academic proletariat, even in the elite universities, must be denied by the professoriat, who have gained richly from the labor of their "students." The professors must continue to believe that those who teach the bulk of the undergraduate classes are privileged crybabies destined to become the new privileged caste. Strikes, demonstrations, and other militant activity are expressions of graduate students' flirtation with outworn ideologies of class and class struggle and not to be taken seriously. These professors are not only indifferent to the new graduate assistants' unions, they are hostile to them. In effect, they take the position of the administration and its corporate trustees because they identify themselves as its supplicants.

Some who are acutely aware that they hold the last good job in America believe that their best chance to preserve it lies in becoming what the infamous Yeshiva decision alleges: that faculty in private schools are managers and therefore ineligible for union protections under the law. It is not merely that they are highly paid and enjoy the prestige of institutions standing at the pinnacle of the academic system. Their identities are bound up with their ornamental role. To break with the institution on behalf of graduate students would acknowledge that higher education *at all levels* is being restructured and that they may be the last generation of privileged scholars. This admission would prevent them from playing their part in closing the gates.

The Yale struggle is only the most publicized of a growing movement whose main sites are in state research universities. The University of Iowa, the University of Michigan, the University of California at Berkeley, Los Angeles, and San Diego, the State University of New York at Binghamton, and the University of Wisconsin are among the dozen major universities with graduate assistants unions, many of them affiliated with conventional blue-collar organizations such as UAW, as well as AFT. In many cases the AFT or AAUP contract covers adjunct faculty, but graduate assistants must organize separately.

But academic unionism has, in general, not yet addressed the very core of the crisis: the restructuring of universities and colleges along the lines of global capitalism. Most of us are situated in less privileged precincts of the academic system. We have witnessed relatively declining salaries and the erosion of our benefits. And like many industrial workers we have been driven into an impossibly defensive posture and are huddled in the cold, awaiting the next blow. We know that full-time lines are being retired with their bearers, that more courses are taught by part-timers at incredibly low pay and few if any benefits. We are aware of the tendency of elite as well as middle-tier universities toward privatization and toward aligning the curriculum with the job market, and we are experiencing the transformation of nearly all the humanities and many social sciences into services for business, computer technology, and other vocational programs.

In short, although more highly unionized than at any time in history, academic labor has not yet devised a collective strategy to address its own future. We know that the charges against us—that university teaching is a scam, that much research is not "useful," that scholarship is hopelessly privileged—emanate from a Right that wants us to put our noses to the grindstone just like everybody else. So far we have not asserted that the erosion of the working conditions for the bulk of the professoriat is an assault on one of the nation's more precious resources, its intellectuals. Guilt-tripped by mindless populism, whose roots are not so far from the religious morality of hard work as redemption, we have not celebrated the idea of thinking as a full-time activity and the importance of producing what the system terms "useless" knowledge. Most of all, we have not conducted a struggle for universalizing the self-managed time some of us still enjoy.

III

Siting Specifics, Striking Back

Education, Job Skills, or Workfare

The Crisis Facing Adult Literacy Education Today

Emily Hacker and Ira Yankwitt

To acquire literacy is more than to psychologically and mechanically dominate reading and writing techniques. It is to dominate these techniques in terms of consciousness. . . . Acquiring literacy does not involve memorizing sentences, words or symbols—lifeless objects unconnected to an existential universe—but rather an attitude of creation and re-creation, a self-transformation producing a stance of intervention in one's context.—Paulo Freire, "Literacy As Action for Freedom"

Above is a vision of the purpose of literacy education espoused by Brazilian educator Paulo Freire and other advocates for literacy as a means of achieving critical consciousness and personal and political empowerment. Many literacy programs around the world have been founded according to Freire's vision. Currently in the United States, however, the ability for programs to maintain this ideal is being challenged. A brief overview of the federal role in shaping adult literacy policy over the last few decades provides a critical context for understanding the current crisis in literacy education. Prior to the 1960s, there were some public and private efforts toward raising adult literacy levels, but none were conducted on a large scale. In the 1960s, however, two opposing political perspectives on related social issues emerged, resulting in increased public attention to and funding for adult literacy programs.

Spurred by the civil rights movement and the "war on poverty" of the 1950s and 1960s, the Left began to pay increased attention to social issues such as poverty, hunger, health, and education. At the same time, the Right had growing concerns about joblessness, welfare dependency, and the "culture of poverty"—a deficit theory that classified the poor as disorganized, immoral, rootless, and irresponsible, with bad parenting skills, unstable relationships, and low self-esteem.[1] This period also saw the beginning of the rise of computer technology in the workplace, which raised new questions about the meaning of literacy for adults. The Adult Education Act of 1966 (AEA), the first major federal commitment to adult literacy education, emerged in the context of these social changes.

The AEA brought a national focus on increasing adult literacy skills and provided states with the funds to develop and run literacy programs. Although the major hope driving the effort to pass the AEA for many legislators was that it would reduce unemployment and welfare dependency, there were few restrictions attached to the funding defining who could attend literacy programs or for what purposes the adult wished to improve his or her literacy level.

The economic downturn that began in the early 1970s and has continued throughout the 1990s has been responsible for both corporate and industrial downsizing as well as a shift in political and cultural views about poverty and immigration. Over the past twenty years, political and public opinion about poor and immigrant adults (who make up a large percentage of students served in literacy programs) has grown increasingly negative. Amendments and revisions to the AEA made during the 1980s and 1990s reflect these shifts. For example, the AEA has grown narrower in its definition of who can be classified as an adult literacy student and what he or she may study. AEA funds are now broken up into separate categories for programs serving welfare recipients, workers, single mothers, prisoners, and the homeless.[2]

These recent amendments to the AEA require literacy programs to define specific goals, such as moving people from welfare to work, reducing crime, and increasing job skills.[3] To be eligible for any government funding, literacy programs are being asked to take on many new responsibilities, including job development, placement, and training, as well as to report to government agencies on student attendance and employment status. With the pressure of meeting job placement rates, many programs feel they can not afford to work with adults with the lowest skills. Catherine Stercq points out that in this movement toward short-term, employment-focused adult education, "illiterate persons may be excluded from social and occupational integration programs because it may not be 'profitable' to rehabilitate them. This means relegating to the fringes those who are no longer needed or who can be done without."[4]

Some of these challenges to literacy programs and students are directly related to recent changes in national welfare policy, from the Family Support Act of 1988 to the Personal Responsibility Act of 1996, in which "the criterion through which the government has apparently judged education has become economic efficiency rather than effective education."[5] These new and required components of adult literacy education are being used as adjuncts to welfare reform. Adult literacy programs, many of which have their roots in the social movements for economic justice and educational equity, now find themselves part of the movement to "end welfare as we know it."

In 1988, Congress passed the first federal legislation that officially connected adult literacy education with welfare reform. The Family Support Act and Job Opportunities and Basic Skills program (JOBS) stressed the important role education and training had to play in the effort to move adults off the welfare rolls and into the job market, especially for adults with less than a secondary school education. This new legislation gave funding to states to develop programs that would provide literacy education, job training, and other support services to recipients of Aid to Families with Dependent Children (AFDC), the federal welfare program for single parents.[6] JOBS is the umbrella program for the educational and vocational training programs created in response to the Family Support

Act. In August 1996, President Clinton signed the Personal Responsibility Act (PRA). The shift in public opinion about welfare during the last eight years is evident in the much lower status education has been given in the new bill. Among its provisions, the PRA limits public assistance recipients to two years of education and job training. After that, they must participate in workfare. But the bill also gives individual states the freedom to limit access to education and training at an earlier point or to replace this option completely with workfare, as some states have already done.

Where education is still an option for public assistance recipients, it comes with many new rules and limitations associated with welfare policy. For example, many traditionally voluntary adult literacy programs have been required to become mandatory programs. They have had to make curricular shifts as well, toward content centered on preparing welfare recipients for the workforce. In addition, literacy programs have been required to comply with welfare regulations for limiting time of study and reporting on their students' attendance and job status.

These last conditions have created serious ethical dilemmas for many adult educators, uncomfortable with playing the role of "welfare cop." These changes led a director of a literacy program in New York City to reflect: "Most of us receive funding and support from institutions whose goals sometimes contradict our own. How do we respond to those institutions and still remain accountable to ourselves and to our students? Who is to determine what we do when faced with this contradiction? As teachers and administrators, we realize that we have a responsibility to continually question who we are actually serving. We have to challenge ourselves or else fall victim to the bureacracies that attempt to dictate to us and our students."[7]

As a consequence of these policy changes, many adult learners, regardless of their literacy levels, prior work experience, English proficiency, or progress achieved, are being forced out of community-based literacy programs and into workfare or "job search" programs. Those adults who can still enroll in literacy classes often now find themselves in classes with "work-centered" curricula, where they may be taught lessons such as proper dress and social/behavior skills for work instead of the language and literacy skills the students may have been seeking. Henry A. Giroux, who has examined this trend in literacy education, states that "literacy in this perspective is geared to make adults more productive workers and citizens within a given society. In spite of its appeal to economic mobility, functional literacy reduces the concept of literacy and the pedagogy in which it is suited to the pragmatic requirements of capital; consequently, the notions of critical thinking, culture and power disappear under the imperatives of the labor process and the need for capital accumulation." [8]

Well into the second decade of severe government cutbacks for social services and education, it is becoming clear that "the effect on the schools of educational spending reductions, increased unemployment, and falling real wages has been to reduce their 'democratic' side and make them increasingly oriented toward reproducing the relations of capitalist production and its class division of labor." [9] Lawrence Mead, a social policy analyst, contends that the public has grown increasingly adverse to what it considers "voluntary joblessness" and "believes welfare recipients should return to the menial jobs they used to do, and much of the pressure behind Workfare stems from this." [10]

The assumptions in Mead's statement—that the poor are lazy, unmotivated, and could easily find jobs if they only wanted to—are at the foundation of current welfare policies that replace education and job training with workfare. The reality behind these assumptions, though, tells a markedly different story. Roberta Roth, in the 1995 research study *Welfare That Works: The Working Lives of AFDC Recipients*, found that 43 percent of welfare mothers work substantial hours, mostly, however, in low-wage, unstable jobs. Half of those women cycle in and out of the lowest-wage sectors of the labor market, and the other half have steady incomes but at such low wages that they must combine them with welfare. [11]

Now, instead of policies that would improve the wages and working conditions of these jobs, we have workfare, which has the opposite effect on the low-wage sector of employment. In New York City, while city employees by the thousands are being offered the choice of buyouts or layoffs, the Human Resources Administration is sending welfare recipients to those same city offices to fulfill their workfare hours. Currently, there are approximately 37,000 welfare recipients in New York City's workfare program. The majority of these workers are concentrated in departments like parks, sanitation, and general services doing heavy manual labor, while others are working in agencies like the welfare department itself doing "human service" and clerical work. The Giuliani administration has stated that by the end of 1997 its goal is to have over 85,000 welfare recipients participating in workfare, and under the new federal guidelines New York City will need to place a projected 130,000 AFDC recipients into workfare by the year 2002.[12]

Although existing state law mandates that welfare recipients' individual preferences be taken into account when assigning them to an education, training, or work activity, nearly all new welfare recipients are assigned to six months of workfare before they are permitted to participate exclusively in school. Moreover, despite the state law that maintains the welfare department cannot interfere with a recipient's education or training if he or she is making satisfactory progress,[13] some recipients who have been attending literacy classes for over two years while on welfare are being forced to leave their classes to participate in at least six months of work.

At a City Council hearing on workfare in October 1996, officials from the Welfare Department insisted that they are not indiscriminately assigning recipients to workfare, even though between April and June of 1996 they placed over eleven thousand recipients in workfare and only approximately two thousand recipients in other types of education or training. When presented with the case of a woman in her mid-forties who speaks both Spanish and English, reads Spanish at a fifth-grade level, and reads no English at all, city officials contended that by performing maintenance work for six months this woman would enhance her "employability" more than if she spent her days learning how to read and write English.[14] With New York City's two-year time limit on educational activities now reflected in federal law, it is highly likely that beginning in the fall of 1997, literacy programs will start to see a large percentage of their ten thousand students on public assistance being pulled out of classes for workfare. Of course, welfare recipients could still, theoretically, attend school on their own time in the afternoons or evenings. Without additional money for child care and transportation expenses, however, such a scenario is extremely unrealistic.

Public sentiment in support of workfare tends to be rooted either in the punitive notion that welfare recipients should be forced to *pay* for their benefits by engaging in demanding physical labor, or in the paternalistic notion that welfare recipients should be asked to *take responsibility* for their support by providing services to the community. The political rhetoric that the Giuliani administration employs to justify its wholesale assignment of welfare recipients to workfare contends that "work experience," more than any other form of education or training, provides the best means to move public assistance recipients from welfare to self-sufficiency. Yet while administration officials are quick to assert that their workfare program has succeeded in moving recipients from welfare to work, in 1995 only 250 of the 75,000 workfare participants who cycled through 25,000 workfare slots obtained paid jobs in the agencies in which they worked.[15] Given that New York City has shifted from an industrial to a technological economy, and given that by the year 2000, 86 percent of all jobs will require a high school education,[16] why would the Giuliani administration remove welfare recipients with limited reading, writing, and English language skills from literacy programs and place them into workfare slots that lead to neither a marketable skill nor a paying job?

The answer to this question may be purely financial. During the last two decades New York City has been in a state of recurring economic crisis. After the city went bankrupt in the mid-1970s, the Koch administration embraced a postindustrial model of economic growth that emphasized residential and commercial development and facilitated the transformation of New York City into a service-based economy. Real estate developers, investment firms, and high-income households were offered a variety of subsidies and tax breaks, all designed to keep businesses in the city, promote white-collar job growth, and encourage speculation in the local real estate market. Yet while the city provided a twenty-year property tax abatement to almost anyone constructing a high-rise office building, it did next to nothing to support manufacturing or encourage industrial construction. Consequently, the city's industrial infrastructure degenerated, factories closed, and manufacturing jobs were lost, all at a quicker pace than global economic forces alone would have produced. Moreover, during the recession of the early 1990s, the service sector bottomed out, and New York City lost an additional 360,000 jobs, plummeting the city into its current unemployment crisis, in which over 710,000 people are competing for approximately 90,000 available jobs.[17]

As a result of generous tax breaks for the wealthy and a high level of need among the unemployed, New York City's annual tax revenues regularly fall short of its projected expenses (in 1996, the city's budget gap was over $2 billion). Workfare offers a partial solution to the city's financial problems by enabling the city to replace higher-wage, unionized workers with welfare recipients who earn as little as one-fifth the compensation and receive no benefits or collective-bargaining rights. In fact, it costs New York City only 14 percent of the wage of an average full-time clerical worker ($12.32 an hour) to have a welfare recipient in the workfare program perform the same tasks.[18]

Since Mayor Giuliani took office in January 1994, the city has downsized its workforce by approximately twenty-nine thousand municipal workers. While the administration claims that none of these workers have been replaced by any of the city's thirty-seven thousand workfare participants—that would be illegal under federal law—virtually all the work these employees once performed is now being performed by welfare recipients. Indeed, in some cases whole city departments are relying almost exclusively on the labor of workfare participants. The Parks Department, for example, now has three times the number of workfare participants as it does paid employees, and many paid employees resent workfare participants for filling the jobs of their friends.[19] Seen in this light, it does not seem unreasonable to conclude that the city is using workfare as a means of cutting labor costs, weakening municipal labor unions, and closing its budget gap. With a surplus labor force of 130,000 A F D C recipients by the year 2002, there is no telling how many municipal jobs will be cut or how many concessions municipal labor unions will be forced to make.

Aside from providing savings for local governments in the ways described above, the workfare provisions and lifetime limit in the federal Personal Responsibility Act may be profitable for businesses as well. Among the ideas that policymakers are considering are placing workfare participants in private sector positions, diverting welfare grants to employers who agree to pay recipients a wage that is slightly higher than their public assistance benefit,[20] and providing tax breaks and subsidies to businesses that hire welfare recipients once their time limit expires. Such policies would, of course, lead to the displacement of unsubsidized private sector employees, depress wages in the low-income labor market, and, in general, transform the social welfare program into a corporate welfare program without ever changing the funding stream.

Conspicuously absent in the recent debate over welfare reform and workfare is the idea codified in the Family Support Act of 1988 that education is the key to gainful employment. One might suspect that this is because with corporate flight, downsizing, the shift to a high-tech labor market, and the aftermath of a recession from which major urban centers such as New York City have never recovered, policymakers and business-people fear that it is not in their long-term interest to have an educated, employable populace with high expectations to secure jobs that simply do not exist. It may, however, be in their short-term interest to have an undereducated, impoverished reserve army of labor that is economically dependent on its own indentured servitude.

The image of adult literacy education as a workforce preparation and adult literacy students as exploitable surplus laborers is a far cry from Freire's vision of adult education as critical consciousness-raising and adult learners as empowered political actors. One challenge facing adult literacy practitioners today is how to continue to facilitate the intellectual and creative development of their students while meeting funding requirements that mandate a focus on the acquisition of narrowly defined job skills. This conflict between programmatic integrity and economic necessity will continue to plague adult educators as long as they are forced to rely on government funding for the survival of their programs and as long as the notion of "education for its own sake" continues to be undermined by ideological attacks.

A more immediate issue confronting adult literacy practitioners is how to support welfare recipients in their pursuit of personal growth and self-realization at a time when they are being denied access to education and relegated to dead-end workfare jobs. While this essay reflects the authors' experience as literacy workers in New York City, the issues raised are concerns for adult education programs across the country. With the passage of the Personal Responsibility Act, welfare recipients will, at best, be permitted to participate in two years of education before being forced into workfare and, at worst, will not be able to participate in education or training at all. Literacy workers must unite to combat the myths and stereotypes that government officials invoke to rationalize these welfare reform policies, and must work alongside other activists and advocates to champion the idea that education is a right to which everyone is entitled.

Notes

1 Arlene Fingeret, *The Illiterate Underclass: Demythologizing an American Stigma* (Ann Arbor, Mich.: University Microfilms International, 1982), 70, 71.

2 U.S. Congress, Office of Technology Assessment, *Adult Literacy and New Technologies: Tools for a Lifetime* (Washington, D.C.: U.S. Government Printing Office, 1993), 139.

3 Elena Cohen, Susan Golonka, Rebecca Maynard, Theodora Ooms, and Todd Owen, "Literacy and Welfare Reform: Are We Making the Connection?" in *National Center on Adult Literacy Technical Report*, TR94-16 (Philadelphia: National Center on Adult Literacy and Family Impact Seminar, 1994), 16.

4 Catherine Stercq, *Literacy, Socialization, and Employment* (Hamburg, Germany: UNESCO Institute for Education, 1993), 32.

5 Peter Jarvis, *Adult Education and the State: Towards a Politics of Adult Education* (London: Routledge, 1993), 47.

6 Cohen et al., "Literacy and Welfare Reform," 16.

7 John Gordon, "Welfare and Literacy," *Literacy Harvest* 4 (winter 1995): 12.

8 Henry A. Giroux, *Theory and Resistance in Education: A Pedagogy for the Opposition* (New York: Bergin and Garvey, 1983), 14.

9 Martin Carnoy and Henry M. Levin, *Schooling and Work in the Democratic State* (Stanford: Stanford University Press, 1985), 15.

10 Lawrence Mead, *The New Politics of Poverty: The Nonworking Poor in America* (New York: Basic, 1992), 143.

11 Roberta Spalter Roth, *Welfare That Works: The Working Lives of AFDC Recipients* (Washington, D.C.: Institute for Women's Policy Research, 1995).

12 The Personal Responsibility Act requires that by the year 2002, 50 percent of each state's AFDC recipients must be in work programs. It is estimated that New York State will have approximately four hundred thousand AFDC recipients, 65 percent of whom will reside in New York City.

13 New York, *Social Service Law*, secs. 335(2)(a) and 336-a(5)(a), enacted by the state legislature in 1990 to comply with the federal Family Support Act of 1988. Expanded on in 18 NYCRR sec. 385.5(d).

14 Meg O'Regan, executive deputy commissioner, Human Resources Administration, and Seth Diamond, deputy commissioner, Office of Employment

Services, testimony before the City Council General Welfare Committee, October 7, 1996.

15 Liz Krueger and John E. Seley, "The Return of Slavery: Lessons from Workfare in New York City," *Dollars and Sense*, November/December, 1996, 31.

16 New York State Education Department, Office of Workforce Preparation and Continuing Education, untitled memo, December 21, 1995.

17 Robert Fitch, *The Assassination of New York* (New York: Verso, 1993). Current unemployment figures are based on New York State Department of Labor statistics for November 1996.

18 A Home Relief recipient (single person on welfare) receives about $5,570 a year in cash grant, shelter allowance, and food stamps. Many Home Relief recipients are performing workfare jobs that would earn a full-time worker $25,000 to $30,000 a year plus benefits. The cost to the city per month for a Home Relief recipient is $176. Home Relief recipients work 104 hours per month, costing the city $1.69 per hour. The cost to the city per month for an AFDC mother with two children is $144. AFDC recipients currently work 80 hours per month, costing the city $1.80 per hour.

19 The Parks Department currently has approximately twenty-five hundred paid employees and over seventy-five hundred workfare workers.

20 Governor George Pataki, *Welfare Reform Memorandum and Proposed Legislation*, November 13, 1996.

In Defense of CUNY

Bart Meyers

By virtue of its history, size, and location, the City University of New York (CUNY) contributes an interesting chapter to the chronicle of growth and contraction, attack and resistance in public higher education. Formed in the early 1960s by the combination of New York City's municipal colleges—including City College established in 1847, Hunter College in 1869, Brooklyn College in 1930, and Queens College in 1937—CUNY inherited a record of outstanding achievement in undergraduate education. Since its formation, CUNY has added a graduate school with doctoral programs, a law school, a medical school, community colleges, and additional senior colleges. Currently, there are 206,500 full- and part-time students enrolled, making CUNY one of the largest public universities in the United States.

Open Admissions

Although a public university in a city with a history of de jure ethnic group integration, CUNY and its constituent colleges had, for the most part, served European American students with relatively few students from other ethnic groups finding their way in. The civil rights movement of the 1950s and 1960s and the leftist political movement of the 1960s transformed the white and largely Jewish composition of CUNY's student body. During the 1968–69 academic year, a groundswell of pent-up demand at CUNY produced a militant campaign on the City and Brooklyn campuses for an open admissions policy that would promote ethnic integration. Students of color led the struggle, but it was joined by a substantial number of European American students and some faculty.

Unwittingly, this campaign partially paralleled a plan for open admissions in CUNY championed by a segment of the corporate-political elite who understood the benefit of using an institution supported by tax revenues to train workers for the private economy. Their plan, however, differed crucially from the students' open admissions project. While the students demanded open admissions at all levels of the university, that is, for both community and senior colleges, the elite plan called for channeling previously excluded students solely into the community colleges. A campaign of rallies, speeches, broadsides, building seizures, fires set in buildings, confrontations with college administrations and police, and arrests resolved the differences largely in favor of the students.

Between 1969 and 1975, CUNY experienced its most rapid growth. New units were added, already existing units expanded enrollments, the student body diversified along class and ethnic lines, and the faculty increased its numbers significantly. At the same time, the political excitement of the era continued to manifest itself on the campuses, primarily in continued militant protest against the Vietnam War, antiracist and feminist actions, and the establishment of ethnic and women's studies departments and programs.

The Fiscal Crisis

By 1975–76, when the deficit financing and inflation associated with the Vietnam War and the Organization of Petroleum Exporting Countries (OPEC) oil shocks, among other factors, had jolted the U.S. economy and threatened to end its post–World War II expansion, the resulting fiscal crisis spelled the end to CUNY's expansion and the beginning of its forced contraction. Besides, the university had a student body whose demographic characteristics no longer resembled those of the political-corporate elite and which was much too politically unruly for them.

Despite the high-sounding rhetoric issuing from New York's City Hall and from the governor's mansion about the fundamental importance of supporting public higher education, the city and the state cut CUNY's budget and in the fall of 1976 ended a history of nearly 130 years of free tuition. Over a period of years, this policy had what must have been its intended effect of substantially reducing the enrollment of full-time students at the senior colleges.

1991–1992

During the 1991–92 academic year, the governor proposed and the legislature voted for a cut in CUNY's budget that was deeper than usual, leading CUNY's board of trustees to impose a tuition hike and to retrench faculty. Students and faculty organized on campuses and formed CUNY-wide, ad hoc protest organizations: the CUNY Coalition of Students (CCS) and the CUNY Coalition of Concerned Faculty and Staff (CCCFS), respectively. Their joint demonstration in the spring of 1992 through lower Manhattan's financial district was large and spirited. Still, the budget cuts stood, and CUNY's Board of Trustees remorselessly implemented the tuition hike and faculty retrenchment.

Although the student and faculty ad hoc organizations soon wilted, a subgroup of fifteen CCCFS members formed around a legal strategy for the defense of CUNY. Since 1982, when it assumed full funding of CUNY's senior colleges and graduate school, New York State had funded operations at the State University of New York, with its predominantly white student body, at a level substantially higher than the comparable operations at CUNY, at which people of color made up two-thirds of the student body in 1992. Modeled on a successful federal lawsuit in Mississippi, the group brought an equal opportunity lawsuit in state court against the governor, lieutenant governor, comptroller, and the legislature. The lawsuit charged that the state discriminated against students of color through its unequal funding of the two universities. Although successful at the first judicial level, the case was eventually lost in appellate court.

Still, the effort was not wasted. The multiethnic lawsuit group developed a great deal of information about CUNY and funding of the university, while establishing working relations of trust and respect among its members. It was also able to resuscitate the largely moribund CCCFS in order to meet the challenge of another crisis at CUNY.

1995–1996

In 1995, Governor George Pataki, who had run on a platform of unleashing market forces and contracting government programs, proposed to cut $158 million from the previous year's $616 million budget, a record reduction of 26 percent.[1] New York City mayor Rudy Giuliani, not to be outdone, proposed to reduce the city's support for CUNY as well. In a particularly nasty measure, Giuliani refused to permit approximately ten thousand students on welfare to satisfy their newly required workfare requirements at CUNY, making impossibly difficult their scheduling of school, work, and family.

The governor's proposed budget would have required the dismissal of one thousand full-time faculty (25 percent of the total) and one thousand part-time faculty. To soften the process of forcing faculty out of CUNY, the governor pushed through an early retirement incentive for faculty that explicitly ruled out hiring replacements. The budget proposal, if enacted, would have necessitated the cancellation of ten thousand class sections. Finally, in an attempt to reverse the gains of the 1960s in class and ethnic integration of the student body, Pataki proposed two measures that would put college attendance beyond the reach of many CUNY students.[2] He wanted a tuition increase of $1,000 per year (a 41 percent increase over the $2,450 level of the previous year's tuition) and an end to the SEEK, College Discovery, Educational Opportunity, and the Higher Educational Opportunity Programs that served seventy-one thousand full-time and nine thousand part-time educationally and financially disadvantaged students, who were primarily people of color.

Over student and faculty protests, the CUNY Board of Trustees did not wait for legislative action on the governor's budget and precipitously declared a state of financial exigency. This declaration authorized Chancellor Ann Reynolds to retrench faculty. At the same time, the board passed a number of resolutions. It authorized a tuition increase; stipulated for the first time that students must complete remediation and ESL work within their first year at CUNY or be forced out; and reduced the number of credits needed for graduation from 64 to 60 for the community colleges and from 128 to 120 for the senior colleges, thus rationalizing a reduction of faculty. For faculty, it demanded an increase in instructional productivity (that is, larger classes) and announced that it would reexamine faculty workloads for negotiation of the next faculty contract.

The board's authorization of retrenchment and its other resolutions provided an opportunity for the chancellor to reinvigorate her earlier attempt to restructure and further centralize her control over the colleges. Her market-driven plan called for the elimination of low-enrollment departments (for example, French, German, physical education) at some of the colleges, while pushing for a new community college (at a time of dramatically shrinking budgets!) with a curriculum tied to the employment needs of business. The plan would terminate faculty from affected departments, leaving students to make time somehow for extensive travel on the New York subway system to other CUNY units to complete their coursework.

Not surprisingly, the chancellor's restructuring plan provoked another fight-back movement among students and faculty that, although rancorous and often divided, was also broadly based and often militant. The main student group was the CCS, which reformed as an ad hoc coalition of already existing and newly formed campus groups. The CCS set about organizing its main event—a rally in New York's City Hall Park and a march to Wall Street—with an energy and creativity that eventually contributed greatly to a turnout of as many as twenty thousand.

A number of fault lines, however, opened up within this new coalition. Many of the students did not know each other well. The difficulties this created for working together were exacerbated by ethnic tensions and political differences, some of which were bounded by the rigid lines of sectarian political groups. Righteously convinced of the justice of its demands, the CCS was loathe to compromise its principles. Asserting that citizens have the right to demonstrate peacefully where they please, the CCS refused to negotiate a parade permit with the police for the march to Wall Street. The CCS was also reluctant to include elected politicians as speakers at the rally, believing them all to be opportunists who would push their own agendas rather than the needs of CUNY.

The possibility of broad unity revolved around the ad hoc nature of the CCS and its politics. The University Student Senate (USS), a largely passive organization with neither inclination nor capacity to organize a large demonstration and used to working at the top with politicians, bridled at a rival center of student activity, rejected CCS's politics, and refused to join forces in building a common resistance against the cuts. Similarly, the leadership of the Professional Staff Congress (PSC), the union that represents the instructional staff of CUNY, felt much more comfortable lobbying politicians than taking politics to the streets, especially CCS's politics. The PSC leadership, despite efforts by members of the nascent New Caucus,[3] declared that it did want to work with CCS students but only with those students associated with the legitimate USS. The PSC and the USS then proceeded to line up the support of the Black and Puerto Rican Caucus of the New York State Legislature.[4]

On March 16, 1995, one week before the demonstration planned by the CCS and the CCCFS, the PSC and the USS held a rally and march to protest the budget cuts. Approximately forty-five hundred students and faculty participated. Some activists had feared that it would be small and suggest weakness to the governor and the legislature. In fact, it received little publicity and almost certainly reduced the numbers for the demonstration the following week on March 23.

Nonetheless, the March 23 mobilization was a success. The CCS organized the participation of hundreds of high school students, whose future education depended on a viable CUNY. The CCS and the CCCFS—whose members endorsed the rally despite the CCS's decision not to get a police permit for the march — had stirred up interest and enthusiasm on most of the CUNY campuses, and large contingents arrived with floats, banners, and signs to loud cheers at City Hall Park. The CCCFS organized a feeder march of one thousand faculty in academic robes and mortarboards that came over the Brooklyn Bridge.

The police deployed an overwhelming force to meet the demonstrators. On motorcycles they revved their engines and circled the park; on horseback they herded the demonstrators; and on foot, in riot gear, they prevented exit from the park.

Meanwhile, discipline on the rally stage broke down. The student chairperson, protected by her colleagues, assumed total control, determining capriciously who was allowed to speak. When a large contingent of demonstrators attempted to march out of the park, the police penned them up in a small space and allowed no movement. As the police pushed the students back, incidents occurred, and when an officer went down with a coronary, the other police, apparently motivated by the incorrect belief that the stricken officer had been attacked, surged into the crowd. The rest of the afternoon turned into a police riot.

Students, faculty, administrators, the media, and people in downtown Manhattan paid intense attention to the rally and its demands. Evaluations differed. Some believed that it had gotten out of hand, that the CCS was to blame, and that it was a setback for CUNY. Some felt that they could not work with the CCS in the future because of its lack of discipline. Others asserted that without the numbers that the CCS and CCCFS had mobilized and the disorder that had materialized, the demonstration and CUNY's needs would have been invisible. Many regretted the lack of a broader unity. Most held some combination of the above opinions.

When the legislature finished its protracted negotiations, it approved cuts that deeply wounded but did not kill CUNY outright as the governor's proposals would have done. Instead of a $158 million budget cut, the legislature voted a reduction of only $100 million. Rather than increasing tuition $1,000 per year, the chancellor and the board now saw their way clear to raise it only $750 per year. The chancellor and the board proceeded with retrenchment, but because 617 faculty and higher education officers had chosen early retirement, they retrenched fewer faculty and staff than had originally been feared.[5]

The remaining episode of defending C U N Y against the 1995–96 budget cuts occurred in the courts. After the legislative budget restorations, the increased revenue from higher tuition, and the savings from early retirements, C U N Y's 1995–96 budget was virtually the same as its budget for the previous year. It did not appear that C U N Y was, after all, in a state of financial exigency, which under C U N Y's own bylaws must exist in order to institute retrenchment. On this basis, the University Faculty Senate and the P S C brought and won a court decision at the first judicial level to overturn the board's actions. C U N Y appealed this decision and won its case, permitting the retrenchment to proceed.

1996–1997

While the court actions described above were proceeding, Pataki's multi-year program of tax concessions to the wealthy continued to erode the state's tax base. Therefore, the governor proposed once more to cut C U N Y's budget for the 1996–97 academic year. His plan authorized a tuition increase as well as a reduction in student aid, which would have forced many poor students out of C U N Y. Moreover, faced with another significantly reduced budget, C U N Y's Board of Trustees again declared a state of financial exigency so that retrenchment of faculty could proceed.[6]

This time around the resistance differed critically. The C C S was reincarnated as the Student Liberation Action Movement (S L A M). The S L A M leadership concluded that they could organize on their own terms a massive and successful campaign based on their contacts from the previous year and their record of having organized a large, militant demonstration. With even greater insistence on their principles of the previous year, they refused to tolerate an event in which elected officials, even if they accepted all the event's politics, played any role at all. Although S L A M now agreed to secure a parade permit from the police, they were unwilling to compromise on the route of march with any other group.

This rigidity made it impossible to establish any coalition with the U S S, which had a newly elected and more open leadership. The C C C F S was unavailable as a partner for several reasons. First, too many of its members were unwilling, after the previous year's experience, to cooperate with SLAM. Second, the approach of working in constantly forming and decomposing ad hoc groups seemed unproductive. Third, most of the activists from CCCFS were now devoting their energy to working with the New Caucus of the PSC. They concluded that CUNY could best be defended by working in an organization with resources, a formal responsibility for defending the instructional staff, a relationship to CUNY defined by the PSC-CUNY contract, and the possibility of making common cause with other workers' organizations in the city.

The Student Liberation Action Movement approached the New Caucus to work with it, but the caucus told SLAM leaders that they should deal with the entire PSC, which the New Caucus hoped to bring along. The New Caucus by this time had won elections at additional campuses and now led six of the college chapters (Baruch College, Borough of Manhattan Community College, Brooklyn College, City College, La Guardia Community College, and Queens College), having won every election that it had contested. No longer a small minority within the PSC, the New Caucus persuaded PSC leadership to confer with SLAM in a joint effort to organize a major demonstration for the spring. Unfortunately, SLAM's rigid refusal to negotiate with anyone the terms of the event, particularly the issues of politicians speaking and the route of march, made PSC participation impossible.

The group's increasingly strident rhetoric isolated it. Therefore, the march through Manhattan's streets on March 21, 1996, drew no more than one thousand students and faculty. Rather than presenting a powerful movement for CUNY's defense, the march demonstrated weakness.

Fortunately, the tide both nationally and in the state had turned against unremitting cuts in social services. Responding to this sentiment, the legislature partially restored CUNY's funding, obviating the need for a tuition increase and preserving intact student financial aid. Faculty retrenchment was blocked; however, the lines of retirees were again withdrawn from the university.

As the 1996–97 academic year drew to a close, contradictions emerged within CUNY management. With the expiration of their terms, members of the Board of Trustees appointed by former governor Mario Cuomo left, and new Giuliani and Pataki appointees replaced them. Consistent with the right-wing assault against public services, Anne Paolucci and Herman

Badillo, the new board chairperson and vice-chairperson, respectively, trumpeted that CUNY was failing in its mission of higher education. The board argued that the chancellor's shortcomings lay at the center of the problem.

The board charged that the chancellor presided over degraded standards for student performance, anemic graduation rates, and excess funding of remediation. It asserted that community college graduates often had not mastered English and demanded that this mastery be demonstrated by scores on a controversial CUNY exit exam. Indeed, only days before commencement at Hostos Community College, the board insisted that the graduating students take the CUNY exam and be denied their degrees if they failed it. In fact, few did fail it.

The board's charges were laid at the chancellor's door, and the relentless criticism finally drove out Reynolds, effective September 15, 1997. When the 1997–98 academic year began, CUNY had no chancellor, management was in disarray, and the future course of CUNY was in doubt.

The New Caucus of the PSC

As the crisis receded during the spring 1997 semester, SLAM's forces dissipated. The faculty union organizing effort accelerated, however. In its platform approved at the founding convention on December 2, 1995, the New Caucus declared:

1995–1996 is a critical year in the history of CUNY and our union. Public higher education in New York is under attack—by the government, by the media, by conservative ideologues, and by a university administration intent on consolidating its power and undermining faculty governance.

More than ever, we need organization and resources to defend our livelihoods and profession, to protect the education of our students, and the dreams of hundreds of thousands of New Yorkers for a better future. The Professional Staff Congress—given its financial means, its professional and labor affiliations, and its eight-thousand member base—is the institution best placed to defend CUNY.

The statement went on to explain why it was necessary to form a caucus to vie for power within the union:

But the PSC's leadership group, the City University Unity Caucus (CUUC) is not up to the task. CUUC has become a closed elite that monopolizes virtually all decision-making, that removes membership from policy debates that are the lifeblood of the union, and that equates loyalty to itself as loyalty to the union.

In May 1994, even before the official founding of the New Caucus, the Brooklyn College chapter held a well-attended citywide meeting on part-time faculty in CUNY that began the process of formulating its policy. Like other U.S. universities, CUNY depends on cheap, part-time faculty labor, with more than half of the classes at some units taught by part-timers. Dependence on this large and growing segment of the faculty threatens the existence of the professorate as well as students' access to continuing association with faculty or participation in research and scholarship.[7]

The New Caucus believes that a successful defense of public higher education depends on unity and on mobilizing the entire instructional staff to be active in this fight. This can happen only if the union organizes the unorganized (primarily, part-time faculty) and if the union is committed to "bringing up the bottom," that is, improving the pay, benefits, and working conditions of the most badly treated segments of the workforce (that is, part-time faculty, college laboratory technicians, and lecturers).

Since its consolidation, the New Caucus has spearheaded a CUNY grievance against increasing class size. It gathered the evidence for the court case that enjoined the CUNY administration from proceeding with the 1995–96 retrenchments and related actions. It has rejuvenated moribund campus chapters and transformed them into active defenders of CUNY, its faculty, and its students. In the functioning of the citywide union, however, the New Caucus has only limited effect because it is a minority within the PSC, and the CUUC votes down, often summarily, its resolutions at the delegate assembly.

In April 1997, the New Caucus ran a slate for the twenty-one central offices of the union (president, first vice-president, secretary, treasurer, and so on). The CUUC caucus won the election by a margin of two to one, maintaining its majority in the delegate assembly and its control of the union's central office.

The New Caucus believes that for an organization only one-and-a-half years old, it did well in the first contested P S C election in twenty-three years. It developed a C U N Y-wide operational capacity, achieved recognition, forced a discussion of issues, and, perhaps most important, made contacts at campuses throughout C U N Y for future electoral efforts. As the fall 1997 semester began, the New Caucus renewed the process of organizing its forces for assuming the direction of the union and for the defense of C U N Y.

Notes

This article will appear in *Radical Teacher*, no. 53 (in press).

1 Huge cuts in all social service areas accompanied the reduction of C U N Y's budget. Pataki had proposed and the state legislature had voted a massive tax reduction program that gave maximum benefit to the wealthy taxpayers of the state.

2 In the fall of 1994, a third of C U N Y senior college students and almost one-half of community college students came from households with incomes of less than twenty thousand dollars per year. Approximately a third of the students worked full-time, and another third worked part-time. A fifth of the senior college students and almost a third of the community college students supported children ("Undergraduate Student Experience Survey," C U N Y Office of Institutional Research and Analysis, 1994).

3 The New Caucus is a progressive, activist caucus within the P S C. By spring 1995, it had won elections on only two campuses and was a minority force within the P S C and thus could not direct its policy.

4 Referred to as the Black and Puerto Rican Caucus, this group met irregularly, and although it had significant political strengths, it could not pull out a large number of people for a demonstration in the streets. Moreover, by this time the Puerto Rican legislators who had formerly met with the caucus were no longer doing so.

5 The chancellor and the board removed from C U N Y the lines of both those faculty and staff who retired and those who were retrenched. Furthermore, even with the ameliorating effect of retirements, many instructional staff were retrenched, for example, 168 instructional staff at senior colleges. The tuition increase constituted a move toward privatization. In the 1989–90 academic year, student tuition contributed 21 percent of the community college

budgets, while in 1996–97 the percentage covered by tuition swelled to 43 percent. The comparable figures for the senior colleges for the same years are essentially the same, 20 percent and 44 percent.

6 At that point, the lower court had not yet found that the board's declaration of financial exigency for the 1995–96 year (on the basis of the governor's proposal but prior to the legislative vote) violated CUNY bylaws and was, therefore, illegal.

7 The PSC has a contractual right to a dues checkoff for all members of the instructional staff. Under CUUC, the PSC exercises this right for all instructional staff except part-timers. Naturally, this practice leads full-time faculty and staff, whose dues are collected anyway, to join the union, but few part-time faculty, whose dues are not automatically collected, choose to join. In fact, under the CUUC leadership, part-timers are rarely informed of their right to join the union, and obstacles are put in the way of their obtaining membership cards. The caucus occasionally makes noises, especially at election time, about the importance of part-time faculty's issues, but in the absence of a significant part-timer membership to pressure it, CUUC does little or nothing for this segment of the instructional staff. Instead of fostering unity within the membership ranks, it abandons a large and growing segment and therefore encourages the administration to employ this cheap labor force rather than hire professors. Similarly, CUUC does little to bring up the pay scale or to improve the working conditions of other badly treated constituent groups (for example, college laboratory technicians and lecturers). These CUUC policies reduce the size and unity of the PSC and erode its power.

Faculty, Students, and Political Engagement

Jeremy Smith

Did you, too, O friend, suppose democracy was only for elections, for politics, and for a party name? I say democracy is only of use . . . there that it may pass on and come to its flower and fruits in manners, in the highest forms of interaction between men, and their beliefs—in religion, literature, colleges, and schools— democracy in all public and private life.—Walt Whitman, *Democratic Vistas*

Think about the kind of world you want to live and work in. What do you need to know to help build that world? Demand that your teachers teach you that.— Peter Kropotkin, quoted in Paul Goodman, "The Duty of Professionals"

In 1978, Irving Kristol and other prominent neoconservative activists launched the Institute for Educational Affairs (IEA). With an initial budget of four hundred thousand dollars, and major support from corporations such as Coca-Cola, Dow Chemical, General Electric, and K-Mart, the IEA began promoting scholarship that defended corporate interests and provided intellectual justifications for capitalism. The goal of IEA grantees, such as the Ethics and Public Policy Center, was to research and assess "the attack on the multinational firms by university groups and so-called public interest lobbies."[1] The IEA's program also included career promotion for conservative assistant professors and graduate students and the publication of books and a network of "alternative" student newspapers.

The IEA was followed by a series of organizations dedicated to mobilizing intellectual opinion in favor of market capitalism and "Western civilization." Accuracy in Academia recruited students and professors to spy on progressive faculty and then used the information to compile a database on "left-wing propagandists." The National Association of Scholars (NAS) was founded in 1987 to assist faculty in organizing conservative caucuses within professional organizations and against multicultural and feminist programs and affirmative action. By 1992, NAS had fourteen hundred members and a budget of $708,000.[2]

By 1993, corporations and right-wing philanthropies were pumping at least $20 million a year into campus-based think tanks, endowed "free enterprise" chairs, student and faculty organizations, research centers, and curricula based on "Western" values.[3] By the mid-1990s, the revamped IEA—which in 1990 changed its name to the Madison Center for Education Affairs—has an estimated annual budget of $3.5 million.

The Progressive Faculty Response (or Lack Thereof)

When I began college in 1988, the term "political correctness" was just appearing in op-eds and books. By the time of the Gulf War, progressives were constantly on the defensive. The right-wing juggernaut had arrived.

As an undergraduate student activist, I was reluctant to challenge faculty to be more politically engaged. First, I was intimidated. Second, when I did try to recruit faculty to the movement, many of them said that their activism was expressed solely and sufficiently through teaching or publishing; still others felt that activism was incompatible with academic "objectivity"; others said that they just didn't have the time. Many of them, I knew, shared my convictions; I was therefore puzzled by their apathy and inactivity. If right-wing faculty could be so organized and visible, why then couldn't progressive faculty respond in kind?

One night, during a strategy session with two graduate student leaders on campus, I expressed a desire to begin organizing faculty through our student organization. My comrades looked aghast. "They can organize themselves," I was told. But year after year, I waited in vain for progressive faculty to take public action on university downsizing, racism, and tuition increases. While some faculty did act as individuals, they never acted as a group and so were never powerful or even influential. At best, they were merely interesting.

In the winter of 1995, in the wake of Republican congressional victories and a wave of antiabortion terrorism in Florida and Massachusetts, I joined the staff of the Center for Campus Organizing (CCO), a national clearinghouse based in Cambridge, Massachusetts. Within weeks of my arrival, hundreds of campuses were alive with protests centered around the House Republican Contract with America. From New York to Ohio to California, faculty, administrators, and students worked together to speak out against cuts to education and social welfare. In February 1995 the CCO issued a call for a nationally coordinated Day of Campus Action against the Contract with America, which involved more than one hundred campuses. It is estimated that twenty-five to thirty thousand students and at least three thousand faculty participated directly in demonstrations, teach-ins, or pickets. The nationwide protests were a rare example of faculty and even administrators acting outside their institutional roles, for themselves and in solidarity with students.

While faculty who participate in protests such as the Day of Action against the Contract with America have been and continue to be criticized for violating their "professional trust," I have come to feel that they are in fact acting as authentic professionals by refusing to conform to expectations that are defined by fundamentally conservative ideological forces. Paul Goodman writes that "since it is the genius of our society to co-opt the professions to subserve money and authority, for a professional to be authentic means to be in conflict. And since the system of institutions is interlocked and centralized, it is impossible to be in conflict without being gradually involved with general reform and even revolution."[4]

The CCO, almost alone among campus organizations, actively cultivates cooperation between faculty and their students. The CCO's full-time, paid staff is composed entirely of current or recent students, with an average age of approximately twenty-four. The eight-person board of directors, along with an extensive network of advisory boards, is composed primarily of scholars from universities all over the country. In addition, the vast majority of CCO's paying members are faculty, and we maintain a network of activist faculty through an e-mail discussion list called CAN-FAC.[5] Faculty are also the primary readers of CCO's journal, *Infusion*, and many of its other publications. Prominent academics on CCO's chief advisory board include Frances Fox Piven, Mel King, and Nobel laureates Bernard Lown and George Wald.

CCO has benefited from the ferment of the 1990s among both teachers and students. But during the three years of our existence, CCO has wrestled with the same practical questions that have vexed student movements since at least the 1960s: What is the state of higher education, and how does it affect our means and ends as a social movement? What is the role of students, faculty, and other members of the campus community in social change movements, and what are the prospects for cooperation between these disparate groups? What vision and long-term political goals do we collectively embrace in our short-term political struggles? And, finally, what strategies and issues will help us to achieve our long-term goals?

The Right, Corporations, and the University

"Political correctness" was not an act of God; it was an extremely effective propaganda tool created by right-wing think tanks, disseminated by a well-funded, right-wing campus press, publicized in books and op-eds by right-wing journalists and scholars, and later adopted by many so-called liberals. *Politically correct* was not a description of a movement but a tool for discrediting anyone who raised issues of human equality and environmental justice.

The political correctness campaign was also intended to generate doubts about the intellectual and social viability of new student populations (women, blacks, Hispanics) and is directly linked to attempts to shrink the student population by slashing financial aid and raising tuition. Heather MacDonald of the right-wing Manhattan Institute argues that the City University of New York (CUNY), with its grand working-class and immigrant traditions, "has a very radical affirmative action program for unqualified minority students. . . . College is a privilege; if [budget] cuts mean these unqualified students are no longer able to go to college, that would be a good thing." [6] Trinity College professor Paul Lauter points out that "access [to higher education] can be restricted only if one can . . . argue that restriction is a function of economic forces beyond our control and if one can somehow make college politically suspect." [7] That argument was political correctness, joined with the campaign against budget deficits.

The flip side of the political correctness campaign is "corporate correctness"—the fundamental restructuring of colleges and universities to serve the needs of private enterprise. As politicians and their corporate sugar daddies have cut federal and state funding for education, colleges have turned increasingly to friendly corporate relations departments to fund basic programs. This process, which began in earnest in 1980 with the election of Ronald Reagan, has escalated to a point where university presidents often sit on multiple corporate boards.

This is fine with big business, which has turned to universities for research, cheap labor, and cultural influence. The downsizing of academia has paralleled corporate downsizing: because companies are cutting employees and reducing job training and recruitment, big business has demanded that universities develop more "job-based" curricula, producing students who are better indoctrinated and more technically proficient.

Universities have developed internship programs and curricula in response to corporate advice and financial assistance. The Ford Corporation has worked with five universities to develop a "Ford curriculum." At Arizona State, graduate students are working for American Express to develop computer programming. The president of Lehigh University told the *New York Times*, "These corporations are ever more competitive . . . and they're saying, 'We can't afford to hire someone and then take two years training them how to function—you have to do it.' I've been in higher education a long time, and I've never seen such fundamental change in undergraduate education as what I'm seeing now." [8]

The result is bigger classes, schemes to shorten matriculation and en-roll more students, cutbacks on tenure and salaries, the elimination of "unprofitable" courses and departments with low enrollment, and the commodification of research and writing.

This situation, of course, is part of the much-noted, worldwide trend toward the decline of nation-states and the rise of transnational capital. Universities are becoming disengaged from serving the cold war defini-tion of the "national interest" and are attaching themselves to corporate interests. The resulting crisis in higher education has been paralleled in the wider society by falling wages, welfare cuts, the breakup of communi-ties, huge increases in the prison population, and the commercialization of cultural expression.

Resisting Attacks on Higher Education

In October 1996, the Center for Campus Organizing and Teachers for a Democratic Culture convened a meeting of faculty to discuss this situa-tion. The conference, held at the Massachusetts Institute of Technology (MIT), was unusual for two reasons: first, it was not an intellectual exer-cise but a gathering of activists interested in concrete strategic problems; second, the planning and publicity was carried out at the initiative of stu-dents by both students and faculty connected to the Center for Campus Organizing.

At the meeting (which received favorable coverage in the Chronicle of Higher Education), speakers and participants advanced an analysis very similar to the one I have just made. "The same forces that are trying to bring down the standard of living of American workers are trying to de-stroy higher education," said Michael Zweig, a professor of economics at the State University of New York at Stony Brook.[9] While the discussion was often unfocused, a few key issues emerged, which I highlight below:

—Educational downsizing. According to polls for the recent presidential election, education ranked as voters' number one concern, and Clinton won largely on the strength of a (slightly) better education policy. Standing up against cuts that will hurt both workers and the quality of education—and advocating an education that will be relevant and accessible to working- and middle-class families—offers tremendous potential for building coalitions both on and off campus.

—*Federal and state budget priorities.* The Right has succeeded in defining the parameters of debate on public budgets by turning capital gains and corporate taxes, the military, and a balanced budget into sacred cows. Progressives can wrest it back by presenting constructive alternatives, such as progressive tax policy, moderate budget deficits as a tool of economic growth, and incremental cutting of the military budget with incentives for industries that convert from war to civilian production. Budget issues can be raised by campus groups in the context of struggles around tuition, pay cuts, the elimination of tenure, and the dumbing-down of education.

—*Access to education.* Faculty, students, and campus workers must refuse, in word and deed, the idea that education is a road to privilege. By fighting for affirmative action, financial aid, low or no tuition, and multicultural programs, we can ensure that everyone feels able and welcome at different levels of higher education. It is also necessary to extend support to primary and secondary education, because children and teenagers need equality of education in order to reach a "higher" education.

The conference also highlighted the need for an organized labor movement on the corporate campus. Student participants from the 1996 AFL-CIO Union Summer, activists in the spring 1995 CUNY struggle, and veterans of the Yale strike were on hand to describe the potential (and pitfalls) of cooperation between academia and labor. One model of cooperation is the Academic Committee for Workplace Justice, which collected four hundred signatures from academics around the country for a letter that was sent to Yale president Richard Levin, urging the Yale administration to bargain in good faith with its striking clerical, technical, service, and graduate employees. Another model is the Center for Campus Organizing's work with the Jobs with Justice coalition and the national AFL-CIO on organizing labor conferences for students, recruiting young people into Union Summer, editing publications for the AFL-CIO on student-labor organizing, and cocreating the New England Student Labor Solidarity Network.

The MIT meeting was part of a larger CCO strategy to organize faculty and students as part of the same national movement. As a national organization, the Center for Campus Organizing can do what more "decentralized" networks cannot: raise money from large philanthropies, concentrate resources around specific campaigns, create a sense of national movement among members and advisers, and implement coordinated strategies.

Merging Theory and Action

The situation is clear: conservative academics, at the behest of corporate power and the religious Right, have consciously organized to narrow the parameters of campus debate and limit access to education. Progressive academics, if they are to gain lost ground and then advance, must respond in kind and in alliance with groups inside and outside academe, including labor and the local community.

This campaign to free the university from corporate and military interference and turn it toward building a better world is long overdue. If we are serious about creating an educational system that is popular, democratic, socially responsible, relevant, and relatively independent of money and power, then we must act to defend that vision.

The merger of theory with action is an old goal, perhaps the oldest in the history of the Left. The tension between ideals and the material world is the engine that drives our movement. Progressive academics, if they want to be worthy of the name, must express their theoretical work through direct action and political engagement.

For some professors, this is a bitter pill to swallow. Questions arise: What about our careers? We have tenure and job security to think about. We must publish serious scholarly work, and that takes time and dedication that can be undermined by political activism. Also, what about my professional obligations to be scholarly and objective?

My response is as follows: When paper workers in Decatur, Illinois, went out on strike for two grueling years, don't you think they were concerned with their job security and families? When black students sat down in Southern lunch counters to protest segregation, don't you figure they had other interests to pursue? And when students and their teachers spoke out against injustice in places like South Africa and El Salvador, isn't it possible they were afraid for their futures, even their very lives?

The times demand activism, and activism, unfortunately, involves trade-offs. It also involves uncomfortable (for some, excruciating) questions: How are "professional standards" shaped by power and money? How are they shaped to maintain the status quo? Does my status as an academic divorce me from the way most people live? How does the academic rat race restrict my freedom to think and then act on my thinking?

The point is not that professors should harness themselves to political movements; nor is it that they should reject their professional status in favor of a more "proletarian" lifestyle. I am instead pleading with academics to act as what Paul Goodman calls "authentic professionals"—women and men who are autonomous, ethical, iconoclastic, and unwilling to lower their standards for the sake of status. Professors must engage in the conflict with power that authenticity demands—not just in the realm of ideas but in practical politics as well.

What, then, are the practical implications of faculty activism? What, concretely, can they do?

The Needs of the Student Movement

The young people now entering the movement are arriving on the defensive. The big priorities are fighting the right wing in Congress and on campus, protesting tuition increases and declining educational access, and defending the gains of the civil rights and feminist movements. For the most part, students are organizing without guidance or outside support—unlike their right-wing counterparts.

We cannot yet speak of a broad and effective student movement that commands the enthusiasm and loyalty of even a "prophetic minority" of young people, but we can take note of the prerequisites for such a movement: a core of highly committed and knowledgeable leaders, primarily veterans of feminist and environmental struggles; the existence of well-developed, largely autonomous national organizations; and social contradictions that are pushing many young people to question the status quo.

At the Center for Campus Organizing, involving faculty in a "student" organization was initially seen as insurance against the usual instability of student groups. We worked to link student and faculty through our local networks and on a national level. Faculty, we felt, could provide experience, maturity, and knowledge to young student activists. This much turned out to be true. As CCO has matured, however, we have also discovered a natural political alliance between the two groups, as well as a source of financial support.

While it is an article of faith among fund-raising professionals that academics are notoriously low donors to political and service organizations (relative to income), they do have far more financial resources than students and youth. Newer youth-led social change organizations, such as CCO or YouthAction, rely disproportionately on philanthropic foundations for financial support, sometimes for as much as 90 percent of their funding, with only small numbers of paying members. As a result of direct-mail campaigns and organizing, faculty memberships now supply the bulk of CCO's small nonfoundation income.

Because discontinuity is a fact of life for student organizations (and because students have limited emotional and political experience), it is absolutely essential for them to have mentors. By attending the occasional meeting, speaking at events, and being available to student leaders, faculty advisers can provide institutional memory, a friend in the faculty union, and continuity from year to year.

The value of a strong faculty adviser was illustrated to me during a visit to Lehigh University, where during the 1980s there had been a potent activist organization called the Progressive Student Alliance (PSA). After the Gulf War, the PSA faded briefly from the campus scene, until its faculty adviser, Professor Ted Morgan, imparted it to a new generation of students. The last time I was there, the PSA was doing excellent work on campus.

The Need for Self-Organization

In addition to mentoring student activists, faculty have a responsibility to fight for their own interests while showing solidarity with the interests of other workers. This demands organization and strategy.

There are eight concrete things that faculty can do to get organized:

1. *Support local and national campus organizations.* Faculty have deeper pockets and more personal maturity than their students, who do not always see the need

to part with movie-and-pizza money. Therefore, they have a responsibility to provide monetary support to the local and national organizations that speak out for progressive education.

2. *Join a labor union and support labor.* Faculty and janitors are both employees; it is only a question of one feeling superior to the other. If you institution has a faculty union, then join; if it doesn't have a union, then organize one. In addition, respect the labor of those who clean the toilets, change the light-bulbs, and type department correspondence. When they strike, refuse to cross picket lines, and give to strike funds.

 Labor has political and financial muscle as well; they can mount serious campaigns that will assist faculty and students with their on-campus struggles. It is also important for students to learn to use the tools of a labor movement, to help them survive in twenty-first-century America.

3. *Form progressive caucuses within departments and professional groups.* Politics, as the saying goes, starts with the person next to you. Talking to other academics, administrators, and campus workers—one-on-one and through mediated forums—is the first step in creating community and raising questions about institutions and disciplines.

4. *Build a student movement, and link it to the community.* The staff and board of the Center for Campus Organizing, using the New Left and right-wing student movements as models, have discussed the following strategies for rebuilding a student movement:

 —Bring students on different campuses together regionally or nationally to develop the sense of participation in a national movement.

 —Introduce students to administrative and fund-raising skills for maintaining membership organizations while still in school. This will help campus organizations sustain themselves and equip students to contribute to the stability of grassroots nonprofit groups after they graduate.

 —Connect young people with paid internships, apprenticeships, and entry-level jobs in the social justice movement.

 —Link youth training, electoral efforts, and community groups so that the volunteer base for a political campaign can be used between elections and so that electoral campaigns do not have to start from scratch.

 —Weave activism into the fabric of everyday life, instead of exalting it to heroic proportions and making it the property of the vanguard.[10]

 —Bring students into contact with young people who are not in college, particularly those in the poorest and most oppressed sectors of our society. This grounds them and gives them a sense of what is at stake.

—Form a mass radical national organization, along the lines of Students for a Democratic Society, which can develop a nationwide progressive voice on campus, link disparate campus constituencies, and develop a common program for educational reform.

—Develop allies off campus who can provide resources, political muscle, and a place to go after graduation. In the 1990s, potential allies include philanthropic foundations, labor, and the progressive nonprofit sector.

5. *Expose the antidemocratic agenda of the corporate and religious Right.* Faculty have credibility and access to the media that many progressives do not have; through op-eds and media appearances, they can explain how and why right-wing economics, social policies, and cultural vision will make all our lives more difficult and boring than they already are. Conservatives have gone a long way on small ideas; we need only to take measurements on exactly how small they are.

6. *Organize across different institutions and geographic boundaries.* Struggles that confine themselves to one campus, one city, or one state are doomed to failure, because the problems are nationwide. Organizing that pits the Ivy League against large public schools, or four-year universities against community colleges, is ultimately self-defeating. Alliances are formed on two levels: informally through one-on-one relationships between leaders, and in formal cooperation between organizations. They are expressed through joint action and shared resources and manifest in the power to influence attitudes and public policy outcomes.

7. *Build coalitions outside of campus.* When a university downsizes, who gets hurt? The lost jobs and slashed salaries affect both the campus and the community outside of campus. In addition, working people have a stake in maintaining quality and access to education.

8. *Integrate political struggle into daily life.* Go to demonstrations when they are called; sign petitions; get arrested once in a while; get involved with the community.

The Need for Ideas

Last year, I was drinking beer with the editor of a well-known magazine of cultural criticism, who is also a professor of history in Chicago. I told him, "T——, your magazine is really great for pointing out how old forms of rebellion are co-opted. But what about suggesting new forms of rebellion? We know what has failed; now we have to ask what will succeed."

His reply was telling: "Right now, it's soft-headed to think about new forms of rebellion. The triumph of global capital is so complete that it is useless to imagine a better society."

Now, I think he had a point, but I don't think that it's a very useful point. We all know that things are bad. Describing exactly how bad they are is both cathartic and useful, but if we stop there then we have not gone forward. T—— was also speaking with the voice of privilege. It is well and fine for college professors to say that rebellion is pointless, but many people in our society have no choice but to rebel. Their survival depends on their ability to say "No" to exploitation, racism, sexism, colonialism, and daily alienation.

I am sorry to say that many academics are in a similar state of mind, which I can only liken to shadowboxing in a floodlit room. When numerous progressive academics at Yale University crossed picket lines, they were expressing a cynicism that infects their students and gives strength to a strikebreaking administration.

The apathy and cynicism of academics are enemies that must be fought. Yes, we have experienced defeats, and it is hard to know where to strike back. But we can't shrink from rebellion or from imagining alternatives to oppression.

I have often thought that faith means admitting "I don't know" and then proceeding as though you do. Our lives are based on faith—not because we are lemmings but because we are human. Despite all evidence to the contrary, I have to believe that human beings of different races and cultures can find ways to work together; that men and women can coexist and give each other strength; and that violence, which will be used for as long as it is useful, will become obsolete. Most of all, I have to believe that we can replace authoritarian economics, both socialist and capitalist, with a system that will allow women and men to survive and reach their full potential.

A larger vision and a shared program are necessary in the short-term struggle because they assist people of different classes and races in understanding one another's needs and provide a basis for working together. Common ideas, carried by common interests, can bring disparate communities together for a common struggle.

It does not need to be pointed out that academics and independent intellectuals are, if not the generators, then at least the receptacles, interpreters, and disseminators of the ideas that will carry us forward. Academic research, particularly in economics and the social sciences, needs to be popularized and put to use by social movements. Ideas—technological, social, economic—are the basis for a better world; to matter, they must be learned, taught, and tested in the real world. Only when academics perform this function can they legitimately claim to be authentic professionals.

Notes

1 Sara Diamond, "Endowing the Right-Wing Academic Agenda," in *The Guide to Uncovering the Right on Campus*, ed. Rich Cowan and Dalya Massachi (Cambridge, Mass.: Center for Campus Organizing, 1994), 14.

2 Ibid., 14.

3 Joel Bleifuss, "Doing Right by the Campus Left," *In These Times*, January 22, 1995, 12.

4 Paul Goodman, "The Duty of Professionals," in *Drawing the Line: The Political Essays of Paul Goodman*, ed. Taylor Stoehr (New York: Free Life Editions, 1977), 173.

5 To contact the Center for Campus Organizing, e-mail cco@igc.apc.org; www.cco.org; phone 617-725-2886; or write CCO, 165 Friend St., #1, Boston, MA 02114.

6 Paul Lauter, " 'PC' and the Attack on Higher Education," in *The Guide to Uncovering the Right on Campus*, ed. Cowan and Massachi, 29.

7 "Quote Unquote," *Infusion* 1 (spring 1996): 15.

8 Kirk Johnson, "In the Changed Landscape of Recruiting, Academic and Corporate Worlds Merge," *New York Times*, December 4, 1996, B13.

9 Scott Heller, "Educators on the Left Organize to Fight Attacks on Academe, Which They See as Part of a Bigger Effort to Divide Society," *Chronicle of Higher Education*, October 11, 1996, A12.

10 The first five items in this list are drawn from an unpublished article by Rich Cowan, "Developing a Youth Strategy: Lessons from the Right."

Need a Break from Your Dissertation?
Organize a Union!

William Vaughn

Unions Are a Grad's Best Friend

I am a union goon. No one says so to my face, but I'm sure that's what some of my friends must be thinking. For the past five years, I've worked to bring union representation to the approximately fifty-four hundred graduate employees of the University of Illinois at Urbana-Champaign (UIUC). The union to which I proudly belong, the Graduate Employees' Organization (G.E.O.), won a representation vote 1,633 to 906 in April 1997. For reasons I'll explain presently, this has not meant immediate recognition from our employers at UIUC. Our fight continues, just as it does on campuses across the country. In the hopes of making those efforts easier and more sustainable, I'd like to share what I've learned from my time in the UIUC campaign. If I can't quite incite you to fanaticism, I'll at least try to demonstrate why you *should* become a goon: not because you'll have any opportunities to rough somebody up but because, with the state of graduate employment nationwide, sooner or later you'll have to learn to take a punch.

Like many of my colleagues in the English program, I came to UIUC because of the assistantship I was offered. As a nontraditional applicant (my undergrad degree is in advertising), I felt fortunate to receive any kind of support for my studies. In our department, those entering the M.A. program are typically guaranteed seven years of funding, whereas those admitted into the Ph.D. stage are guaranteed six. For most people, that means one year of teaching one course per semester, followed by five or six more of teaching two per term (followed by—no, I won't get into the *"visiting* teaching associate" or "postdoc" situations here; that's another article). One can typically expect to get *some* time off during one's years in the program, especially within the dissertation stage, but the thing to stress here is that most grad employees in our program hold assignments equivalent to what a professor holds, except that we are credited with two-thirds appointments, whereas professors are—mysteriously— described as being *full-time.* I guess it's because of all the extra energy we have (that is, we can teach three classes, even grading-heavy introductory writing classes, in the same time it takes a professor to manage two).

I want to stress here that most English grad employees *do* feel lucky to get this level of support. One of the signal aspects of the G.E.O. is that it arose not out of some cult of the oppressed but rather from a genuine sense on the part of most teachers that what they were doing was *work,* plain and simple, and that, furthermore, we deserved the same rights as anyone else who worked for the university. This is an important point and bears elaborating on. A school such as UIUC simply couldn't function without the labor of its teaching, research, and graduate assistants (not to mention the many so-called hourly employees, whose working conditions are worse yet). In my own department, for example, graduate employees perform approximately two-thirds of the undergraduate teaching (so *that's* why they are called two-thirds appointments). If you want to radicalize a group of people, place them in a radical situation. The G.E.O. was born in the English department because the circumstances of our work are so extreme. But the union flourished because what we experienced in English was just one point on a continuum of vital labor performed by grad employees.

So You've Decided to Form a Union

It is your status as an employee, then, that makes a union the right solution to your problems. At UIUC, those problems were inadequate health coverage and the lack of such things as a standardized, impartial grievance procedure or contracts that specified terms and conditions of employment. Of course, we weren't being paid all that well either, and some grad employee unions have been able to win significant salary hikes for their members. But money was never the principal issue for the G.E.O., in part because it can become a (misleadingly) divisive issue (well-off grads, and there are some, will accuse you of income leveling). You'll have to decide what is important to your population. Learning those issues should be one of the key purposes of the many conversations you will have as you organize.

Whatever those issues turn out to be, though, and however you formulate them as reasons for voting union, there are at least five reasons why you should not begin a campaign. The first reason is *trendiness*. Face it—I wouldn't be writing this piece and you wouldn't be reading it if grad employee unions, and academic labor issues in general, didn't happen to be "hot" at the moment. That's all well and good, and we in the movement appreciate whatever support and attention we can garner, but building a union, as somebody once put it, is the toughest job you'll ever love. If you are not sufficiently committed to it and if your potential membership is not primed for your message, being trendy will not get you very far. This is perhaps less of a problem for those starting a drive than it is for the activists you'll need to be developing. Realize that a lot of people will *say* they want to help, and may mean it sincerely, but don't be surprised when some of them seem more interested in being associated with something cool than with actually making it work. This may seem like a trivial concern, but you will be battling apathy and indifference from day one, and you especially need to guard against it among your core activists.

But the trendiness problem extends beyond just the laxity of your alleged supporters. Is your campus *as a whole* ready for a campaign? It takes a lot of education to convince people they should want a union, perhaps especially when those people themselves are highly educated and think of unions as a "working-class" phenomenon. Plus, you don't want to be starting your card drive before you have substantial—ideally, universal—name recognition and know what issues are going to motivate people (in other words, what issues are important to them). These things take time. The G.E.O. existed for two years before we began our drive. We used that time to learn from the people we wanted to represent, to build our name recognition, and to develop our leadership and activists. Don't try to jump-start the process because you are anxious to cash in on a trend. On a small campus, you may need less time, but when you are dealing with fifty-four hundred employees and an even greater number of grad students as a whole, you must be willing to be patient.

Another reason not to unionize is because you expect to get some *benefits*. I know, I know—you thought that was the only reason people ever did it. But remember that you are part of a terminal workforce, and unless you're just beginning grad school when you start your union, the chances are quite good that you won't be around when people start benefiting from that first contract. In Illinois we are subject to a particularly noxious piece of (anti-)labor law, which prevents us from organizing in a way that would obligate our employer to recognize us. We're still fighting the ruling that screwed us, but those kinds of court battles drag on for years. Otherwise, we'll either have to get the legislation rewritten (Ha!) or *compel* our administration to deal with us. Whatever happens will take still more time.

Schools in such states as New York and California have had to fight similar long-term wars of recognition. Of course, you may be lucky and work in a state with favorable labor law. And it's quite often the case that an administration will start throwing bones to ward off a campaign, so you might see some benefits that way. (At UIUC, that's how we got our dental plan.) But you can't rely on such successes, so my advice is to generate your enthusiasm out of something other than the prospect of tangible benefits: the rightness of what you're doing; the prospect of benefits for *future* workers; and the experience of intangible benefits you'll accrue from building something with other people. Those may sound a bit lofty and implausibly noble, but for many of us, that's why we became educators in the first place. If you can explicate a poem to a roomful of people who are not tangibly rewarding you at that moment, because you believe the meaning of that poem can be important to them, if not now but someday, then you can certainly build a union for the same reasons.

But whatever you do, don't build one out of a sense of *ownership*. That is, don't put so much of yourself into the cause that you obscure both the equally legitimate claims of fellow and future employees and the best interests of the union in the abstract. Another name for this problem is "founder's disease," and it often impedes the development of new leadership, because people are intimidated or put off by those who seem to wield greater authority simply because they were there first. Just as important, though, a false sense of ownership can wind up costing you in the same ways as will an unjustified expectation of benefits. Building a union should be an empowering, not an embittering, experience. Keep your perspective. You only own one share, and just as you can't take all the credit for the successes, you shouldn't take all the blame for the setbacks.

The fourth reason not to unionize is because you're invested in a *single issue*. (Here I mean something like a benefit; recognition, your real goal, is a more abstract concept.) Several things can go wrong here. One is that you may be the only one pushing that particular issue. Another is that the issue may be addressed prior to achieving recognition (for example, the dental plan at UIUC)—then what do you do? Perhaps most important, what if the driving force behind a campaign is a core of people animated by one specific goal? Eventually, those people are going to move on. Then what happens, if you haven't sufficiently inculcated in your membership a respect for what unions are about? I have in mind here a specific case of a union that won recognition rather quickly and easily but still didn't have a contract two years later because the membership could not enforce their victory. They had been led by a small group with one specific goal; when that group—and their issue—departed, they left behind no organization to carry on the general business of the union, which meant that the activists who remained had no basis by which to mobilize—or, more important, to *increase*—their membership. In other words, they were faced with the prospect of having to rebuild the union from the ground up, even though they'd won their election. Don't make this same mistake!

The final reason not to form a union is because you're *unhappy with grad school.* There are plenty of reasons to believe that having clear boundaries between your work and your scholarship will improve your life. By the same token, your adviser may breathe easier as well. But a union won't make you like your adviser more; it won't improve the quality of your dissertation; and it won't make your campus town look more like New York or Chicago. It goes without saying that grad school is a stressful—and, unfortunately for some, even traumatic—experience. Some of that is to be expected, some not. But a union serves you in your capacity as an *employee.* If you don't like being in grad school, organizing a union can certainly distract you, but it's never going to solve the underlying problem. I've seen enough bitter people in my seven years as a grad student to know what this kind of life can do to you. And I've read testimonials from union activists that say more about their unhappiness with Ivy League culture than they do about addressing employment concerns.

As an organizer, I welcome all the help I can get. So I'd never refuse assistance from someone who was motivated more out of distaste for graduate school than dissatisfaction as a worker. But, invariably, people who are grounded in that kind of bitterness either burn out quickly or communicate too much of what is really bothering them to those they are attempting to recruit. And at that point such activists are hurting the union.

Clearly, the near pathological climate among grad students faced with a relentlessly dismal job market does intersect with the large-scale academic labor crises of which grad employee unions are one method of redress. So there is a legitimate employment-related basis for much of the bitterness I describe here. But I strongly suspect that people who are unhappy in grad school aren't going to be much happier as professors. They *may* be happier as union organizers, in which case I would urge them to quit cold turkey and concentrate on the thing they love. But don't expect a union to remake the structure of academia at large or your department in particular. Don't organize to punish someone; do so to reward the people who deserve it.

Before the Beginning

Because unions are such a good idea for graduate employees, don't be surprised to learn that previous generations of your peers have tried to start one. This was definitely the case at UIUC, where interest in unionizing dates back as far as the early 1970s, those heady days when the unions at Madison and Ann Arbor first began to coalesce. But interest is one thing, and actually building a union, quite another. While there had always been individuals interested in addressing the employment concerns of graduate students, and even earlier incarnations of the G.E.O., the move to unionize didn't begin for real until the fall of 1993, and the formal step of conducting an authorization card drive didn't commence until two years after that. What took so long?

There are three enemies to a nascent graduate employee union. The first is *isolation*. Although I can't speak for those proto-activists of the early 1970s, I know from our experience twenty years later that a movement takes off—literally, but also in terms of excitement and energy—only when people from various disciplines come together. You can't build a union out of one department, and the longer the interest remains within that one discipline, the easier it is to burn out or just turn bitter. It is not just the difficulty of resolving employment issues at the department level but also that suffocating sense of specialization we've all felt when, no matter how much we like and respect our colleagues, we long for an academic worldview with different tricks, new perspectives. The inevitable sense of sameness you can get from your home department militates against the urgency for change that a union can afford.

Given that, it shouldn't be surprising that a lot of the energy for new unions comes out of such programs as American studies, cultural studies, and geography, which are themselves intellectually volatile at the moment and open to people who court new ways of thinking. Similarly, one of the best ways to find other interested union activists is by participating in interdisciplinary bodies or programs. People with the intellectual curiosity and need to expand the boundaries of their own field are ripe for the kind of interdisciplinary work that organizing represents. Here at UIUC, for example, the Unit for Criticism and Interpretive Theory has been a crucial nexus for G.E.O. activism, because it is a space where people from different disciplines come together to share new approaches and ideas. Look for opportunities like this on your own campus, and if they don't exist, make them happen. You'll profit intellectually and from an organizing standpoint.

Yet having said this, I'm sensitive to the charge that I argue for a kind of vanguard or at least imply that some grad employees are better suited for union organizing or leadership. On the first point, I would emphasize that I'm talking here of what it is like to *start* a union. While diversity is an ongoing concern for any such organization, it's simply the case that the initial energy for a grad employee union will tend to come from certain places—that is, from among the disciplines represented by the readership of this volume. Once you have a viable organizing unit together, though, you definitely need to get beyond that early cell, and you will discover interest in places you never thought possible.

As for who makes the best organizers and leaders, I can only fall back on what I've seen within the G.E.O. and other unions. Some of our earliest members were from physics, and among our current officers are a law student, a mechanical engineer, and a kinesiologist. But the vast majority of active *organizers* has always come from a relatively small pool of disciplines: English, history, sociology, philosophy—you get the idea. It's not worth belaboring the reasons why—and I'll repeat, perhaps defensively, you *must* and *will* find supporters from all across campus—but some kind of disciplinary skew figures to be inevitable in your organization. You can combat that trend, but you're unlikely to defeat it entirely.

I would simply stress here the tremendous boost I felt when we first started to connect with *anyone* who wasn't from English. Whether we added these people through classes or other social pursuits (for example, food co-ops, political organizations, and so on) we had in common, newsgroups or other electronic meeting places, or plain old-fashioned flyering, it was an incredibly energizing and validating experience just to be together in the same room for the first time. More than four years later, many of these people are still active in the G.E.O. That's a testament both to the rightness of the cause and to the bonds you are able to forge when people from different backgrounds come together for a common purpose.

Which brings us to the second enemy of nascent unions, *indecision*. What do you understand your purpose to be? An earlier incarnation of the G.E.O., from whom we borrowed our name, never took the formal step of becoming a union. They accomplished a number of things for grad students and grad employees alike, and they even collected dues for a while, but they never affiliated with an international or took the kinds of steps that would have made it possible to negotiate terms and conditions of employment. The result was that they died out, leaving an important legacy but no real basis from which to resurrect the movement.

You may think this is a trivial point. Of course you want to form a union. But it is one thing to build an organization to serve the interests of graduate students/employees and another to constitute that group as a union. One of the first things you should do when you apprise yourself of the conditions of your campus is investigate existing mechanisms for addressing your concerns. You'll almost certainly find something, whether it's graduate representation in student government, some sort of advisory council to your graduate college, or the many associations of grad students within given departments. All these bodies are capable of doing some good, and at the very least, they'll allow you to network with active grad students, some of whom will be supportive and others of whom should at least allow you to use their group's meetings to disseminate your message.

But none of these entities is a *union*. None has the legal standing by which to obligate your employer to bargain with you over terms and conditions of employment. Nor can you achieve that with some ad hoc association of vaguely disgruntled graduate employees, no matter how well they call attention to themselves or how effectively they can advocate a single issue on behalf of their constituents. You will be tempted—and many of your members/supporters/contingent supporters will urge you— to use your organization to win immediate benefits for graduate employees. And there are sound rhetorical, organizational, and self-motivational reasons for following this plan. But every moment you spend using your hypothetical union to service its hypothetical membership is time you could have been using to build a real union that could win *guaranteed* benefits.

This is no small issue. As I said, there are sound reasons for wanting to accomplish something short of formal recognition and the contract such recognition can make possible. But the circumstances of organizing a grad employee union constitute a viciously zero-sum game. You are already having to juggle the responsibilities of work and scholarship. You are a necessarily transient employee. Organizing, for all that it can invigorate, is a seriously taxing pursuit over the long term. Now add partner and maybe family responsibilities. Where are you also going to find the time to be winning prerecognition benefits for your not quite union members? And even if *you* can come up with the extra hours, how many other people can? This is one of the most difficult compromises you'll be faced with, and I'm not saying you should organize only around representation, but think about it this way: if you win something without getting it signed into a contract, what have you really won? And if you accomplish a lot of little things but do not build an organization that will outlast you, what have you really accomplished? Only an instantiated, formally recognized union can negotiate binding contracts and endure beyond the passing interests of a small core of motivated leaders. You owe it to yourself to emphasize recognition; that's what deciding to unionize means.

But there is one more hurdle you'll have to overcome. I usually refer to this as the problem of a "meeting culture," but to maintain consistency with the other two barriers, I'll call this one *discussion*. You will guard against this barrier even after you have expanded past isolation and resolved your indecision, because if there's one thing graduate students are good at, especially graduate students in the humanities, it is laboring over trivial distinctions. You would not be in grad school if you did not excel at this behavior. And the very interdisciplinarity that you will need to propel your movement brings with it a potential for endless haggling over issues far less consequential than the choice to unionize.

I first heard this phenomenon described by an organizer for the American Federation of State, County and Municipal Employees (AFSCME). The anecdote he told concerned an organizing campaign for grad employees, which foundered in part because the group was spending too much time arguing over what color their flyers should be. The context of the story, which he told during the period when we were auditioning affiliates, was the reluctance many internationals feel about working with grad employee locals, whose members are often better at hashing out the fine points of insignificant details than they are at enacting the larger goals that subsume such minutiae.

Think about it for a moment. Hasn't your whole graduate experience depended on your ability to make fine distinctions among arguments and interpretations? Haven't you been rewarded for carving out your own niche, however tiny, and ridiculed when you resorted to vast and obvious generalizations? Well, folks, if nothing else, a union is a vast and obvious generalization. Its *members* are distinct, and the contracts it can win should be specific to those members' (collective) circumstances, but as an idea, a union is a pretty transparent thing. So transparent that you may be tempted to look through and past it to the details on which you've been trained to concentrate. *Resist that temptation!*

Look, for all I know, the A F S C M E guy's story was apocraphyal. Yet it contained a kernel of truth, one at which, to extend the metaphor, the G.E.O. has continued to gnaw throughout its history. You will never overcome this barrier decisively, because you will never entirely unlearn the skills you have so assiduously accumulated. So let me finish this point with two anecdotes of my own, the veracity of which I can attest to. The first has to do with a union that, as I write, has just affiliated with an international. At a conference held just before they made their decision, a representative from this union described their circumstances. He listed about eight different committees they had formed. Now, having worked with this union before, I knew that they could count maybe two dozen hard-core activists. I don't know what those committees thought they were doing, but if they met at all regularly, they were certainly dissipating the energy of the two dozen people who could have been out organizing. It's not that there aren't issues to research and other work to be done. But the most important thing you'll ever do for your union is talk to and recruit new members, educate them and hear their concerns, and organize them into a body that can win and maintain representation rights.

The second anecdote comes out of that same conference. A representative from a different union, one in a much more preliminary stage of organizing, was describing their current activities, which he summarized as amounting to weekly three-hour meetings. Now, I can be pretty blunt at these gatherings and don't always ingratiate myself with my peers. This time, though, I bit my tongue. Because I remember what it was like starting out, and I remember why it took us two years to get to the card drive. At the same time, I know how much time you can squander having endless bull sessions, rehashing personal grievances, trading witticisms, and just enjoying the company and commiseration of your peers. None of those is necessarily related to building a union, however. Grad employee unions are tremendous social resources for their members, and you can never oversell that benefit, but—everybody, repeat after me—the time you spend discussing, grousing, joking, and socializing is time you could have spent organizing. The thing is, you can discuss, grouse, joke, socialize, *and* organize—in fact, that's exactly what organizing is. You just do it with *new* people, around whom you can build an organization, instead of with the same ones you already know. The people you know are already in the union. Meet new people, and make the union bigger.

The Organizing Model

So you know you want a union—now what? One first step would be to collect information from existing grad employee unions, most of which maintain web sites or at least have e-mail addresses through which you can request information (see the Appendix). These will both give you ideas about how other unions are constituted and what they do and supply you with some important anecdotal information you will need when you encounter skeptics during your organizing. Nothing refutes misperceptions like the facts, and while facts and statistics alone won't win your election, they will make your job a lot easier. So collect 'em, trade 'em, and share 'em with your friends.

You'll also need facts about your own campus; such as how many grad employees there are, where they work, what they do, how much they earn, and so forth. You may already know this information for your own department, but for programs for which you do not yet have a contact person (that is, a supporter or potential organizer), you'll have to try other methods. Often, if it's just departmental information you need, the secretaries, who may themselves be unionized, will provide you with what they know. Inevitably, though, you'll encounter resistance, and especially at the grad college level, you're unlikely to get such information simply by asking for it. If there exists some sort of advisory council of grad students or other body for funneling concerns from grads to the administration, the people in charge of these may be of help. Otherwise, you may wind up having to file for the documents under the Freedom of Information Act, details of which you can get from the office you're requesting through.

Why do you need this information? Because ultimately you will be contacting *all* the people described on those lists, and you need to know who they are and where to find them. In addition, it helps to know about disparities in income, workload, and the like to see if there are obvious issues around which you should or should not organize. Ultimately, you'll get this information much more proximately and meaningfully when you are out talking with people, but even before you begin that process in a big way, it helps to know the terrain a little. Which is the last reason you need the basic information about grad employees: because you want to ascertain the magnitude of the task ahead of you. Many unions, for example, don't represent most research assistants, because courts have determined that the "work" of such grads, when it approximates or equals their dissertations, does not constitute work after all (in the way that, say, teaching or administrative duties *do* count as work, because they are not necessarily related to one's scholarship). You will need to know the various percentages of assistantships, where they are concentrated, and so on.

There is one additional category of information you will need to investigate, and to which I have already alluded: the various groups and associations of grad students, as well as any body that mediates between students/employees and the university. You need this information for two reasons. First, with regard to graduate student groups specifically, these will become prime means of contact for you. You need to get on the agenda of such groups so that you can attend their meetings and explain what you're trying to do. You may also find that the leaders and activists within such organizations will become active in the union. Second, concerning those mediating bodies, you need both to familiarize yourself with how information flows and decisions get made at your school and to learn how to explain the inadequacies of those mechanisms when you're organizing. One question you'll face again and again is, Why a union? In other words, someone may agree with you about the pressing need to address specific issues, but they may not understand why a union is the best means of so addressing them. You need to be able to demonstrate why the alternatives won't work. And just the fact that you've bothered to educate yourself about such alternatives will add credibility to your case—you won't come off as a fanatic about unions but as someone who has weighed the options and made the smart choice.

One other reason to do this kind of research is that it may tell you something historically about other efforts to improve conditions for grad employees, union-oriented or otherwise. At UIUC, for example, there is a body called the Graduate Student Advisory Council (GSAC). It exists at the pleasure of and reports to the Graduate College and mainly concerns itself with academic affairs. But it has, periodically, attempted to affect areas such as health coverage. When the G.E.O. first began, one of my tasks was to attend a GSAC meeting, find out what they did, and let them know what we were about. In the course of that meeting, I mentioned that two of the benefits we hoped to win were eye and dental coverage. Several GSAC members promptly informed me that we were wasting our time because they had made such proposals themselves in the past, proposals that went nowhere (literally, as I was to learn years later, when the administrator in charge of negotiating our health package confessed that the Graduate College had never forwarded the proposals drafted by GSAC; this is what allowed her to say that we were only now receiving dental coverage because we had never before expressed any interest in it). That's a good factoid to have handy when someone says, "Sure I'd like to get my teeth cleaned, but do we really need a union for that?"

So now you're awash in information. You've learned about other unions, and you know something about how your school operates. From this point on, a lot of your energy is going to be devoted to two things: running meetings and talking to people. Sure, you'll need to be writing (posters, announcements, press releases, general propaganda), as well as planning and coordinating events (rallies, demonstrations), and there's always some kind of research to be done. But the bulk of what it means to operate a grad employee union amounts to going to meetings where the policy is formed and organizing members (that is, surveying, recruiting, or mobilizing them for an action). In the early days of the G.E.O., the first responsibility belonged to the Steering Committee, and the second, to the Organizing Committee. There were—and are—other standing committees, but these, or some rechristened version thereof, are the only regularly meeting bodies in the union. Today, they're known as the Coordinating Committee and the Stewards' Council ("steward" being the name for a department representative/organizer).

Some people, and I would count myself among them, would argue that a union really needs only *one* such body. I believe this for two reasons. First, the exigencies of grad school life militate against finding enough different people to supply two committees' worth of hard-core volunteers. Second, organizing, as a practice, is a fairly straightforward thing, such that once you know how to do it, you don't need to spend a whole lot of time talking about it to other organizers. The lesson here is to keep things simple. You may be tempted to create a committee to do everything, but before you get caught up in a maelstrom of committee generation, ask yourself these four questions: (1) Does that task (for which you're forming the committee) need to be done right now? (2) Does it need to be done by a group of people, or can one person handle it? (3) Are there enough individuals to staff the committee reliably? and (4) Will the task to be addressed be ongoing or terminal? If the answers are "yes," "a group," "yes," and "ongoing," you would perhaps be justified in forming a committee. But be aware that the rhetorical act of constituting a group for a specific purpose often occludes the actual work done by that group. Let me give you an example. For years, the G.E.O. has allegedly had a "publicity" committee, but most of the publicity for the union continues to be done by staff and individual volunteers. In that instance, the vital need for a product has overcome the inertia of just thinking "the committee" will handle things. But there are other, similarly empowered groups whose work is not taken up as quickly. Remember that you're always having to combat apathy; you teach a dangerous lesson to both activists and general members when you create entities within the union that don't really do anything or aren't held accountable for what they do. And there is only so much energy you can devote to accountability anyway.

However you decide to constitute yourselves, it is imperative that when you do come together, either in some sort of executive committee or in terms of a full-scale membership meeting, that you know how to manage such affairs efficiently. Graduate students excel at the seminar model for discussion, but if you allow that format to reign in your meetings, you will not only waste huge amounts of time but also breed much unnecessary and detrimental resentment (because you lack rules for what is an appropriate contribution). Adapt the following advice to fit your specific circumstances, but train yourselves to follow *some* rules. There's nothing more frustrating than having only a limited amount of time to devote to something you believe in and then frittering that time away in pointless discussion.

First, make sure you have an agenda for every meeting. You can always call for additions and announcements at the start, but a little foresight will prevent a great deal of chaos. Second, have rules for how the meeting is to be run, and appoint someone to enforce them. (Ultimately, you may want an elected parliamentarian to perform this function; early on, rotating the responsibility may be the best way to instill the discipline in the greatest number of members.) Robert's Rules of Order are complicated but can be modified; regardless, you need some way of policing how discussion takes place, how decisions get made, and who determines when you've wandered off the topic. Third, be sure to have a recording secretary to take notes. (Here again, you can begin by sharing this task, but as with the parliamentarian, the G.E.O. currently elects individuals for this position.) Finally, have a time limit for the meeting. There are always occasions when you may need additional time, and I can think of several grueling meetings of the G.E.O., such as when we were first drafting and amending our constitution, when I thought it was quite productive to remain together for a marathon session. But if you have a clear sense of your business and you're policing the discussion against extraneous remarks, you should be able to handle most small meetings in an hour and most membership meetings in an hour or hour and a half. The exceptions would be when you're using the time to brainstorm or otherwise generate ideas; if you're doing this too often, you need to prepare further for your sessions by having the early work done beforehand, perhaps by assigning individuals to draft position papers or by using a meeting for the express purpose of developing ideas, and nothing else.

I can't say too often, though, that most of the work of a union gets done outside of meetings, and if you're spending too much time in them, something is wrong. Settle on a structure, agree on responsibilities, and then hold yourselves accountable to both. That way, you can devote most of your energy to the real business of a grad employee union, which is organizing.

All of the above, of course, assumes you have someplace to meet. It's always fun to commandeer classrooms for this purpose clandestinely, but your lives will become much easier the sooner you can arrange regular meeting spaces. If you register as a student group (always a good step before you have formally affiliated), you may receive room rental benefits, in addition to a small budget. But you may not get office space. For that, you might need to apply to some outside agency. For the G.E.O., it was the University YMCA, which despite its name has no swimming pool but does house a number of student groups working for social justice. Look for an organization like that which may be willing to sponsor you, and don't be afraid to approach such a group even if they don't formally offer such sponsorship. You have allies in your community, even if it takes some time to find them.

Among those potential allies are students, professors, and other staff, the last especially if they're unionized. With regard to the first group, you'll need to perform outreach if only to address concerns about how better compensation for grad employees may affect tuition. Our chancellor has specialized in representing the campus as a divisive competition of interests, and there are obvious ways in which a union drive can be characterized unfavorably to undergraduates. You'll need to educate this population by writing articles for the student paper(s) — particularly, rapid responses to the scare stories that may appear there. More important, though, connect with undergraduate organizations and collaborate on issues that affect all students. The G.E.O. has participated in student government elections, spoken before various student groups, and worked with bodies such as Students for Real Democracy on fee issues that hurt grads and undergrads alike.

To date, we've been somewhat less effective in marshaling the support of faculty. We did get about one hundred professors to sign a petition supporting us, and individual professors have helped at rallies and in our legal case, but we've never come up with a comprehensive plan for developing faculty support. In part this is simply because the job of reaching fifty-four hundred grad employees is daunting enough. But even a call to action circulated within my own department by two sympathetic professors failed to generate any real interest. In some cases, the best you can hope for is to keep the faculty from working *against* you. To that end, avoid the divisive rhetoric of our chancellor, and emphasize how clear boundaries between academics and employment serve everyone well. Your rallies, by design, will be raucous affairs, but otherwise don't comport yourselves in ways that allow antiunion faculty to indulge in their worst fears. I feel like an etiquette teacher having to say such things, but honestly, sound arguments and whimsy will win you more respect than unnecessary belligerence. It's not like your organizers are being disappeared by faculty death squads (well, maybe *metaphorically*). So try to adopt a no-first-strike policy. There's no real reason why professors should oppose a grad employee union; if nothing else, don't *give* them one.

More fruitful has been our work with the many other unions on campus. We attend one another's events and monitor our various victories and setbacks. Just as when you discover fellow grads who share your concerns, hooking up with other unions on campus is a way of forging community. And that should be the lesson for all such outreach efforts: recognizing a common purpose, whether that be quality education, high professional standards, or fair labor practices. A little communication can help your effort tremendously, because it's often the case that the various populations on campus don't know the circumstances of grad employment. So connect your fight for fairness to the work of your school at large; that's a message you can take all across your campus, as well as beyond.

Getting Organized

You hear the word "organizing" a lot when you talk to people in grad employee unions. You might think, for all that the word seems simple enough, that it is somehow foreign to your experience. In fact, though, you couldn't function as a graduate student without already knowing how to do most of what you'll be engaged in as an organizer. The majority of what you will do involves one of four practices: *listening, learning, educating,* and *persuading*.

"Listening" means hearing what other grad employees have to say about their working conditions, and recording those concerns. It means being willing to hear something new, rather than selling only your ideas for why a union is necessary. If you've ever attended a lecture, taken notes, and trained yourself to be open to new ways of thinking, you already know a great deal about organizing.

"Learning" relates both to the research you'll have to do when you start the union and the ongoing awareness you'll need to cultivate with regard to the developments that will take place as your campaign progresses. Always remember, you are dealing with a population that is necessarily preoccupied and transient. There's a great deal to know about unions in general, notwithstanding the circumstances specific to your campus. As an organizer, you have to be responsible for that information, in part to make yourself appear credible, but also because a lot of the colleagues you encounter will rely on you as a source. But if you've ever drawn connections between bodies of knowledge, participated in a class discussion, or conducted any research, you've already experienced what organizers need to know.

"Educating" simply means putting that knowledge into practice: explaining the purpose of a union, answering questions about particular goals and principles, and connecting the aims of the union to the needs of the membership. If you've ever given a talk, answered a question in a seminar, or related your scholarly interests to the concerns of your profession, then you've developed skills that are relevant to an organizer.

Finally, "persuading" entails helping potential members recognize common interests, demonstrating the injustices suffered by specific graduate employees, and making the case for a union as the best way to address those common concerns and particular problems. This is the most difficult part of the job, but if you've ever taught a class, developed a thesis, or elaborated an argument, then you already know how to be an organizer.

If I make this appear overly schematic, it's because I know from having trained organizers how forbidding the practice can seem. Even the most committed activists may balk at the prospect of organizing, because it is difficult and too often feels like door-to-door sales. But you are *already* enacting the very skills you need to be a successful organizer and would not be where you are now if that were not the case. Play to your strengths—if you believe in the idea, use what you've learned as a student/teacher/researcher/administrator to make that idea compelling to your peers. And the people you'll be talking to *are* your peers, even if they work in another discipline. You necessarily begin with a lot of common ground, which is more than most door-to-door salespeople can count on.

So now that I've assuaged your fears about the general practice of organizing, what does it look like in its particulars? Let me run you through one scenario, which involves organizing a department from which you have no current members. The first thing you'll need to do is locate the building or buildings where you can find the employees. This isn't always as easy as it sounds: a department may have its business offices in one place, even though many of the students in that program work or teach elsewhere. Let's assume, though, that this is one of those blessedly easy departments where everything takes place under one roof. Locate the main office or, if necessary, the grad office, and after identifying yourself, ask the following questions: Do you have a directory for current students or employees? Are there bulletin boards in this building where I can post notices that might be of interest to them? Do the students/employees have mailboxes, and are they accessible? Are there any places in the building where grad students congregate or particular ways they have of communicating, such that a relevant group might have access? Is there some sort of association of grad students? When do they meet? Who is/are the president(s)?

Basically, you want to know who and where the grad employees are and how you can most easily get in touch with them. When I was first organizing for the G.E.O. and we hadn't formally become a union yet, it was helpful to be able to say I was with "a registered student group." But even if you don't have that cover story, you should be able to get answers to at least some of your questions, and as soon as you have even one member, that person can get you the program directory that will make your life much easier.

Assuming, though, you at least know where the mailboxes are and can deliver to them, your next step should be to "seed" the department by distributing a flyer, brochure, or whatever form of propaganda you've been generating. Remember that one key to winning a drive is *exposures*. Give people some time to acclimate themselves to the idea of a union before you start trying to recruit them as members. You'll find that your encounters run much more smoothly when you have even a little background in common (that is, the information on a flyer) versus when you're literally starting from nothing.

If you're lucky, you'll also have learned by this point whether the program has its own graduate student association or any type of organization that meets to discuss academic and professional affairs. Get on its agenda, give members some printed material ahead of time, and make your pitch. Do some research in advance to learn a little bit about the circumstances of the department, so that you don't make any obvious mistakes in translating what you know about grad employees in general to the specifics in their program.

If no such organization exists, call your own meeting. Follow the relevant procedures for reserving a room and advertise the meeting. You might not draw a soul, but the people who do attend figure to be highly motivated, and even if you can't turn them into organizers, learn as much from them as you can about their program, so that *you* can be a better organizer.

Which raises one of the trickier issues you'll face in building your union: how to assess (potential) personnel. In the G.E.O., we've often had the experience that when we recruit people to become organizers, they say that organizing would be too much work but that they would be willing to talk to their friends, stuff mailboxes, and post flyers. In truth, the best organizers do more than that, but if you accumulate enough people willing to perform the three tasks just named, you're well on your way to victory. Be honest with people about the work involved, aim for the highest level of contribution, but offer less taxing options if they don't seem interested in managing an entire department. Most important, *get a commitment*. Have them hear themselves say what they're going to do. You can never overestimate how busy grad students will be, so hold them as accountable as you can when they agree to help in the effort.

So far, you've mainly been focusing on identifying and recruiting organizers and building name recognition within a department. Eventually, though, you'll start to focus on one-on-one conversations. This is true whether you're organizing purely for membership, as part of a card drive so that you can hold a recognition election, or for the purpose of winning that election. In the last two instances, it's pretty clear what the goal of your encounter should be: either having them sign an authorization card, which is like an individual slice of a petition requesting that an election be held, or having them vote for the union once that election has been approved. For building membership as well, the goal may be discrete—that is, having them fill out a membership card. But often you'll want a stronger commitment than that, such as having them attend a meeting or workshop, participate in some event, or recruit five of their friends to sign cards (which saves you work while building a stronger membership). Regardless, don't ever just talk to people if your only purpose is to talk. (This is the one-on-one corollary to the *discussion* problem that can beset your executive meetings.) Most of your work will be rhetorical, yes, but always be sure to connect an action to your rhetoric. If nothing else, it will help you evaluate the effectiveness of that rhetoric (in terms of how many people follow through on the action); ultimately, though, actions are what make a union strong.

Finally, you should always maintain some kind of record of your encounters. This will help you keep track of your progress, identify key issues, locate potential activists, and determine which messages work for a given program. You may go to the trouble of preparing some kind of "contact information sheet," or you may do this informally. Inevitably, though, a lot of the wisdom of your union will remain trapped in the minds of your membership if you don't have some means of *formally* recording and preserving it. Even something as mundane as the location, number, and delivery rules for a department's grad student mailboxes needs to be spelled out. There's nothing more aggravating than being asked to perform what seems like a trivial task, only to discover that you don't know where the boxes are, how many items to bring for distribution, or which secretary to ask for help. Even the most well-intentioned volunteers will start to balk at your requests if you don't do the small things to make their jobs easier.

Let's Pause Fifteen Seconds to Allow Our
Local Affiliates to Identify Themselves

So far, you've constituted yourselves as a union, you've done your research, and you're beginning to reach out to your potential membership. Congratulations! Now the real work begins. Having built up a certain amount of momentum, you need to continue evolving, and the next stage in the growth process is affiliating. Choosing an affiliate is the most important step your organization will face at this point. And even expressing it that way—that is, as a *choice*—speaks to one of the peculiar features of grad employee unions. Outside of academia, it is often the international union, through its state or local branch, that initiates a relationship with those organizing a new campaign (more pointedly, it is often the existing union that initiates the campaign *itself*). And even in instances where members of the local approach the existing organization, they may face little choice in with whom to affiliate. The odds are good, however, that you *will* face a choice. And while this may prove disconcerting to the traditionalists with whom you may have to deal, it's a valuable opportunity to have, both because the pressure of having to make the right choice will discipline your own group and because the accountability such discretion implies helps keep international unions responsible to their locals, as well as to their membership at large.

But why affiliate at all? Why not preserve the utmost autonomy and run your own campaign, start to finish? The main reason you'll want to affiliate is because of the resources you'll gain, both material and otherwise. As a registered student group or its equivalent, you'll have some sort of budget, but nothing on the scale of what an established union can provide. Similarly, while those in the movement are always glad to share tips and information, it is much easier to access both strategic resources and the bodies to help deploy them when you are connected to other grad employee unions, most of which participate in one or both of the following associations: the Alliance of Graduate Employee Locals, which includes unions affiliated with the American Federation of Teachers, or A FT; and the Coalition of Graduate Employee Locals, which includes all grad employee unions that wish to participate. Always remember that you are embarking on a heinously difficult task and will need all the support you can garner. Affiliating is the best way to garner that support, as well as the legitimacy that will both embolden your movement and strengthen it in the eyes of those with whom you'll ultimately be negotiating your contracts.

As for the specific resources you may obtain by affiliating, aside from greater access to existing grad employee locals, the key categories include training, funding, and staff and legal support. Depending on where you're at when you affiliate, you may profit from having experienced organizers prepare your members for the rigors of a card drive or election, or just help them learn the basics of any organizing scenario. And it goes without saying that a real budget will accelerate your effort; it is difficult to survive on what you are likely to obtain just as a student group or by passing the hat at membership meetings. But even if you could manage the training and funding issues on your own, the help you gain in staff and legal support alone will justify the decision to affiliate. Having paid staff and legal counsel have made all the difference for the G.E.O.: the former were indispensable for both our card drive and election campaign, and the latter has been essential for keeping alive our prospect of formal recognition through state labor law. So while it would be wrong to claim that the G.E.O. couldn't have achieved what it has without affiliating, I can attest both to the mundane and to the overarching ways in which affiliation has made our job much easier.

Assuming I've persuaded you of the merits of affiliation, how do you proceed? First, you should educate yourself about your options. Contact other grad employee locals about the relationships with their internationals. More important, though, find out about the unions already present in your community and on your campus, and learn what you can about the strengths and weaknesses of their state organizations. However much you may like a union because of its politics or nationwide successes, a bad state federation—because it is the state branch with which you'll be in most contact—can doom your relationship from the start. Having said that, though, I would also caution you against basing your judgment on *personal* reactions to the state or local representatives of a union. This can be hard to resist, but for some obvious reasons—for example, you're affiliating with a union, not an individual; those individuals aren't going to be in their jobs forever; charisma isn't everything—you need to police against making a decision based on how glamorous the representatives seem. In some ways, this is another facet of the trendiness pitfall discussed above. You're making a business decision, not a lifestyle choice. Act accordingly.

So now you've targeted a few potential affiliates. Perhaps one is particularly strong already on your campus or has recently waged a successful campaign or both. Perhaps another represents grad employees at a school nearby or in a neighboring state. At UIUC, our choice came down to AFSCME and AFT. AFSCME had recently waged a successful campaign on behalf of the clerical workers, and there are AFT locals at the University of Wisconsin campuses in Madison and Milwaukee and at the University of Michigan. Having narrowed the field to these two options, we proceeded to formulate a set of questions to help us choose between them. In general, the issues you need to address include (1) the level of support you will receive both during and after your organizing drive; (2) the degree of autonomy you will exercise; and (3) how and when dues will be collected, as well as how they are allocated. More specifically, we asked our potential affiliates about such things as their general mission statement; their profile and expectations of us; their experience with grad employee locals; their relations with other unions; our role in determining who our organizers would be; legal expertise; and particular organizing strategies. In all, we posed forty-five questions, and as I indicated, this is the kind of request at which a potential affiliate may balk, simply because they're not used to being quizzed and evaluated this way. Don't let that deter you. Even if you have only one valid option, ask that affiliate what you need to know, and use whatever information you glean to prepare for and negotiate your subsequent relationship. It's a truism, but the more you know, the better.

Up until now I've been presenting this scenario as though you hold all the power, while your meek and hopeful suitors compete to please you. In fact, you may need to *convince* a potential affiliate that you are worth their time. If they're doing their job right, they will have questions for you as well and expectations you'll need to meet before they will commit. Indeed, this may remain true during and beyond the organizing drive. That kind of pressure is both honest and helpful, and if a potential affiliate *doesn't* bring any to bear, you are entitled to wonder how committed they will be or whether they make important decisions as deliberately as they ought. The AFT, for example, wanted us to cultivate five hundred members before formalizing our relationship, and having to meet that goal made us a stronger organization.

At the other end of the spectrum are affiliates that decide *so* deliberately that they decide *against* you. This may be because they feel they lack the proper resources or expertise or see your struggle as too difficult. For example, employees at private universities have had great difficulty in organizing: they have faced a murky legal outlook, and private campuses are often virulently antiunion and wealthy enough to back up that virulence with big bucks. Recent decisions by the National Labor Relations Board favoring the union at Yale may clarify and improve the legal outlook, but I know from being at meetings with AFT officials that even the most aggressive internationals are shy of taking on some schools, either because of the special circumstances presented by private universities or because the law or general climate of a certain state makes organizing at a public campus unusually forbidding. If you're faced with one of these scenarios, you really have only two (nonexclusive) choices: building informal coalitions with the unions already present on your campus, assuming there are any, and *proving* to an international you're worth investing in. In the meantime, network with existing grad employee locals to have them bring pressure on their internationals to work with you. More important, though, *organize!* If the issues are pressing and the membership is energized, you can accomplish a great deal short of formal recognition, plus you'll have something tangible to bring to a potential affiliate that may otherwise be reluctant to deal with you.

But assuming you have internationals that are willing, the next step, and perhaps the most difficult to negotiate, is determining *how* you're going to make your affiliation decision (assuming, that is, you have options). You may opt to decide just within some executive committee; have members or all grad employees vote to confirm/disconfirm the recommendation of the executive committee; or have members or all grad employees choose from among all possible candidates. The first option is obviously the least democratic but potentially the most informed. The other two options are more unpredictable, with an open vote—that is, among all potential candidates, and open to all grad employees, regardless of membership status—being the most chaotic and potentially disastrous (for example, if antiunion activists organized to sabotage it somehow). However you choose to resolve this matter, plan it out beforehand and carefully. This is a huge decision, and you want to make it both wisely and in a way that generates the least amount of rancor (because how you decide this issue is one of the acts that has the potential for creating division among activists, and you'll never have enough of those that you can afford to offend some).

A few final thoughts on affiliation. First, I would encourage you to bargain for selecting paid organizers from within your own local. This is also one reason you don't want to affiliate too quickly. Allow your union to develop appropriately, such that you cultivate skilled organizers *before* you affiliate. This is especially important because you are always going to face the accusation that the union is somehow a *third party* between the grad employees and their employer. Having paid staff who are not or never have been students at your school only feeds that kind of thinking. If no one steps forward and you can't supply your own organizers, then you will obviously have to hire from without. But I for one would be suspicious of any organization that expected to succeed and couldn't come up with its own people. You are going to need massive volunteer labor as it is, and if you don't have *anyone* temporarily willing to trade an academic appointment for a stint as a paid organizer, I'd be concerned about the level of volunteer support as well.

Second, money changes everything. Especially if you are hiring your organizers from within, there may be people who want the jobs and don't get them, and if you don't have a well-defined and impartial mechanism for making those decisions, you'll breed a great deal of unnecessary resentment. Beyond that, there are the consequences of having an increased budget and how spending decisions get made. Here again, a little foresight can save you a great deal of trouble down the line. Finally, don't be surprised if, come election time, your opposition starts negatively characterizing the money you've received—in terms of how it demonstrates who *really* pulls the strings, how much members are going to have to pay back in dues, or some such nonsense. In this instance, perhaps there's nothing you can do but be prepared for such accusations. Just remember that money is not an unalloyed blessing.

The final caution I would offer on this subject concerns the way your members may start to perceive the union after it is affiliated. You deserve to be proud of both interesting an affiliate and making an informed choice. But one of the dangers you face is that even the most dedicated activists may start to feel as though they can contribute less, because now people are being paid to do the work. In truth, even a small staff can accomplish a great deal. But it is neither healthy nor effective long-term for a union to rely on its staff as its primary source of energy. This not only fuels the third-party argument but also renders your union impotent in ways that can cost you even *after* you've achieved recognition. I offer no magic solution to this problem; I simply encourage you to recognize and guard against the tendency. Affiliating will help you in countless ways, but it can't, on its own, make your union work. You're only ever as strong as your membership. Remember that; your employer certainly does.

How to Win an Outside-the-Formal-Framework-of-State-Labor-Law Union Election for Graduate Employees at the University of Illinois by a Margin of 1,633 to 906 (On Two Particularly Beautiful Days in the Middle of April 1997)

Actually, most of what follows should be pretty applicable to your campus as well. I include all the qualifications to remind you that it helps to be precise in how you tailor a campaign. Unions, as I've indicated, are a kind of blatant generalization in the abstract, but successful unions generate their victories out of a precise assessment of their strengths and interests and the obstacles that face them. Perform that assessment, and modify the following advice accordingly.

First, build back from where you want to be, and where you want to be is savoring your victory and gearing up to negotiate a contract. For obvious reasons, everything takes place within the context of a fall to spring academic timetable. Where do you want to be the week before the election, the month before, and so forth? The G.E.O. had to revise its timetable more than once. Initially, we wanted to have assessed all the voters by the end of the fall semester so that we could use the spring to concentrate our energy where it would be most effective (that is, turning out "yes" votes). We fell short of that goal, but we continued to aim for weekly and semester targets, both as a way of making an onerous task more manageable and as a way of motivating organizers with precise expectations.

Next, remember that membership (volunteers) is the key. How are you going to activate members? Use social activities, such as volunteer nights (at which time you prepare mailings, stuff mailboxes, run a phone bank, or chalk the sidewalks), and presentations or cookouts at grad housing to build solidarity and make work fun. Also, construct networks of accountability. And aim to do everything for the union (attend a meeting or rally, organize, create materials) with at least one other person. You'd be surprised how many people will respond, if you just ask them. And that's how you foster membership: by soliciting people to participate and by having expectations for them.

Third, be flexible in your organizing strategies. Different departments require different tactics, as do different periods of the campaign. If something is not working, figure out why and change or scrap it if necessary. We began our election campaign with the Stewards' Council as our principal organizing tool, without having devoted sufficient time to developing that body. Later, we switched to a model in which four teams were each responsible for a quadrant of the campus. And throughout, we phoned people in the evenings, to set up appointments and just to get the word out about the election. Learn from other unions, but also bear in mind the particulars of your campus.

Fourth, when you organize, be nice, but be aggressively nice. Grad employees are busy people. You have to go to them most of the time (to their offices, their labs, their homes), but a surprising number appreciate the effort (and even when they don't, be nice about it). Listen to their concerns, but remember that you need a goal for every contact you make—make sure they're listening by having them agree to something. Even if you can't get them to come to a meeting or commit to help in the effort, try to get them at least to agree rhetorically with one of your points (that is, help them persuade themselves).

Next, repeat this mantra: exposures, exposures, exposures. You can count on accumulating a core of organizers—the kind of people who are just waiting for someone to tell them about a union effort (although you should try to identify these folks *before* both the election campaign and the card drive, one more reason to build your organization deliberately). But once you've skimmed off that cream, you'll have to work much harder to persuade people to give time or even just to support the idea. And most of them won't do so at first. Plan on multiple exposures: several conversations, flyers in their work site, mailings, media accounts, and so on. At UIUC, most people had heard of the G.E.O. before we began the election campaign. Then, during the campaign, they received our monthly newsletter, multiple phone calls, and our building/office/home visits, along with at least one reminder just before the election. Don't get discouraged—you're asking a lot from people, some of whom have no real idea of what unions do. Be patient, but be aggressively patient.

Sixth, remember that nobody ever built a union through e-mail or solely with clever flyers or because they hosted the coolest parties. Do all these things, but talk to people face-to-face. Nicely, in an aggressive sort of way. It's fun. You get to see parts of your campus you might otherwise never experience and learn things from other disciplines you would never have encountered (most of which you'll forget, but it's still fascinating to hear about). I've made friends in physics, plant biology, entomology, and anthropology and learned about the research people were doing in dozens of other fields—all because of the G.E.O. Collegiality. Interdisciplinarity. University. Union. They kind of go together.

Finally, expect opposition. Maybe not today, maybe not tomorrow, but when the big day comes, don't be shocked to find that somebody doesn't want a union. We had some hairy moments between election days when we knew that the polling site where we expected the most opposition was seeing a lot of traffic. It takes a tremendous amount of work to build a union and very little effort to show up one day and vote "no." Don't forget that.

Are You Now or Have You Ever Been an Employee?

Within two weeks of our election victory, we received word that the administrative law judge for the Illinois Educational Labor Relations Board (IELRB) had decided against us. That is, according to (her interpretation of) state law, we didn't qualify as employees and couldn't organize under the Illinois Educational Labor Relations Act (IELRA). (We'd anticipated as much, which is why we didn't wait for the ruling before holding our election.) I was actually the first to find out, because I happened to be in the office when a reporter from the local newspaper called for a reaction to the announcement. Having testified at the legal hearings myself, during which episode the administration attempted to deploy against us, first surreptitiously and then with the law judge's blessing, our confidential (!) student records, I was well positioned to deliver a reaction unfit for the family paper with whose representative I was speaking. Alas, I managed to restrain myself.

We've since appealed the law judge's decision, to the full IELRB. Our argument is twofold. First, in finding that our student status by itself prevents us from qualifying as employees under state law, the judge seems to have contradicted the directions given by the executive director who appointed her. Before any evidence was offered, our administration tried to have our petition for election dismissed. The executive director for the IELRB denied this motion, arguing that hearings needed to be held so as to gather information that went beyond mere enrollment status. Yet the law judge hardly needed the hearing evidence to arrive at the decision she did; instead, she relied on a point we had conceded all along—that we had to be enrolled to hold our positions. Clearly, if that is her argument, she neither heeded the directions she was given nor needed to hear any of our testimony.

We also challenged her definition of the word "student," which is the major sticking point in the relevant legislation. Siding with our administration's call for a "plain and ordinary meaning" of the word, the judge resorts to that hoariest of first-year composition gestures and actually writes a sentence that begins "Webster's defines 'student' as." (To her credit, and unlike that first-year student, she does not *open* her argument with this line.) But after establishing this supposedly "plain and ordinary meaning," she then goes on to carve out a quite extraordinary definition, relative to the IELRA. The judge argues that what "student" really means in Illinois law is something like "those who must be enrolled as students in order to be employees." Of course, this is rank nonsense. We've argued all along that the word in the law is ambiguous, because *we're* ambiguous:

both students *and* employees. Indeed, every such term of classification in the IELRA is defined, *except* "student." But that's what happens with those radical, activist judges: always extending—oops, I mean *excising*— the rights of minorities, workers, and other such riffraff.

So we've appealed, but I honestly don't know what good it will do. My sense is that this campaign will be won on the ground, not in the courts. For too long, progressive forces in this country have relied on judicial decisions to secure their victories. But all it takes is one judge who can't think, or one election that goes the wrong way, and you get a bad decision or a lousy law. In the end, it really doesn't matter whether your campus is public or private or what kind of state or federal law you have to deal with. This country has never given labor anything it didn't fight for. I'm tempted to tell you to take the money you were going to give to lawyers and buy yourself a good pair of shoes. Then get out and start talking to people. Five years of hard work have taught me that there's nothing like waking up in the morning pissed off, but with the means for doing something about it. So get mad, yes—but then, *get organized.*

for J. F., J. J., and V. W., the mothers of the G.E.O.

Appendix: Recognized or Affiliated American and Canadian Graduate Employee Unions

Recognized U.S. Unions

State University of New York (SUNY) System
Graduate Student Employees Union/CWA Local 1188
Central Office
P.O. Box 6415
Albany, NY 12206-0415
phone: (518) 438-7773
fax: (518) 434-1188
e-mail: EC7739@cnsvax.albany.edu

University of California (UC), Berkeley
Association of Graduate Student Employees/UAW Local 2165
2372 Ellsworth

Berkeley, CA 94704
phone: (510) 549-3863
fax: (510) 549-2514
e-mail: agse@netcom.com
web site: http://bmw.autobahn.org/~foo/agse/

University of Florida, University of South Florida, and Florida Agricultural and
    Mechanical University
Graduate Assistants United/NEA
238 Norman Hall
University of Florida
Gainesville, FL 32611
phone: (352) 392-0274
web site: http://www.ucet.ufl.edu/gau/

University of Iowa
UE Local 896—Campaign to Organize Graduate Students (COGS)
20 E. Market St., Suite 210
Iowa City, IA 52245
phone: (319) 337-5074
fax: (319) 337-5111
e-mail: cogs@blue.weeg.uiowa.edu

University of Kansas
Graduate Teaching Assistants' Coalition/AFT Local 4565
web site: http://kuhttp.cc.ukans.edu/cwis/organizations/aegis/public_html/
    index.html

University of Massachusetts—Amherst
Graduate Employees Organization/UAW Local 2322
Campus Center
UMass/Amherst
Amherst, MA 01003
phone: (413) 545-0705
e-mail: geo@oitunix.oit.umass.edu
web site: http://www-unix.oit.umass.edu/~geo/

University of Massachusetts—Lowell
Graduate Employees Organization/UAW Local 1596
Graduate School

One University Avenue
Lowell, MA 01854

University of Michigan
Graduate Employees Organization/A F T Local 3550
527 E. Liberty St., Suite 205
Ann Arbor, MI 48104
phone: (313) 995-0221
fax: (313) 995-0548
e-mail: usergeo@umich.edu
web site: http://www.umic.edu/~taunion/

University of Oregon
Graduate Teaching Fellows' Federation/A F T Local 3544
870 E. 13th Ave.
Eugene, OR 97403
phone: (541) 344-0832
fax: (541) 344-2105
e-mail: gtfforg@efn.org
web site: http://www.efn.org/~gtff/

University of Wisconsin — Madison
Teaching Assistants' Association/A F T Local 3220
306 N. Brooks St.
Madison, WI 53715
phone: (608) 256-4375
fax: (608) 256-2649
web site: http://www.taa-madison.org/

University of Wisconsin — Milwaukee
Milwaukee Graduate Assistants' Association/A F T Local 2169
739 W. Juneau Ave.
Milwaukee, WI 53211
phone: (414) 765-0933
fax: (414) 765-9141

Recognized U.S. Faculty/Graduate Employee Units

City University of New York (CUNY)
Professional Staff Congress/AFT/AAUP
25 W. 42d St.
New York, NY 10036
phone: (212) 354-1252
fax: (212) 302-7815

Rutgers University
Rutgers Council of AAUP Chapters
P.O. Box 10360
New Brunswick, NJ 08906
phone: (908) 445-2278
fax: (908) 445-5485
e-mail: aaup@rci.rutgers.edu

Affiliated U.S. Campaigns

Indiana University at Bloomington
Graduate Employees Association/CWA Local 4730
Indiana University
Poplars 331
Bloomington, IN 47405
phone: (812) 855-7929
e-mail: gea@indiana.edu
web site: http://www.indiana.edu/~gea/

UC, Los Angeles (UCLA)
Student Association of Graduate Employees/UAW
900 Hilgard Ave., Suite 209
Los Angeles, CA 90024
phone: (310) 208-2429
fax: (310) 824-0439
e-mail: sageuaw@ix.netcom.com

UC, Riverside
Coalition of Allied Student Employees/UAW
3595 University Ave., Suite K

Riverside, CA 92501
phone: (909) 369-8075

UC, San Diego
Association of Student Employees/UAW
2166 Avenida de la Playa, Suite E
La Jolla, CA 92037
phone: (619) 454-0170
e-mail: aseuaw@igc.apc.org

UC, Santa Barbara
Association of Student Employees/UAW
P.O. Box 22704
Santa Barbara, CA 93121
e-mail: ucsbase@netcom.com
web site: http://www.west.net/~ucsbase

UC, Santa Cruz
Association of Student Employees/UAW
1362 Pacific Ave., #207
Santa Cruz, CA 95060
phone: (408) 423-9737

University of Illinois at Urbana-Champaign
Graduate Employees' Organization/AFT
University YMCA
1001 S. Wright St.
Champaign, IL 61820
phone: (217) 344-8283
fax: (217) 344-8281
web site: http://www.cen.uiuc.edu/~volker/geo.html

University of Minnesota
Graduate Student Organizing Congress (GradSOC)/AFT
1313 5th St. SE
Room 330B
Minneapolis, MN 55414
phone: (612) 379-5950 or (612) 379-5951
web site: http://www.geocities.com/collegepark/quad/7779

Wayne State University
Graduate Employees Organizing Committee/AFT
e-mail: geocwsu@taiga.com
web site: http://www.taiga.com/geocwsu

Yale University
Graduate Employees and Students Organization/HERE
Federation of University Employees/HERE
425 College St.
New Haven, CT 06511
phone: (203) 624-5161
web site: http://www.cris.com/~unions/geso.html

Recognized Canadian Unions

Carleton University
CUPE Local 2323
510 Unicentre
Ottawa, Ontario
K1S 5B6 Canada
phone: (613) 520-7482
fax: (613) 520-4378
web site: http://www.carleton.ca/cupe2323/

Dalhousie University
CUPE Local 3912
c/o CUPE Nova Scotia
308-7071 Bayers Rd.
Halifax, Nova Scotia
B3L 2C2 Canada
web site: http://fox.nstn.ca:80/~cupens/ns-3912.html

Lakehead University
CUPE Local 3905
University Centre 2019B
Lakehead University
Thunder Bay, Ontario
P7B 5E1 Canada

phone: (807) 343-8438
fax: (807) 346-9546

McGill University
Association of Graduate Students Employed at McGill
McGill University, Suite 2401
2020 University St.
Montreal, Quebec
H3A 2A5 Canada
phone: (514) 598-2295
fax: (514) 598-2476
e-mail: agsem@leacock.lan.mcgill.ca
web site: http://www.web.net/~agsem/

McMaster University
CUPE Local 3906
Wentworth Hall Room B108
McMaster University
Hamilton, Ontario
L8S 4K1 Canada
phone: (905) 525-9140, ext. 24003 or ext. 24852
fax: (905) 525-3837
e-mail: cupe3906@mcmail.cis.mcmaster.ca

Ontario Institute for Studies in Education
CUPE Local 3907
252 Bloor St., W Room 8-104
Toronto, Ontario
M5S 1V6 Canada
phone: (416) 926-4728
e-mail: cupe@oise.utoronto.ca

Simon Fraser University
AUCE Local 6/Teaching Support Staff Union
AQ 5130
Simon Fraser University
Burnaby, BC
V5A 1S6 Canada
phone: (604) 291-4695

fax: (604) 291-5369
e-mail: tssu@sfu.ca
web site: http://www.sfu.ca/tssu

University of British Columbia
CUPE Local 2278
6371 Crescent Road
Vancouver, BC
V6T 1Z2 Canada
phone: (604) 224-2118
fax: (604) 224-2118
e-mail: cupe2278@unixg.ubc.ca

University of Guelph
CUPE Local 3913
University Centre, Room 534
University of Guelph
Guelph, Ontario
N1G 2W1 Canada
phone: (519) 824-4120, ext. 6268
e-mail: cupe3913@uoguelph.ca
web site: http://www.uoguelph.ca/~cupe3913

University of Manitoba
CUPE Local 3909
Room 136, St. John's College
Box 101, University Centre
University of Manitoba
Winnipeg, Manitoba
R3T 2M5 Canada
phone: (204) 474-8804
fax: (204) 275-1498
web site: http://www.mbnet.mb.ca/cupe3909/

University of Regina
CUPE Local 2419
122 Campion College
Regina, Saskatchewan
S4S 0A2 Canada

Organize a Union!

phone: (306) 525-5874
fax: (306) 585-1333

University of Toronto
CUPE Local 3902
229 College St., Suite 304
Toronto, Ontario
M5T 1R4 Canada
phone: (416) 593-7057
fax: (416) 593-9866
e-mail: qp3902@gpu.utcc.utoronto.ca
web site: http://www.interlog.com/~qp3902/

York University
CUPE Local 3903
EOB 104
York University
Downsview, Ontario
M3J 1P3 Canada
phone: (416) 736-5154
fax: (416) 736-5480
e-mail: cupe3903@yorku.ca
web site: http://www.yorku.ca/org/cupe/cupe3903.htm

My thanks to Jon Curtiss of the Madison-TAA for permission to reprint the above.

Index

Contributors

Stanley Aronowitz teaches sociology and directs cultural studies at the City University of New York Graduate Center. His more recent work includes *Death and Rebirth of American Radicalism* (1996); *The Jobless Future*, with Bill DiFazio (1994); and *Post-Work: The Wages of Cybernation*, coedited with Jonathan Cutler (1997).

Jan Currie is Associate Professor in the School of Education at Murdoch University, Australia. She has recently published in *Melbourne Studies in Education*, *Australian Educational Researcher*, *Discourse*, *Australian Universities' Review*, and *Women's Studies International Forum*. She has received three ARC grants over the past five years on award restructuring and disadvantaged workers, the changing nature of academic work, and gender and organizational culture. She is coeditor with Janice Newson of *Globalization and Universities: Critical Perspectives* (in press).

Zelda Gamson is Professor of Education and the founding director of the New England Resource Center for Higher Education at the Graduate College of Education, University of Massachusetts, Boston. She has written *Higher Education and the Real World* and *Liberating Education* and has coauthored *Black Students on White Campuses* (with Marvin W. Peterson and Robert T. Blackburn); *Academic Values and*

Mass Education (with David Riesman and Joseph Gusfield); and *Revitalizing General Education in a Time of Scarcity* (with Sandra Kanter and Howard London).

Emily Hacker is a Ph.D. candidate in the English education program at New York University and a former president of United Literacy Workers.

Stefano Harney is Assistant Professor of Sociology at the College of Staten Island, City University of New York. He is author of *Nationalism and Identity: Culture and the Imagination in a Caribbean Diaspora* (1996) and of a forthcoming critique of public administration.

Randy Martin is Professor and Chair of the Social Science and Management Department at Pratt Institute. He is author of *Critical Moves: Dance Studies in Theory and Politics* (Duke, 1998) and coeditor with Toby Miller of *Competing Allegories: The Global and Local Cultures of Sport* (1998).

Bart Meyers is Professor of Psychology at Brooklyn College. His recent work has appeared in the *Journal of Political and Military Sociology* and *Science and Society*. Currently he is researching the Vietnamese defense against the American air war. He is a member of the New Caucus of the Professional Staff Congress, the union that represents the City University of New York's instructional staff.

David Montgomery is Farnam Professor of History at Yale University. He is author of numerous studies in labor history, most recently, *Citizen Worker*, and is currently completing an examination of religion and the labor movement in the nineteenth century.

Frederick Moten is Assistant Professor, Department of Performance Studies at New York University. He is presently working on a book titled "Event Music" that examines the representation of music in Afro-American writing.

Christopher Newfield is Associate Professor of English at the University of California, Santa Barbara. He is the author of *The Emerson Effect: Individualism and Submission in America* (1996); the coeditor, with Avery Gordon, of *Mapping Multiculturalism* (1995); and the coeditor, with Ronald Strickland, of *After Political Correctness: The Humanities and Society in the 1990s* (1995).

Gary Rhoades is Professor and Director of the Center for the Study of Higher Education at the University of Arizona. His *Managed Professionals: Unionized Faculty and Restructuring Academic Labor* was published in 1998.

Sheila Slaughter is Professor in the Center for the Study of Higher Education at the University of Arizona and the author of numerous books and articles. Her most recent book, coauthored with Larry L. Leslie, is *Academic Capitalism: Policies, Politics, and the Entrepreneurial University* (1997).

Jeremy Smith is a 1994 graduate of the University of Florida and the former director of the Campus Alternative Journalism Project at the Center for Campus Organizing (CCO). Jeremy has also worked with Massachusetts Jobs with Justice and the AFL-CIO Organizing Institute on youth and student organizing. He now works as development director of *Dollars and Sense* magazine and serves on the CCO's board of directors. His articles have appeared in Z *Magazine, Labor Notes*, and other publications.

Vincent Tirelli is a doctoral candidate in the Political Science Program at the City University of New York Graduate Center and an Adjunct Instructor at Brooklyn College. He is currently writing a dissertation on higher education politics and the part-time workforce. He is also the coordinator of the Adjunct Project, an undertaking sponsored by the Doctoral Student Council at the Graduate Center.

William Vaughn recently completed a dissertation titled "The Sublime and the Dutiful: Ethics and Excess from Edwards to Melville." He is currently at work on a book about the graduate labor movement.

Lesley Vidovich, Ph.D. student, began her career as a secondary science teacher and curriculum developer and then moved to the university sector in the early 1990s, where she has been teaching in the area of politics and sociology of education. She is currently completing research for her Ph.D. dissertation at Murdoch University titled "A Policy Trajectory Study of the Effects of Changing Accountability Requirements on Australian Higher Education." She coauthored, with Janice Dudley, *The Politics of Education* (1995).

Ira Yankwitt is an adult literacy educator in New York City and is currently vice-president of United Literacy Workers.

Library of Congress Cataloging-in-Publication Data

Chalk lines : the politics of work in the managed university / edited by Randy Martin.

p.   cm.

Includes index.

ISBN 0-8223-2232-3 (cloth : alk. paper). — ISBN 0-8223-2249-8 (pbk. : alk. paper)

1. College teachers—United States.   2. Universities and colleges—United States—
Administration.   3. Education, Higher—Political aspects—United States.
4. College teachers' unions—United States.   5. College teachers—United States—
Political activity.   I. Martin, Randy.   II. Social text.

LB2331.72.C53   1998

378.1'2023'73—dc21   98-21278